State Sovereign Immunity

Recent Titles in Reference Guides to the United States Constitution
Jack Stark, Series Editor

The Right to the Assistance of Counsel
James J. Tomkovicz

Prohibited Government Acts
Jack Stark

Constitutional Remedies
Michael Wells and Thomas A. Eaton

State Sovereign Immunity

A Reference Guide to the United States Constitution

Melvyn R. Durchslag

Foreword by William P. Marshall

REFERENCE GUIDES TO THE
UNITED STATES CONSTITUTION, NUMBER 3
Jack Stark, *Series Editor*

PRAEGER

Westport, Connecticut
London

Library of Congress Cataloging-in-Publication Data

Durchslag, Melvyn R., 1940–
State sovereign immunity : a reference guide to the United States Constitution / Melvyn R. Durchslag ; foreword by William P. Marshall.
p. cm.—(Reference guides to the United States Constitution, ISSN 1539-8986 ; no. 3)
Includes bibliographical references and index.
ISBN 0-313-31348-2 (alk. paper)
1. States rights—United States. 2. Governmental liability—United States—States. I. Title. II. Series.
KF4600.D87 2002
342.73'02—dc21 2002067837

British Library Cataloguing in Publication Data is available.

Library of Congress Catalog Card Number: 2002067837
ISBN: 0-313-31348-2
ISSN: 1539-8986

First published in 2002

Praeger Publishers, 88 Post Road West, Westport, CT 06881
An imprint of Greenwood Publishing Group, Inc.
www.praeger.com

Printed in the United States of America

The paper used in this book complies with the Permanent Paper Standard issued by the National Information Standards Organization (Z39.48-1984)

10 9 8 7 6 5 4 3 2 1

I dedicate this book to my only real love, my wife and family.

Contents

Series Foreword

JACK STARK

One can conceive of the United States Constitution in many ways. For example, noting the reverence in which it has been held one can think of it as equivalent to a sacred text. Unfortunately, most of its devotees have had less knowledge and even less understanding of the document than they have had reverence for it. Sometimes it is treated as primarily a political document and on that basis has been subjected to analysis, such as Charles Beard's *An Economic Interpretation of the Constitution of the United States*. One can plausibly argue that the Constitution seems most astounding when seen in light of the intellectual effort that has been associated with it. Three brief but highly intense bursts of intellectual energy produced, and established as organic law, most of the Constitution as it now exists. Two of those efforts, sustained over a long period of time, have enabled us to better understand the document.

The first burst of energy occurred at the Constitutional Convention. Although some of the delegates' business, such as the struggle between populous and nonpopulous states about their representation in Congress, was political, much of it was about fundamental issues of political theory. A few of the delegates had or later achieved international eminence for their intellects. Among them are Benjamin Franklin, Alexander Hamilton, and James Madison. Others, although less well known, had first-rate minds. That group includes George Mason and George Wythe. Many of the delegates contributed intelligently. Although the Convention's records are less than satisfactory, they indicate clearly enough that the delegates worked mightily to constitute not merely a polity—but a rational polity that would rise to the standards envisioned by the delegates' intellectual ancestors. Their product, though brief, is amazing. William Gladstone called it "the most wonderful work ever struck off."

Despite the delegates' eminence and the Constitution's excellence as seen from our place in history, its ratification was far from certain. That state of affairs necessitated the second burst of intellectual energy associated with that document: the debate over ratification. Soon after the convention adjourned, articles and speeches (some supporting the Constitution and some attacking it) began to proliferate. A national debate commenced—not only about the document itself but also about the nature of the polity that ought to exist in this country. Both sides included many writers and speakers who were verbally adroit and steeped in the relevant political and philosophical literature. The result was an accumulation of material that is remarkable for both its quantity and its quality. At its apex is the *Federalist Papers*, a production of Alexander Hamilton, James Madison, and John Jay that deserves a place among the great books of Western culture.

Another burst, although not as impressive as the first two but highly respectable, occurred when the Bill of Rights was proposed. Some delegates to the Constitutional Convention had vigorously asserted that such guarantees should be included in the original document. George Mason, the principal drafter of the Virginia Declaration of Rights, so held, and he walked out of the convention when he failed to achieve his purpose. Even those who had argued that the rights in question were implicit recognized the value of adding protection of them to the Constitution. The debate was thus focused on the rights that were to be explicitly granted, not on whether any rights ought to be explicitly granted. Again many writers and speakers entered the fray, and again the debate was solidly grounded in theory and was conducted on a high intellectual level.

Thus, within a few years a statement of organic law and a vital coda to it had been produced. However, the meaning and effect of many of that document's provisions were far from certain; the debates on ratification of the Constitution and the Bill of Rights had demonstrated that. In addition, the document existed in a vacuum, because statutes and actions had not been assessed by its standards. The attempt to resolve these problems began after Chief Justice John Marshall, in Marbury v. Madison, asserted the right of the U.S. Supreme Court to interpret and apply the Constitution. Judicial interpretation and application of the Constitution, beginning with the first constitutional case and persisting until the most recent, is one of the sustained exertions of intellectual energy associated with the Constitution. The framers would be surprised by some of the results of these activities. References in the document to "due process," which seems to refer only to procedures, have been held also to have a substantive dimension. A right to privacy has been found lurking among the penumbras of various parts of the text. A requirement that states grant the same "privileges and immunities" to citizens of other states that they granted to their own citizens, which seemed to guarantee important rights, was not held to be particularly important. The corpus of judicial interpretations of the Constitution is now as voluminous as that document is terse.

As judicial interpretations multiplied, another layer (interpretations of interpretations) appeared, and also multiplied. This layer, the other sustained intellectual effort associated with the Constitution, consists of articles, most of them published in law reviews, and books on the Constitution. This material varies in quality and significance. Some of these works of scholarship result from meticulous examination and incisive thought. Others repeat earlier work, or apply a fine-tooth comb to matters that are too minute even for such a comb. Somewhere in that welter of tertiary material is the answer to almost every question that one could ask about constitutional law. The problem is finding the answer that one wants. The difficulty of locating useful guidance is exacerbated by the bifurcation of most constitutional scholarship into two kinds. In "Two Styles of Social Science Research," C. Wright Mills delineates macroscopic and molecular research. The former deals with huge issues, the latter with tiny issues. Virtually all of the scholarship on the Constitution is of one of those two types. Little of it is macroscopic, but that category does include some first-rate syntheses such as Jack Rakove's *Original Meanings*. Most constitutional scholarship is molecular and, again, some fine work is included in that category.

In his essay, Mills bemoans the inability of social scientists to combine the two kinds of research that he describes to create a third category that will be more generally useful. This series of books is an attempt to do for constitutional law the intellectual work that Mills proposed for social science. The author of each book has dealt carefully and at reasonable length with a topic that lies in the middle range of generality. Upon completion, this series will consist of thirty-seven books, each on a constitutional law topic. Some of the books, such as the book on freedom of the press, explicate one portion of the Constitution's text. Others, such as the volume on federalism, treat a topic that has several anchors in the Constitution. The books on constitutional history and constitutional interpretation range over the entire document, but each does so from a single perspective. Except for a very few of the books the special circumstances of which dictate minor changes in format, each book includes the same components—a brief history of the topic, a lengthy and sophisticated analysis of the current state of the law on that topic, a bibliographical essay that organizes and evaluates scholarly material in order to facilitate further research, a table of cases and an index. The books are intellectually rigorous (in fact, authorities have written them) but, due to their clarity and to brief definitions of terms that are unfamiliar to laypersons, each is comprehensible and useful to a wide audience, one that ranges from other experts on the book's subject to intelligent non-lawyers.

In short, this series provides an extremely valuable service to the legal community and to others who are interested in constitutional law, as every citizen should be. Each book is a map of part of the U.S. Constitution. Together they map all of that document's territory that is worth mapping. When this series is complete, each book will be a third kind of scholarly work that combines the macroscopic and the molecular. Together they will explicate all of the important constitutional topics. Anyone who wants assistance in understanding either a topic in constitutional law or the Constitution as a whole can easily find it in these books.

Foreword

William P. Marshall

In 1793, a fledgling United States Supreme Court decided the case of Chisholm v. Georgia. The subject matter of this case might strike the modern observer as tame. The question in *Chisholm*, after all, was only the relatively technical jurisdictional issue of whether the federal courts had the power to entertain contract claims brought against states by out-of-state citizens.

But the controversy created by the case was as fervent as any generated by the individual and criminal rights decisions of our current era. The Court's holding that states could be subject to suit fell upon the nation, as the historians' claim, with a "profound shock" and reaction that followed was swift. The Congress immediately proposed, and the states quickly ratified, the Eleventh Amendment. The amended Constitution now provided that "[t]he judicial power of the United States shall not be construed to extend to any suit in law or equity, commenced or prosecute against one of the United States by Citizens of another State, or by Citizens of any Foreign State." *Chisholm* was reversed.

The passage of the Eleventh Amendment, however, only begins the story. Two hundred years after its ratification, the meaning and significance of the Eleventh Amendment remain unclear. The United States Supreme Court decisions interpreting the amendment have fluctuated widely and have compounded legal fiction upon legal fiction. There is neither consensus on the historical meaning and intent of the provision nor on the policies and considerations that would guide its interpretation and application. The only thing certain about the Eleventh Amendment, in short, is that its meaning and application remain entirely unresolved.

Meanwhile, the stakes in the Eleventh Amendment controversy continue to rise. The debate over the Eleventh Amendment has become shorthand for the debate over the meanings of federalism and state sovereignty. The issues presented in the Eleventh Amendment debate are as basic as the definition of statehood and the supremacy of federal law. What is the relationship of the rule of law to the sovereignty of states? To what extent may the Congress subject state governments and state treasuries to suits by individual citizens? When are states immune from the applications of civil rights laws? The significance of the answers to these and other questions surrounding the Eleventh Amendment cannot be overstated. They implicate the very structure of American government and the central meaning of the Constitution itself.

Into this picture steps this very important book by Professor Melvyn Durchslag. This book is as comprehensive as it is illuminating. Durchslag traces the history of the Eleventh Amendment's promulgation. He addresses the pre-amendment understandings of the constitutional Framers and of the Court in the case that gave rise to the amendment's passage, Chisholm v. Georgia. He navigates us through the maze of the judicial decisions interpreting the provision, while simultaneously alerting us to the external and internal inconsistencies inherent in the cases. He comprehensively advances the competing sides in the policy debates. He provides invaluable insight into how Eleventh Amendment law may continue to develop.

The debates over the structural issues of American constitutional law, of which the Eleventh Amendment is a significant part, are unlikely to abate in the foreseeable future. Constitutional law is in a period of fundamental reformation, and the Eleventh Amendment cases are at the core of this process. Professor Durchslag's treatise, however, provides the necessary insight and analysis from which a meaningful understanding of Eleventh Amendment law—past, current, and future—can effectively be obtained.

Acknowledgments

Several of my colleagues encouraged me to undertake this venture despite my initial doubts. Whether Jon Entin, Eric Jensen, Bob Lawry, Max Mehlman, and Calvin Sharpe were correct in doing so remains to be seen. In addition, I could not have completed this project without the invaluable research and editorial assistance I received from my research assistants over the past two and one-half years. I list them in alphabetical order: John Allota, Jamie Campbell, Rob Hahn, Heather Lang, and Carrie Nixon.

A special thanks, however, is reserved for two people. First is my wife, Susan, who has had to put up with more than my usual state of preoccupation. Second is my friend and erstwhile colleague, Bill Marshall, who not only has written the Foreword and read and commented upon an early draft of this book, but, more importantly, continues to stimulate my interest in federalism generally and the Eleventh Amendment in particular.

Introduction

The Judicial Power of the United States shall not be construed to extend to any suit in law and equity, commenced or prosecuted against one of the United States by Citizens of another State, or by Citizens or Subjects of any Foreign State.

The Eleventh Amendment to the United States Constitution was the first amendment ratified after the Bill of Rights. The significance of the timing of the Eleventh Amendment lies in its subject matter, federalism—the legal and political relationship between the federal government and the states.

The seeds of the Eleventh Amendment were sown in the Constitutional Convention. As most who are even vaguely familiar with the founding period know, the Constitutional Convention of 1787 was rife with controversy. Some, like the disputes between the large and small states, and whether slaves could be counted in the census, were contests between states for influence in the new Union. But it was the fear that the yet-to-be-formed federal government would displace the states as the dominant political force and, in so doing, trample the rights of individual citizens that dominated the Constitutional Convention of 1787 and formed the core of the Anti-Federalist opposition to ratification. Moreover, the division between those who wanted to create a new, strong national government and those who desired merely to tinker with the Articles of Confederation, was not at all regional in nature. While Alexander Hamilton of New York (who actually left the Convention not long after it convened and returned only six days before its end) is often described as the nationalist, some of the most ardent and influential nationalists, in fact, came from Southern states. It was they, not their northern brethren, who most distrusted the states.

Citing, among other practices, the states' confiscation of land, prevention of the collection of legitimate pre-war debts (a practice that is directly pertinent to the

Eleventh Amendment), and issuance of worthless paper "money" (declared to be legal tender), Southern nationalists, led by James Madison and Edmund Randolph of Virginia and Charles Pickney of South Carolina demanded explicit restrictions on states. The most radical proposal was offered by Pickney and seconded by Madison. It called for the Senate to be empowered to veto any legislation enacted by the states it deemed to be "'improper.'"[1] While this proposal was soundly defeated, the Convention did adopt a series of explicit restrictions on states now contained in Article 1, § 10. These include prohibiting states from coining money or issuing Bills of Credit, passing bills of attainder (legislative declarations of guilt), and abrogating contractual obligations (the fear here was states enacting debtor relief/bankruptcy laws).

The nationalists won the initial round of the states' rights debate, not only in the Convention where their influence predominated, but also in the state ratification conventions, albeit not without some significant difficulty. The Constitution of 1787, however, was incomplete, not only for the reason most often cited, the absence of a Bill of Rights, but also because the contours of federal power remained largely undefined. The former was rectified in 1791 with the ratification of the first eight amendments, which afforded individuals protection from actions of the federal government.

Two other amendments were ratified at the same time, the Ninth and the Tenth. While the first eight amendments largely prohibited the federal government from infringing on specific individual rights, the Ninth and Tenth Amendments cast a far wider net. Designed to appease those who feared that the national government would displace the states as the dominant political force, these amendments confirm, albeit in different ways, that the federal government is a government of *limited* and *defined* powers. Unlike the Articles of Confederation, however, these latter two amendments consciously did not limit federal authority to only those powers *expressly* enumerated in Article 1, § 8. To have done so would have restricted the new government in much the same way as it was restricted during the period of Confederation. The government of the United States would have been doomed to failure. The cost of the decision to express the limited nature of the federal government and leave the contours of its delegated powers undefined is that today, some 215 years later, the line that divides federal authority from state authority seems immune from precise definition.

It should come as no surprise then that the first constitutional amendment after the Bill of Rights would continue the dominant refrain of the Constitutional Convention, the ratification debates, and the Ninth and Tenth Amendments, and federal usurpation of state prerogatives. Indeed the decade in which the Eleventh Amendment was ratified, the last decade of the eighteenth century, saw some of the most vicious and divisive states' rights disputes in our history.[2] The decade began with a proposal by Alexander Hamilton, then Secretary of the Treasury, to have the federal government assume the states' remaining unpaid Revolutionary

War debts. While certainly a benefit to many states, those like Virginia, which had largely paid their debts, objected to being taxed to retire the debts of other states. More importantly, many viewed Hamilton's proposal as transferring still greater authority from the states to the central government. Despite Madison's early objections to Hamilton's proposal, the Congress enacted the bill. The congressional action prompted an immediate rebuke by the Virginia legislature, led by the ardent anti-federalist Patrick Henry. The reason—paying the Revolutionary War debts by the states was not enumerated in the Constitution as a federal authority. Paying a state's debt was therefore the sole responsibility of the state notwithstanding that these debts were incurred in a national effort to wrest control from the British Crown. Put differently, Patrick Henry and the Virginia Legislature assumed that unless *expressly* authorized by the Constitution, the federal government had no authority to act.

Following on the heels of the federal assumption of state debts dispute came the controversy over creating the First Bank of the United States. Again, the one time nationalist, James Madison led the congressional opposition to the bank, using the same arguments cited by Patrick Henry in the debt assumption controversy—Congress did not have the express power to create a bank corporation, or any other corporation for that matter, and thus if such a corporation was to be created it must be done by the states. Despite those objections Congress enacted the legislation. The debate then shifted to the executive branch where both Attorney General Edmund Randolph and Thomas Jefferson advised President Washington to veto the legislation because it infringed on state power. Alexander Hamilton, arguing the other position, relied on Article 1, § 8, Clause 18, which grants Congress the power to "make all Laws which shall be necessary and proper for carrying into Execution the forgoing Powers...." This clause, he argued, gave Congress the ability to select the means *appropriate* to the ends denominated as federal by the Constitution, including the power to establish a banking corporation. Washington, whether persuaded by Hamilton's legal interpretative arguments or not, signed the legislation.

Two other states' rights (or anti-federal power) disputes during this decade deserve mention. First was the Whiskey Rebellion in which refusals to pay the federal tax on whiskey had to be met with a force of federalized state militiamen. This aroused the ire of states' rights republicans who objected to the conscription of their soldiers in the effort of a national cause, particularly one that did not threaten their states directly but related only to the refusal to pay a federal tax. The other dispute was more serious. It involved a perceived threat of war with France (with which many republicans expressed more than a casual affinity) and ultimately an idea (never acted upon) by Alexander Hamilton to use federal force to seize the Louisiana Territory from Spain, an ally of France. Hamilton's proposal would have required marching federal troops through Virginia and North Carolina, an idea those states found antithetical to their sovereignty. The Union may have been saved by Thomas Jefferson who persuaded Virginia not to secede over this issue.

But two more disputes, one that began in the early years and one that closed the decade, had effects well beyond the others. The latter was the congressional enactment of the infamous Alien and Sedition Acts in 1798. Enacted by a federalist Congress and signed by a federalist president (John Adams), the most controversial of these statutes was the Sedition Act, which imposed criminal penalties for uttering "false, scandalous, or malicious" statements about the federal government, the President, or the Congress. Today, we find the Sedition Act to be a reprehensible restriction of free speech. But in 1798 the objection was that it created a *federal* crime for activities not directly germane to any of the specific authorities denominated in the Constitution to be matters of federal concern. The statute was problematic, therefore, because it infringed the sovereignty of the states, and not (at least not directly) that it was an undue restriction on individual liberty. The states' rights issue prompted two resolutions, one drafted by Thomas Jefferson for the state of Kentucky and the other by James Madison for the state of Virginia. Both asserted, as a foundational principle, that the Union was a compact, not of the citizens of the nation, but of the sovereign states. The Union could therefore only act for peace and prosperity of the *states*.

The Kentucky Resolution was rather temperate, arguing little more than what had been asserted in the Bank and debt assumption disputes regarding the lack of federal power to act with respect to a matter not expressly authorized by Article 1. Madison's Virginia Resolution went one step further; it introduced interposition, the doctrine (later to become the legal raison d'étre of the secession that led to the Civil War) that the states could independently defy any exercise of federal authority that, *in their judgment*, was a threat to the state's sovereignty and to the rights of its citizens. The specific issue of the Sedition Act and federal authority to promulgate general criminal laws died due to both the inability of Madison and Jefferson to persuade any other state to enact a similar resolution and the subsequent election, in 1800, of Thomas Jefferson as President and a republican Congress.[3]

The other dispute, the one that prompted the Eleventh Amendment, began in the early part of the decade with a suit in the United States Supreme Court by a group of Dutch bankers against the state of Maryland. Unlike the Sedition Acts, which prompted an angry response from the usual cast of anti-federalist characters, protests over the simple filing of the bankers' lawsuit were both widespread and vehement. As the eminent historian, Forrest McDonald, wrote:

"An anonymous Philadelphia newspaper article ...declared that if the actions were maintained, 'one great National question will be settled—that is, that the several States have relinquished all their Sovereignties, and have become mere corporations,...for a sovereign State can never be sued or coerced by the authority of another government.' Another writer asserted that the actions 'involved more danger to the liberties of America than the claims of the British Parliament to tax us without our consent.' They would lead 'to the consolidation of the Union for the purpose of arbitrary power, to the downfall of liberty and the subversion of the rights of the people.'" "(Y)et another predicted that 'if the sovereignty of the States is to be thus annihilated, there must be a consolidated Government and a standing army.'" 4

Strong words, yet these were fully in accord with the views of Patrick Henry, James Madison, Thomas Jefferson, and others who had opposed other national efforts during this first full decade of the Republic. But this time the republicans won; they secured an amendment to the United States Constitution. Indeed this amendment was the first, and one of only three in our history, adopted in specific response to a ruling by the United States Supreme Court. The others are the Sixteenth Amendment that validated the graduated income tax and the Twenty-Sixth Amendment that granted eighteen year olds the right to vote. (The Fourteenth Amendment overruled the Court's infamous decision in Dred Scott v. Sanford (1857), but it had broader purposes.) This work attempts to define the scope and legal dimensions of that republican political victory. As will become painfully obvious, however, this is not an easy task. It may indeed be an impossible task. Two–hundred years after its ratification, the Eleventh Amendment continues to be a work in progress and is likely to continue to be so for quite some time.

At first blush, the Eleventh Amendment seems straightforward enough, albeit somewhat obtuse to those unfamiliar with the nuances of federal judicial authority. Article 3 of the U.S. Constitution allows federal courts to decide "*all* cases...arising under (the) Constitution, the Laws (and Treaties) of the United States...(and) to controversies between a State and a Citizen of another State...." As will be detailed in the first section of Part I, this language, particularly the last clause, prompted strong objections from anti-federalists who feared that the states would be held to account for their actions to unelected, life-appointed federal magistrates. Their predictions proved to be correct. In 1793, the United States Supreme Court held that the language of Article 3 meant precisely what it said—a state could be sued by a citizen of another state. The Eleventh Amendment, in what seems to be a clear textual expression, removes this possibility. Appearances, however, are oftentimes deceiving.

Supreme Court Justice Felix Frankfurter is reputed (but never with a direct citation) to have sarcastically quipped, "only when the history is ambiguous should one refer to the plain language of the [Constitution]." While he was directing his sarcasm at a misguided approach to statutory interpretation, Justice Frankfurter might just as easily have been describing the Court's Eleventh Amendment jurisprudence since 1890. In that year the United States Supreme Court decided Hans v. Louisiana (1890), in which it relied heavily on history, or at least its version of history, to extend the Eleventh Amendment's proscriptive reach well beyond its rather limited text.

While it is the nature of the beast that constitutional history is closely bound to constitutional interpretation, rarely is history consistently at center stage as it is with the Eleventh Amendment. Unlike other provisions of the Constitution, legal scholars (not just historians) have written volumes on the historical backdrop of the Eleventh Amendment and with every change in the Court's interpretation, and there have been many, more commentary is produced.[5] What has sparked, and continues to spark, the interest of both historians and lawyers is that the Supreme Court has taken an amendment whose text is clear and unambiguous (thus the reference to Justice Frankfurter) and has used a profoundly contestable history to alter its meaning. The fact that the textual revisions wrought by the *Hans* Court's history have survived 110 years of interpretation, is made all the more remarkable because the Court in *Hans* may itself have been motivated by political concerns or at least by a recognition of political reality.

Justice Bradley, the author of *Hans*, had served as the fifth and, ultimately, the tie-breaking vote on the Election Commission appointed by Congress to advise it about the electoral outcome of four contested states in the 1876 election. As reported by legal historian John Orth, Justice Bradley, an ardent supporter of federal authority, had originally decided to declare his support for the election of Samuel Tilden, the Democrat, but later decided to concur with his Republican brethren and support the electors of the Republican Rutherford B. Hayes. As Professor Orth notes, "(t)he price of Southern acquiescence in the decision of the Electoral Commission was . . . self government for the South,"[6] the end of Reconstruction, that is. With the election of Hayes and the end of Reconstruction, federal troops were removed from the South and the Congress, once controlled by firebrand radical Republicans, was in no mood to reimpose federal authority over recalcitrant states. A Supreme Court judgment forcing Louisiana to make good on its bonds would thus be unenforceable. So why should the Court maintain fealty to a text when the result would be an order it knew would not be complied with and which it could not execute? [7]

Judicial decisions, enmeshed this deeply in "the politics of the day," ordinarily have a short shelf life. But the Court's Eleventh Amendment history, revisionist or not, has not only survived 110 years of interpretation, but, like a tropical storm stalled over warm water, it has actually gained strength and momentum with the years. Since 1890, the Court has extended the Eleventh Amendment to include suits in admiralty (admiralty is not a "suit in law or equity") (*Ex parte New York,* 1911); to suits by foreign sovereigns (Principality of Monaco v. Mississippi, 1934); to explicit abrogation of sovereign immunity by Congress under its admitted Article I powers (Seminole Tribe of Florida v. Florida, 1996); to explicit attempts at congressional abrogation of state sovereign immunity in state courts (Alden v. Maine, 1999); and, most recently, to federal administrative agency claims against states instituted by private individuals (Federal Maritime Commission v. South Carolina Ports Authority, 2002). On the other hand, the Court has rejected claims of constitutional sovereign immunity in appeals from state courts to the Supreme Court when the state is a party (Cohens v. Virginia, 1821); in suits filed against states by the federal government (United States v. Texas, 1892); in suits by other states (Rhode Island v. Massachusetts, 1832); in suits by private citizens against states in the courts of other states (Nevada v. Hall, 1986); in suits against state offices to enjoin their continuing violations of federal law (*Ex parte Young,* 1908); and, in a case decided the same day as *Hans*, in suits against political subdivisions of the states (Lincoln County v. Luning, 1890).

There is the argument that the history recited in *Hans,* such as it is, has, over the years, become increasingly less important to Eleventh Amendment jurisprudence as the venerability of *Hans* itself has taken over as the guiding principle through the doctrine of *stare decisis* (the doctrine that admonishes courts to decide current cases consistently with prior decisions). To paraphrase Justice Scalia, *Hans* has become part of our constitutional culture (Lucas v. South Carolina Coastal Council, 1992). History may therefore be unimportant to our modern understanding of the Eleventh Amendment and therefore not deserving of either recapitulation or debate. However, the Supreme Court has continued to debate both the particulars and the significance of that history. The Court's current majority relies upon early history to defend the notion that the Framers would have been "profoundly shocked" had they realized that states could be sued by individuals in federal court, a notion that is at the heart of Hans v. Louisiana.[8] And the current dissenters, who have consistently constituted at least three and most often four members of the Court, have increased their calls to reconsider Hans v. Louisiana largely because of its shaky historical foundation. The early history of the Eleventh Amendment thus remains important.

Part I discusses the historical backdrop of the Eleventh Amendment. This task is accomplished in three sections. The first analyzes what was perceived to be the greatest threat to the states from the newly proposed federal judiciary—that it would become the forum in which states would be sued by individuals for debts incurred fighting the Revolutionary War. The second section, in a detailed fashion, discusses both the Constitutional Convention of 1787 and the more lively debates over the scope of federal judicial power in the state ratifying conventions. Finally, Part I concludes with the detailed historical analysis with a discussion of the United States Supreme Court's decision in Chisholm v. Georgia (1793), the decision that resulted in the Eleventh Amendment.[9] In addition, this section discusses the short history of the adoption of the Eleventh Amendment. While divided in three parts to make it more manageable, the history can only be understood as an uninterrupted continuum and should be read as such. Only by doing so can one begin to piece together the rather confusing puzzle that resulted from Chisholm v. Georgia's holding that Article 3 allowed a South Carolina citizen to sue the state of Georgia in federal court for money owed for the purchase of military equipment for the Georgia militia.

Part II, the Analysis, analyzes and critiques the jurisprudence of the Eleventh Amendment. It is presented more or less chronologically, starting with United States v. Peters (1809), and leading up to the watershed year of 1890 and the Court's decision in Hans v. Louisiana. Eleventh Amendment jurisprudence is then discussed topically, analyzing in detail four separate (but not distinct) doctrinal aspects of the Eleventh Amendment. The concluding section is an assessment and critique of the current jurisprudence. Ultimately however, one's final judgment of the Court's performance in interpreting the Eleventh Amendment must rest on how defensible its interpretation of the historical/political events leading to that amendment are. This is not because of any belief that the Framers' intent is *the*, or even *a*, legitimate method of constitutional interpretation, but because the Court's own opinions leave us no choice. The Court's reading of history is either its salvation or its poison.

NOTES

1. Forrest McDonald, *States Rights and the Union: Imperium in Imperio, 1776–1876* (Lawrence: University Press of Kansas, 2000) 18.
2. McDonald, *States* 28–43.
3. Bernard A.Weisberger, *America Afire: Jefferson, Adams, and the Revolutionary Election of 1800* (New York: Harper Collins, 2000).
4. McDonald, *States* 35.
5. The two leading treatises are Clyde E. Jacobs, *The Eleventh Amendment and Sovereign Immunity* (New York: Doubleday, 1972) and John V. Orth, *The Judicial Power of the United States: The Eleventh Amendment in American History* (New York: Oxford University Press, 1987). There are, in addition, numerous articles. I list only several here. Akhil Reed Amar, "Of Sovereignty and Federalism," 96 *Yale Law J.* (1987) 1425; Martha A. Field, "The Eleventh Amendment and Other Sovereign Immunity Doctrines (Part I)," 126 *University of Pennsylvania Law Rev.* (1977) 515; William A. Fletcher, "A Historical Interpretation of the Eleventh Amendment: A Narrow Construction of an Affirmative Grant Rather than a Prohibition of Jurisdiction," 35 *Stanford Law Rev.* (1983) 1033; John J. Gibbons, "The Eleventh Amendment and State Sovereign Immunity: A Reinterpretation," 83 *Columbia Law Rev.* (1983) 1889; Lawrence Marshall, "Fighting the Words of the Eleventh Amendment," 102 *Harvard Law Rev.* (1989) 1372; and James E. Pfander, "History and State Suability: An 'Explanatory' Account of the Eleventh Amendment," 83 *Cornell Law Rev.* (1998) 1269.
6. Orth, *Judicial* 54.
7. Orth, *Judicial* 74–80.
8. The "profound shock" theory of the Eleventh Amendment, as will be discussed later, holds that the Framers of the constitution would have been "profoundly shocked" at the notion that states could be sued by individuals in federal courts. The earliest scholar to defend this theory was Charles Warren. Charles Warren, *The Supreme Court in United States History, Vol. 1* (Boston: Little, Brown and Co., 1922) 91.
9. U.S. Constitution, art. 3, sec. 2, clause 2.

PART I

HISTORY

English and American Law Before the Constitutional Convention

STATE INDEBTEDNESS AND ASSUMPTIONS OF SOVEREIGN IMMUNITY

Whether one reads the Eleventh Amendment broadly to confer both an immunity from liability[1] *and* a prohibition on congressional authority to abrogate that immunity[2] or narrowly to prevent the exercise of federal judicial authority against states only when the plaintiff is a citizen of another state or a foreign nation,[3] all agree that the Eleventh Amendment was intended, *to one degree or another,* to preserve (or restore) the states' sovereign immunity. Immunity from what kinds of suits and by whom is the subject of Part II of this volume. For present purposes, it is important to understand that immunity from suit extends only to those political bodies that can claim the status of "sovereignty." In its broadest sense, sovereignty is "the ability...to prescribe the rules of order and behavior for others...without having (1) to look to higher authority as a source of power or (2) to be subjected to the oversight of that higher authority."[4] Whether stemming from the often cited adage that "the King can do no wrong" or from the more conceptual notion described by Justice Holmes that, "there can be no legal rights as against the authority that makes the law on which the right depends" (Kawananakoa v. Polyblank, 1907) is, for these purposes, unimportant. What is important is that sovereign immunity is a legal doctrine that holds that a state or nation, as the case may be, possessed of its own independent powers, cannot be sued and thus be made accountable to others for exercising those powers in an allegedly unlawful manner.

Sovereign immunity has a long tradition in Anglo-American jurisprudence dating back to the twelfth century. By the time of the reign of Henry III (1216–1272), it was clear that the Crown could not be sued *eo nomine* (in his own name).[5] It is often asserted that the reason for the inability of an individual or, more appropriate to its historical context, a subject, to sue the "state" is that "the King can do no wrong." But it appears that while this may have been the doctrine in theory, the practice was quite the opposite. As Clyde Jacobs establishes, the Crown was regarded as the "fountain of justice" and was therefore required, both by law and conscience, to provide remedies to its subjects who felt aggrieved by the Crown's mis- or maladministration.[6] It was during the reign of Henry III's son, Edward I (1272–1307) that remedies against the Crown to enforce its obligation to do justice first developed.[7] A number of procedures evolved during these years by which an individual could sue the Crown, even in its own name. Most commonly used was the Petition of Right, whereby an individual could petition the Crown seeking whatever redress it thought appropriate to undo the alleged wrong. Since the Monarch did not have the time or inclination to personally review each petition, a specially appointed commission, the Privy Council, or the Chancellor reviewed petitions at the behest of the Monarch. Most importantly, Petitions of Right, certainly by the eighteenth century, were granted or denied on the basis of law, not on the basis of whim, caprice, or expediency. The individual responsible for reviewing the petition conducted a preliminary factual investigation and, based on that investigation, determined whether the petitioner had a right to the relief sought. If so, he "endorsed the petition that right be done."[8] If the facts were contested, the case was then tried before a commission to determine the facts. If the law was in dispute, the matter was referred to one of the Crown courts, the King's Bench, the Chancery, or the Exchequer, for final decision.[9] The salient point about these procedures is that they were just that, procedures and no more. Up to and including the end of the eighteenth century, sovereign immunity was "largely a legal conception, which determined the forms of procedure in some cases but did not seriously impair the subject's right to recovery in accordance with the substantive law."[10] At most, sovereign immunity under eighteenth-century English common law meant that the King or Queen could not *personally* be subject to the processes of the common law courts. It did not insulate the British government from meeting its obligations imposed by law.[11]

Not surprisingly, there is no evidence that the American colonies inherited even the limited immunity the British Crown was afforded by the common law. The colonies, after all, possessed none of the attributes of sovereignty; they were ruled by Britain and had to look to the British parliament for all their power. Whatever authority the colonies possessed was acquired directly from the charters granted by the British Crown and could be revoked by the Crown. This status was recognized in the colonial charters. The charters of Massachusetts, Connecticut, and Rhode Island specifically made those colonies and their Governors answerable to all courts in the "Realm." The colonies of Virginia, New York, Maryland, and Pennsylvania were silent on whether the colony itself or the Governor were similarly subject to suit, but the assumption was that they, like the proprietary corporations they resembled, were.[12]

Judge Gibbons concludes that "(i)n order to support the proposition that a general understanding of state sovereign immunity prevailed at the time of the Constitution's ratification, it must therefore . . . be shown that the state governments that succeeded those established pursuant to colonial charters or proprietary grants considered themselves to be immune from suit."[13] The evidence unearthed by Judge Gibbons fails to support any such claim of sovereign immunity. As he establishes, "not a single eighteenth-century state constitution . . . asserted that the newly created state was not subject to suit. In fact, these texts point in quite the opposite direction."[14] Both Connecticut and Rhode Island adopted as their first constitutions their previous charters. These constitutions specifically subjected them to private suits. Moreover, most state constitutions contained a bill of rights intended to secure basic individual rights for their citizens. The majority of states included among these rights a guarantee of a judicial remedy. Indeed, the constitutions of Pennsylvania and Tennessee coupled the guarantee of a civil remedy in the bill of rights with a grant to the legislature to enact procedures for asserting rights against the government.[15] These provisions, explicit or implicit, were nothing more than a restatement of English common law: "If the plaintiff has a right, he must of necessity have means of vindication if he is injured in the exercise or enjoyment of it. Right and remedy, want of right and want of remedy, are reciprocal."[16]

What later made right and remedy not reciprocal in the United States was a combination of fortuity and self-interest. The fortuity was a change in the form of government after the Revolution that removed the Crown, leaving the former colonies with no supervisory authority. The former colonies were, in a true sense, "sovereigns." American citizens thus lost the avenues in British law that had ensured their rights against the government, such as the Petition of Right and the courts of the Chancery and Exchequer. With some exceptions, most notably Virginia,[17] these fora and procedures were not replaced by American counterparts. This was due largely to self-interest. The new states of the Union had very few funds at their disposal with which to wage a protracted campaign against England, one of the world's wealthiest and most powerful nations. As a consequence, they turned to issuing paper "money" as a means of purchasing the provisions they needed to make the attempt to wage war. With the war finally won, the newly sovereign states were forced to deal with the problem of how to pay back the creditors who had made the victory possible. Professor James Pfander's research indicates that by 1779, the states had issued approximately $210 million in debt securities in order to finance their participation in the Revolutionary War.[18] Much of this "money" was in the hands of foreign states and foreign citizens. Additional debt was purchased at a substantial discount from the initial creditors by domestic speculators hoping to be repaid at par in specie or hard currency.[19] The states understandably resisted opening their court systems to suits by their numerous creditors.[20]

Attempts by the states to retire their debts were mixed. Massachusetts tried, unsuccessfully,[21] to retire its debts by issuing specie and paying for it by enacting high taxes on its citizens. The result was Shay's Rebellion, one of the events that underscored the need for an overhaul of the Articles of Confederation. Other states, such as Rhode Island and a number of southern states, simply issued paper money, avoiding the need to tax its citizenry to repay their Revolutionary War debts. By the late 1780s the states' paper money had become essentially valueless.[22] And when merchants and creditors refused to accept the paper money, laws were enacted requiring them to do so.[23] This was the situation that formed the backdrop for both the ratification of the Constitution and the ratification of the Eleventh Amendment only nine years later.

It is no great surprise that those states with the largest pre-Constitution debt were the most concerned that Article 3 would be interpreted as it was in Chisholm v. Georgia, to permit an individual to sue a state in a federal court. These were also the states most strongly in favor of a constitutional amendment to overturn *Chisholm*.[24] That most states in 1793 supported, even welcomed, the adoption of the Eleventh Amendment says little, however, about the states' understandings of sovereign immunity as a general concept in 1787. It is true that the Revolution did not throw out the baby with the bathwater. But whether the new states had a conception of their sovereign immunity that went much beyond their near panic about pre-Constitution war debts is not clear from their support of the Eleventh Amendment. More importantly, the near unanimous support for the Eleventh Amendment does not, by itself, justify an interpretation that grants a broad *constitutional* sovereign immunity to states, precluding not only the exercise of federal *judicial* power, the historical import of sovereign immunity, but federal *legislative* authority as well. Rather, if there is historical support for a broad sovereign immunity interpretation of the Eleventh Amendment, it must be found in the Constitutional Convention of 1787 and in the Ratification debates in the state conventions.

THE CONSTITUTIONAL CONVENTION AND RATIFICATION DEBATES

The Constitutional Convention

There is no written history of general sovereign immunity that the states had grown to expect under the British system to tell us how the founding fathers believed the conflicts between the states and their numerous creditors should be resolved and in what forum the resolution ought to occur. A look at the records surviving from the Constitutional Convention also has very little to add to the understanding of how the Founders of this country intended to deal with that issue. First, the debates and discussions that occurred at the Constitutional Convention were not officially recorded. The delegates to the convention deliberately did not make official recordings of the debates and discussions so that they would be able to speak and vote their opinions without fear of later reprisal. Nevertheless, some understanding can be gleaned from secondary sources containing the notes and recollections of the delegates. Second, and more pertinent to interpretations of the Eleventh Amendment, there is no mention in the available secondary sources of a debate taking place concerning whether a state can be sued by a private individual in the federal court system. In fact, there is little debate recorded concerning the jurisdiction of the federal courts at all. This leaves us with only one way of determining what the Framers intended to accomplish with the diversity clauses of Article 3, trace how Article 3 and its jurisdictional grants to the federal courts evolved during the summer of 1787.

The brief attempt to govern the country using the Articles of Confederation, which contained no federal judiciary, save for prize and piracy claims, led to near universal agreement that a strong and independent federal judiciary was needed.[25] A federal government with significant, albeit limited substantive powers at the very least, needed an authoritative forum that could provide for uniform interpretation of federal law. The Constitutional Convention officially convened on May 14, 1787, but debate on the structure and form of the new federal government did not begin until Edmund Randolph presented the Virginia Plan on May 29, 1787.[26] The Virginia Plan, believed to have been written by James Madison, consisted of fifteen resolutions. These resolutions called for a strong federal government with the three branches we now have, and provided a broad sketch of the type of government desired by such federalists as Randolph and Madison.[27] The resolution that provided for a national judiciary stated the following:

> 9. Resd. that a National Judiciary be established to consist of one or more supreme tribunals, and of inferior tribunals to be chosen by the National Legislature, to hold their offices during good behavior; and to receive punctually at stated times fixed compensation for their services, in which no increase or diminution shall be made so as to affect the persons actually in office at the time of such increase or diminution. That the jurisdiction of the inferior tribunals shall be to hear & determine in the first instance, and of the supreme tribunal to hear and determine in the dernier resort, all piracies & felonies on the high seas, captures from an enemy; cases in which foreigners or citizens of other States applying to such jurisdictions may be interested, or which respect the collection of the National revenue; impeachment's of any National officers, and questions which may involve the national peace and harmony.[28]

Although the resolution does not mention controversies between a state and citizens of another state or foreigners, it does grant the federal courts jurisdiction over "cases in which foreigners or citizens of other States applying to such jurisdictions may be interested."[29] What exactly is meant by this phrase is unclear. Clyde Jacobs, however, concludes that it was meant to include cases instituted by foreigners or out-of-state citizens.[30] But it is also possible to interpret this clause as the predecessor to the clauses that eventually granted jurisdiction in cases between two states and between citizens of different states. If interpreted in this way, it tells us nothing about Article 3 nor state sovereign immunity.

On June 12, the jurisdiction of the national judiciary as proposed by the Virginia Plan was modified by the Convention. Among other modifications not pertinent to the Eleventh Amendment, the Convention changed the phrase "other States" to "two distinct States of the Union."[31] Regarding the parts establishing jurisdiction, the resolution now read:

That the jurisdiction of the inferior tribunals shall be to hear & determine in the first resort, that the jurisdiction of the supreme tribunal shall be to hear & determine in the first resort, that the jurisdiction of the supreme tribunal shall be to hear & determine in the dernier resort, all piracies, felonies, &c.; cases in which foreigners or citizens of two distinct States of the Union applying to such jurisdictions may be interested, or which respect the collection of the National revenue; impeachment's of any National officers, and questions which may involve the national peace and harmony.

This change removed any possibility that the resolution granted the federal courts jurisdiction over cases between states and citizens of other states or foreigners. Instead, the resolution now gave the federal courts what we now call *diversity jurisdiction*, that is, jurisdiction to hear cases between citizens of different states.

However, one day later, on June 13, on motion of Randolph seconded by Madison, the jurisdiction of the federal courts was again altered. The new resolution read, "[t]hat the jurisdiction of the national Judiciary shall extend to cases which respect the collection of the national revenue, impeachment's of any national officers, and questions which involve the national peace and harmony."[32] The Convention agreed to the resolutions submitted by Randolph, but on June 15, before any further discussion of those resolutions could occur, William Paterson presented an alternative plan, known as the New Jersey Plan. This plan also provided for an independent national judiciary:

5. Resd. that a federal Judiciary be established to consist of a supreme Tribunal the Judges of which to be appointed by the Executive, & to hold their offices during good behavior, to receive punctually at stated times a fixed compensation for their services in which no increase or diminution shall be made, so as to affect the persons actually in office at the time of such increase or diminution; that the Judiciary so established shall have authority to hear & determine in the first instance on all impeachments of federal officers, & by way of appeal in the dernier resort in all cases touching the rights of Ambassadors, in all cases of captures from an enemy, in all cases of piracies & felonies on the high seas, in all cases in which foreigners may be interested, in the construction of any treaty or treaties, or which may arise on any of the Acts for regulation of trade, or the collection of the federal Rev-

enue: that none of the Judiciary shall during the time they remain in Office be capable of receiving or holding any other office or appointment during their time of service, or for thereafter.[33]

Paterson's resolution regarding the federal judiciary, in form, resembled Randolph's first resolution, as it specifically defined those matters over which the United States courts could exercise authority. These matters however, did not include claims where the parties were of diverse citizenship. Moreover, the grant of jurisdiction to the United States courts, both lower and Supreme, was not nearly as expansive as that proposed by Randolph and Madison on June 13.

The Convention did not debate the jurisdiction of the federal courts again until July 18. After this debate Randolph's revised resolution was again changed, now reading "[t]hat the jurisdiction of the national Judiciary shall extend to cases arising under laws passed by the general Legislature, and to such other questions as involve the National peace and harmony."[34] This passed unanimously. After further debate, Madison proposed to revise the resolution to read, "that the jurisdiction shall extend to all cases arising under the National laws: And to such other questions as may involve the Natl. peace & harmony."[35] This was also agreed to by the Convention. This version of Randolph's resolution, as well as that of Paterson, was referred to the Committee of Detail on July 26.[36] The Convention adjourned until August 6 to provide the Committee of Detail enough time to develop a report regarding what they believed to be the best language to express the consensus of the Convention. It is safe to conclude, however, that up to this point, there is nothing to suggest that the state could be sued in United States Courts *except* (1) under laws enacted by the "general legislature" and (2) questions that may involve "national peace and harmony." Yet even in those cases, no resolution contained explicit language regarding the right of an *individual* to sue a state in federal court.

The Committee of Detail was comprised of such notable figures as John Rutledge, Edmund Randolph, James Wilson, Oliver Ellsworth, and Nathaniel Gorham. They, like the majority of the Convention, did not make official recordings of their deliberations. Needless to say, it is quite difficult to determine what took place in the Committee from a distance of over 200 years. However, some of its working papers have survived the years, and these help to show the progression from the resolutions referred to the Committee to the draft that emerged on August 6, 1787. Three of these papers are particularly pertinent to the Framers' understanding of whether state sovereign immunity survived the judiciary article of the Constitution. The first is in the handwriting of Edmund Randolph, with additions by John Rutledge.[37] An early draft of the report of the Committee contains the first explicit mention of jurisdiction over cases between a state and a citizen of another state. The judicial article in this draft states:

5. The Judiciary…

7. The jurisdiction of the supreme tribunal shall extend
   1. to all cases, arising under laws passed by the general [Legislature]
   2. to impeachment's of officers, and
   3. to such other cases, as the national legislature may assign, as
      involving the national peace and harmony,
      in the collection of the revenue
      in disputes between citizens of different states
      [in disputes between a State & a Citizen or Citizens of another State][38]
      in disputes between different states; and
      in disputes, in which subjects or citizens of other countries are concerned [& in Cases of Admiralty Jurisdn]

But this supreme jurisdiction shall be appellate only, except in [Cases of Impeachment. & (in)] those instances, in which the Legislature shall make it original. and the legislature shall organize it[39]

The second document that pertains to state sovereign immunity is actually the second draft of the report of the Committee of Detail. This document, which more closely resembles the finished product, also grants the federal courts jurisdiction over disputes between a state and citizens of another state. In addition, it contains the first express grant of jurisdiction over cases between a state and foreign countries or citizens. The document was written by James Wilson (who was later to serve on the court that decided Chisholm v. Georgia) and also contains additions by Rutledge:

14. ... The Jurisdiction of the Supreme (National) Court shall extend to all Cases arising under Laws passed by the Legislature of the United State; to all Cases affecting Ambassadors [and other) public Ministers [& Consuls], to the Trial of Impeachment's of Officers of the United States; to all Cases of Admiralty and Maritime Jurisdiction; to Controversies between [States,-except those who. regard Jurisdn or Territory, -betwn] a State and a Citizen or Citizens of another State, between Citizens of different States and between [a State or the] Citizens (of any of the States) [thereof] and foreign States, Citizens or Subjects. In Cases of Impeachment, (those) [Cases] affecting Ambassadors (and) other public Ministers [& Consuls], and those in which a State shall be (one of the) [a] Part(ies)[y], this jurisdiction shall be original. In all the other Cases beforementioned, it shall be appellate, with such Exceptions and under such Regulations as the Legislature shall make.[40]

The third document of importance to the discussion of the Framers' understanding of state sovereign immunity is the final report of the Committee of Detail, which was presented to the full Convention on August 6. Article XI, § 3, of the report defined the jurisdiction of the Supreme Court as follows:

The Jurisdiction of the Supreme Court shall extend to all cases arising under laws passed by the Legislature of the United States; to all cases affecting Ambassadors, other Public Ministers and Consuls; to the trial of impeachment of Officers of the United States; to all cases of Admiralty and maritime jurisdiction; to controversies between two or more States, (except such as shall regard Territory or Jurisdiction) between a State and Citizens of another State, between Citizens of different States, and between a State or the Citizens thereof and foreign States, citizens or subjects. In cases of impeachment, cases affecting Ambassadors, other Public Ministers and Consuls, and those in which a State shall be a party, this jurisdiction shall be original. In all the other cases before mentioned, it shall be appellate, with such exceptions and under such regulations as the Legislature shall make.[41]

Although this was the first time the full Convention had been presented with the idea of granting the federal courts jurisdiction over cases between a state and citizens of another state or foreigners, there is no record of discussion or debate over these clauses. Perhaps most revealing of the delegates' feelings on the issue is the fact that while there were other changes made in the Committee of Detail's draft before it was given to the Committee of Style, the clauses "between a State and Citizens of another State" and "between a State or the Citizens thereof and foreign States, citizens or subjects" were not altered.

On September 12, after only two days of work, the report of the Committee of Style was delivered to the Convention.[42] The jurisdiction of the federal courts was set forth in Art III, § 2:

The judicial power shall extend to all cases, both in law and equity, arising under this constitution, the laws of the United States, and treaties made, or which shall be made, under their authority. To all cases affecting ambassadors, other public ministers and consuls. To all cases of admiralty and maritime jurisdiction. To controversies to which the United States shall be a party. To controversies between two or more States; between a state and citizens of another state; between citizens of different States; between citizens of the same state claiming lands under grants of different States, and between a state, or the citizens thereof, and foreign States, citizens or subjects.[43]

This language was not altered in any way before the Constitution was signed, and the Convention adjourned on September 17, 1787; only the punctuation was modified.

Because there are no records of the debates that took place at the Constitutional Convention, it is impossible to determine from the existing documents whether the clauses "controversies between a state and citizens of another state" and "between a state, or the citizens thereof, and foreign states, citizens or subjects," were intended to encompass all cases that literally fell under that definition—or whether, as has been subsequently argued, it was only meant to encompass those cases in which the state was either a plaintiff or had consented to being a defendant. It is also impossible to determine whether it was originally intended that a state could be made to answer in United States courts under the first clause of Art

III, which extends jurisdiction to "cases arising under [the] Constitution [and] laws of the United States."

THE RATIFICATION DEBATES

Article 3 of the proposed Constitution, the judiciary article, was not a major target of Anti-Federalist rhetoric. On the few occasions that Article 3 was attacked, it usually concerned the lack of a provision guaranteeing trial by jury in civil cases or the inclusion of a provision in the second clause of Article 3 granting the federal courts jurisdiction to hear appeals with respect to fact as well as law.[44] Overall, the clauses that granted federal jurisdiction over controversies between a state and citizens of another state or foreigners received relatively little attention. And what attention the so-called diversity clauses did receive does not clearly indicate whether the clauses were understood to allow states to be sued in a federal court.

Pennsylvania

The first five states to ratify the Constitution—Delaware, New Jersey, Georgia, Connecticut, and Pennsylvania—did so within four months after it was proposed. Of these five states, only in Pennsylvania did the clauses extending jurisdiction to United States courts over controversies between a state and citizens of another state or foreigners receive any attention.

Tench Coxe, a Pennsylvanian who was a member of the Annapolis Convention and the Continental Congress, wrote a pamphlet that was published in many newspapers of the day[45] titled *An Examination of the Constitution of the United States of America, by an American Citizen.*[46] In this pamphlet, Mr. Coxe wrote:

> But when a dispute arises between the citizens of any state about lands lying out of the bounds thereof, or when a trial is to be had between the citizens of any state and those of another, or the government of another, the private citizen will not be obliged to go into a court constituted by the state, with which, or with the citizens of which, his dispute is. He can appeal to a disinterested federal court. This is surely a great advantage, and promises a fair trial, and an impartial judgment.[47]

The delegates attending Pennsylvania's ratifying convention also praised the jurisdiction of the federal courts over controversies between a state and citizens of another state or foreigners. In the debates of the convention, James Wilson, a member of the Constitutional Convention's Committee of Detail, and later a United States Supreme Court Justice, said; "'*Between a state and citizens of another state.*' When this power is attended to, it will be found to be a necessary one. Impartiality is the leading feature in this Constitution; it pervades the whole.

When a citizen has a controversy with another state, there ought to be a tribunal where both parties may stand on a just and equal footing."[48]

Wilson did not end his commentary on the Judiciary Article there but added:

> '*Between citizens of different states, and between a state, or the citizens thereof, and foreign states, citizens, or subjects.*' This part of the jurisdiction, I presume, will occasion more doubt than any other part; and, at first view, it may seem exposed to objections well founded and of great weight; but I apprehend this can be the case only at first view.
>
> Though the citizens of a state, and the citizens or subjects of foreign states, may sue in the federal court, it does not follow that they must sue. These are the instances in which the jurisdiction of the United States may be exercised; and we have all the reason in the world to believe that it will be exercised impartially; for it would be improper to infer that the judges would abandon their duty, the rather for being independent.
>
> But when we consider the matter a little further, is it not necessary, if we mean to restore either public or private credit, that foreigners, as well as ourselves, have a just and impartial tribunal to which they may resort? I would ask how a merchant must feel to have his property lie at the mercy of the laws of Rhode Island. I ask, further, How will a creditor feel who has his debts at the mercy of tender laws in other states?
>
> It was thought proper to give the citizens of foreign states full opportunity of obtaining justice in the general courts, and this they have by its appellate jurisdiction; therefore, in order to restore credit with those foreign states, that part of the article is necessary. Further, it is necessary in order to preserve peace with foreign nations.[49]

Five days after Wilson made his comments on the judiciary article to the Pennsylvania convention, Robert Whitehall put forth for consideration a bill of rights and several other amendments to the Constitution. The fourteenth of these amendments proposed some changes to the jurisdiction of the federal courts; however, it did not touch the clauses that gave federal courts jurisdiction over cases between a state and a citizen of other states or foreign countries.[50] This amendment ultimately failed to win the support of the general convention and as such has very little general historical significance. However, combined with the words of Coxe and Wilson, it paints a picture of a convention that fully understood, and approved of, an Article 3, § 2 that granted federal courts the power to adjudicate disputes between a state and citizens of other states and foreign countries.[51]

Massachusetts

The treatment of Article 3 in Massachusetts was slightly different from what transpired in Pennsylvania. In Massachusetts, the clauses granting the federal courts jurisdiction over controversies between a state and citizens of other states and foreigners received no mention whatsoever during the state ratifying convention. Outside of the convention, however, those clauses received considerable commentary from nondelegate pamphleteers. Although the criticism seems to have outweighed the praise, it is clear that all understood Article 3 as allowing citizens of one state and foreigners to be able to sue another state in federal court.

We know that the Massachusetts ratifying convention devoted three days to the discussion of Articles 2 and 3. The incomplete records of these debates, however, do not indicate that there was any discussion on the issue of whether a state could be sued in federal courts by citizens of other states and countries. In the end, the convention ratified the Constitution, by a vote of 187 to 168, with nine amendments.[52] Three of these amendments concerned the judiciary, but none addressed the citizen/state diversity clauses.

Outside the convention, however, these clauses caused quite a stir. Several civic leaders of the time, including Samuel Adams,[53] Silas Lee,[54] and James Sullivan,[55] were opposed to permitting states to be sued in federal courts. This was largely because "holders of state securities who were citizens of other states or foreign subjects would be able to sue the state for payment in federal court."[56]

The clauses were also criticized by the "Letters of Agrippa," one of the most prominent and widely distributed anti-federalist publications in Massachusetts.[57] This publication recognized that Article 3 granted the federal courts jurisdiction over cases in which citizens of one state could sue another state:

> This [judicial] power extends to all cases between a state and citizens of another state. Hence a citizen, possessed of the notes of another state, may bring his action, and there is not limitation that the execution shall be levied on the publick property of the state; but the property of individuals is liable. This is a foundation for endless confusion and discord. This right to try causes between a state and citizens of another state, involves in it all criminal causes; and a man who accidentally transgressed the laws of another state, must be transported, with all his witnesses, to a third state, to be tried. He must be ruined to prove his innocence. These are necessary parts of the new system, and it will never be complete till they are reduced to practice. They effectually prove a consolidation of the states, and we have before shown the ruinous tendency of such a measure.[58]

Although the "Letters of Agrippa" called for the rejection of the Constitution by the state of Massachusetts, when it became apparent that the document was going to be ratified, several amendments were proposed to be ratified with it. Two of these would have specifically precluded federal judicial authority over cases between a state and citizens of another state and foreigners.[59] Neither passed however.[60]

Although there was widespread opposition to allowing citizens of other states and foreigners to sue a state it was far from universal. Thomas Pickering, a noted statesman and a delegate to the Constitutional Convention, defended the diversity clauses. He believed, as did many federalists, that such a jurisdiction forced the United States to be responsible for the actions of all its various parts and citizens, and that providing a forum whereby foreign states and citizens could air their grievances against states and receive some sort of compensation prevented the whole nation from becoming involved in a war because of one state's actions. In addition, like Coxe and Wilson, Pickering believed that fairness dictated a neutral forum in which to adjudicate claims of citizens burdened by laws passed in other states.[61]

Ultimately, it appears that it was the federalists like Pickering, Coxe, and Wilson who won the day. As far as we know, the ratifying convention was not swayed by the heated public discussion and approved Article 3 in its entirety without any debate concerning the relevant clauses.

Virginia

In Virginia, the clauses extending jurisdiction to the federal courts over controversies between a state and citizens of another state and foreigners received a great deal of attention. In part, this resulted from concerns about Virginia's Revolutionary War debt. But in larger part it resulted from the prominence and intellectual power and fervor of federalists and anti-federalists alike. Several of the delegates, some of whom were at the Constitutional Convention, addressed the clauses at Virginia's ratification convention. Although all of the anti-federalists who spoke at the convention against these clauses maintained that they allowed citizens of one state or foreigners to call a state into federal court, the federalists did not, as a group, appear as certain about this conclusion as their adversaries. Some of the federalists denied that Article 3 made the states answerable to such actions, while others accepted, even praised, such an interpretation. This inconsistency in the federalists' position makes it difficult to determine how the Virginia Convention ultimately viewed these clauses, but the actions of the Convention as a whole seem to indicate a consensus that a state, under Article 3, was suable in federal court by a citizen of another state or a foreign nation.

The battle of words that took place at the Convention between the federalists and the anti-federalists was both long and fierce. Leading the anti-federalist attack on the diversity clauses of Article 3, was Patrick Henry:

> It sounds mighty prettily to gentlemen, to curse paper money and honestly pay debts. But apply to the situation of America, and you will find there are thousands and thousands of contracts, whereof equity forbids an exact literal performance. Pass that government, and you will be bound hand and foot. There was an immense quantity of depreciated Continental paper money in circulation at the conclusion of the war. This money is in the hands of individuals to this day. The holders of this money may call for the nominal value, if this government were adopted. This state may be compelled to pay her proportion of that currency, pound for pound. Pass this government, and you will be carried to the federal court, (if I understand that paper right,) and you will be compelled to pay shilling for shilling. I doubt on the subject; at least, as a public man, I ought to have doubts. A state may be sued in the federal court, by the paper on your table.[62]

The next member of the Convention that commented on the issue seems to have agreed with Henry that citizens of another state or foreigners could sue the states in federal courts. However, he reached a different conclusion with respect to the specific issue of the debts owed by the states. George Nicholas, a federalist, attempted to assuage Henry's fears by stating that under Article 6 of the Constitution, payment of such money depended on the will of Congress, just as it did under the Articles of Confederation.[63] Therefore, in order for people to recover the full value of the money, they would have to sue Congress.

Can the supreme legislature be sued in their own subordinate courts, by their own citizens, in cases where they are not a party? They may be plaintiffs, but not defendants. But the individual states, perhaps, may be sued. Pennsylvania or Virginia may be sued. How is this? Do I owe the man in New England any thing? Does Virginia owe any thing to the Pennsylvanian holder of such money? Who promised to pay it? Congress, sir. Congress are answerable to the individual holders of this money, and individuals are answerable over to Congress. Therefore, no individual can call on any state.[64]

When the Convention continued its discussion of the judiciary article the next day, Edmund Pendleton, a federalist and the President of the Convention, praised Article 3's grant of jurisdiction. Referring to Article 3, § 2, Pendleton said, "[w]ithout entering into a distinction of all its parts, I believe it will be found that they are all cases of general and not local concern. The necessity and propriety of a federal jurisdiction, in all such cases, must strike every gentleman."[65]

Such praise elicited a strong response from anti-federalist George Mason. Mason argued that the lack of limitations on the jurisdiction of the federal courts would destroy state governments.[66] Referring specifically to disputes between a state and citizens of another state, he explained:

'To controversies between a state and the citizens of another state.' How will their jurisdiction in this case do? Let gentlemen look at the westward. Claims respecting those lands, every liquidated account, or other claim against this state, will be tried before the federal court. Is not this disgraceful? Is this state to be brought to the bar of justice like a delinquent individual? Is the sovereignty of the state to be arraigned like a culprit, or private offender? Will the states undergo this mortification? I think this power perfectly unnecessary. But let us pursue this subject farther. What is to be done if a judgment be obtained against a state? Will you issue *fieri facias*? It would be ludicrous to say that you could put the state's body in jail. How is the judgment, then, to be enforced? A power which cannot be executed ought not to be granted.[67]

Mason next turned to controversies between a state, or the citizens thereof, and foreign states, citizens, or subjects:

> There is a confusion in this case. This much, however, may be raised out of it—that a suit will be brought against Virginia. She may be sued by a foreign state. What reciprocity is there in it? In a suit between Virginia and a foreign state, is the foreign state to be bound by the decision? Is there a similar privilege given to us in foreign states? Where will you find a parallel regulation? How will the decision be enforced? Only by the *ultima ratio regum*. A dispute between a foreign citizen or subject and a Virginian cannot be tried in our own courts, but must be decided in the federal court. Is this the case in any other country? Are not men obliged to stand by the laws of the country where the disputes are? This is an innovation which is utterly unprecedented and unheard-of. Cannot we trust the state courts with disputes between a Frenchman, or an Englishman, and a citizen; or with disputes between two Frenchmen? This is disgraceful; it will annihilate your state judiciary: it will prostrate your legislature.[68]

Having voiced his opposition to the jurisdiction of the federal courts under Article 3 of the Constitution, Mason proposed an amendment providing, "that the judicial power shall extend to no case where the cause of action shall have originated before the ratification of this Constitution, except in suits for debts due to the United States, disputes between states about their territory, and disputes between persons claiming lands under grants of different states."[69] This amendment would later become part of a broader amendment, ratified by the Convention, concerning Article 3.

In an attempt to assuage the fears of the anti-federalists, James Madison, now a delegate to the Virginia convention, indicated that Article 3 did not mean what the literal reading of the language would seem to indicate regarding state suability in federal courts. He argued:

> Its jurisdiction in controversies between a state and citizens of another state is much objected to, and perhaps without reason. It is not in the power of individuals to call any state into court. The only operation it can have is that, if a state should wish to bring a suit against a citizen, it must be brought before the federal court. This will give satisfaction to individuals, as it will prevent citizens, on whom a state may have a claim, being dissatisfied with the state courts. It is a case that cannot often happen, and if it should be found improper, it will be altered. But it may be attended with good effects.
>
> But this will not go beyond the cases where they may be parties. A *femme covert* may be a citizen of another state, but cannot be a party in this court. A subject of a foreign power, having a dispute with a citizen of this state, may carry it to the federal court; but an alien enemy cannot bring suit at all. It appears to me that this can have no operation but this—to give a citizen a right to be heard in the federal courts; and if a state should condescend to be a party, this court may take cognizance of it.[70]

Madison continued:

> The next case provides for disputes between a foreign state and one of our states, should such a case ever arise; and between a citizen and a foreign citizen or subject. I do not

conceive that any controversy can ever be decided, in these courts, between an American state and a foreign state, without the consent of the parties. If they consent, provision is here made. The disputes ought to be tried by the national tribunal. This is consonant to the law of nations. Could there be a more favorable or eligible provision to avoid controversies with foreign powers? Ought it to be put in the power of a member of the Union to drag the whole community into war? As the national tribunal is to decide, justice will be done.[71]

There is some debate as to the purpose behind Madison's statement. Judge Gibbons claims that, while taken alone, Madison's quote endorses state sovereign immunity, "[i]n context, it becomes more ambiguous, since Madison had also pointed to the need for treaty enforcement and for federal tribunals to enforce treaties."[72] According to Judge Gibbons, Madison's statement could be read in only two ways. First, because Virginia's refusal to honor the Peace Treaty was common knowledge, Madison may have been saying that states can be sued without their consent only by foreign nations seeking to enforce federal treaties. The other possibility is that Madison was simply stretching the truth to persuade fence sitters to vote for ratification. However, Judge Gibbons' assessment of Madison's comments is not universally accepted. Martha Field has argued that Madison did not speak out of any political motivation and that, as such, his statements should be taken at face value. Professor Field concluded that Madison's understanding of Article 3 was that it did not allow states to be sued by either citizens of different states or those of foreign nations.[73]

Whatever Madison believed about the meaning of Article 3, and whatever his motivation for speaking as he did, it obviously did not convince the anti-federalists that the states' sovereign immunity was left intact by the Constitution. Patrick Henry replied to Madison:

As to controversies between a state and the citizens of another state, his construction of it is to me perfectly incomprehensible. He says it will seldom happen that a state has such demands on individuals. There is nothing to warrant such an assertion. But he says that the state may be plaintiff only If gentlemen pervert the most clear expressions, and the usual meaning of the language of the people, there is an end of all argument. What says the paper? That it shall have cognizance of controversies between a state and citizens of another state, without discriminating between a plaintiff and defendant. What says the honorable gentleman? The contrary—that the state can only be plaintiff. When the state is debtor, there is no reciprocity. It seems to me that gentlemen may put what construction they please on it. What is justice to be done to one party, and not to the other? If gentlemen take this liberty now, what will they not do when our rights and liberties are in their power? He said it was necessary to provide a tribunal when the case happened; though it would happen seldom. ... This is a dangerous power, which is thus instituted. For what? For things which will seldom happen; and yet because there is a possibility that the strong, energetic government may want it, it shall be produced and thrown in the general scale of power. I confess I think it dangerous.[74]

Edmund Pendleton, another prominent Virginia federalist, took a different view. Again praising the grant of jurisdiction, he stated that "[t]he impossibility of calling a sovereign state before the jurisdiction of another sovereign state, shows the propriety and necessity of vesting this tribunal with the decision of controversies to which a state shall be a party."[75]

John Marshall, who was to become the second Chief Justice of the United States, weighed in on the side of Madison's interpretation:

> With respect to disputes between *a state and the citizens of another state*, its jurisdiction has been decried with unusual vehemence. I hope that no gentleman will think that a state will be called at the bar of the federal court. Is there no such case at present? Are there not many cases in which the legislature of Virginia is a party, and yet the state is not sued? It is not rational to suppose that the sovereign power should be dragged before a court. The intent is, to enable states to recover claims of individuals residing in other states. I contend this construction is warranted by the words.[76]

Marshall also responded to Henry's claim that such jurisdiction lacks reciprocity for the citizen:

> But, say they, there will be partiality in it if a state cannot be defendant—if an individual cannot proceed to obtain judgment against a state, though he may be sued by a state. It is necessary to be so, and cannot be avoided. I see a difficulty in making a state defendant, which does not prevent its being plaintiff. If this be only what cannot be avoided, why object to the system on that account? If an individual has a just claim against any particular state, is it to be presumed that, on application to its legislature, he will not obtain satisfaction? But how could a state recover any claim from a citizen of another state, without the establishment of these tribunals?[77]

Finally, he addressed the clause granting jurisdiction over controversies between a state and foreigners:

> He objects, in the next place, to its jurisdiction in controversies between a state and a foreign state. Suppose, says he, in such a suit, a foreign state is cast; will she be bound by the decision? If a foreign state brought a suit against the commonwealth of Virginia, would she not be barred from the claim if the federal judiciary thought it unjust? The previous consent of the parties is necessary; and, as the federal judiciary will decide, each party will acquiesce. It will be the means of preventing disputes with foreign nations. On an attentive consideration of these points, I trust every part will appear satisfactory to the committee.[78]

Many scholars have criticized the interpretation given by John Marshall, arguing that it was neither an accurate statement of the meaning of Article 3, nor did it persuade his convention colleagues.[79] This they claim is demonstrated by the Virginia convention's adoption of an amendment severely limiting the jurisdiction of the federal courts and incorporating Mason's earlier proposal. Had the

Convention accepted the Madison/Marshall interpretation of Article 3, no amendment would have been necessary. The remainder of the debate over the meaning of Article 3 would seem to confirm that Madison's and Marshall's claims failed to influence their colleagues.

The very next day, June 21, the anti-federalist William Grayson disputed John Marshall's interpretation:

> A state may sue a foreign state, or a foreign state may sue one of our states. This may form a *new*, American law of nations. ... My honorable friend, whom I much respect, said that the consent of the parties must be previously obtained. I agree that the consent of foreign nations must be had before they become parties; but it is not so with our states. It is fixed in the Constitution that they shall become parties. This is not reciprocal. ... There is no reciprocity [sic] in this, that a foreign state should have a right to sue one of our states, whereas a foreign state cannot be sued without its own consent. The idea to me is monstrous and extravagant. It cannot be reduced to practice. Suppose one of our states objects to the decision; arms must be recurred to. How can *a foreign state be compelled to submit to a decision?*[80]

Later that day, the Federalist, Edmund Randolph also rejected the interpretation offered by his Federalist ally, John Marshall:

> Suppose justice was refused to be done by a particular state to another; I am not of the same opinion with the honorable gentleman. I think, whatever the law of nations may say, that any doubt respecting the construction that a state may be plaintiff, and not defendant, is taken away by the words *where a state shall be a party*. But it is objected that this is retrospective in its nature. If thoroughly considered, this objection will vanish. It is only to render valid and effective existing claims, and secure that justice, ultimately, which is to be found in every regular government. It is said to be disgraceful. What would be the disgrace? Would it not be that Virginia, after eight states had adopted the government, none of which opposed the federal jurisdiction in this case, rejected it on this account?[81]

Following the comments by Randolph and Grayson, there was no further debate or discussion of the diversity clauses in Article 3, § 2.

On June 27, the Virginia convention ratified the Constitution with a proposed bill of rights and twenty other proposed amendments attached. One, the fourteenth amendment, proposed limiting the grant of jurisdiction to the federal courts in the Constitution in cases in which the state was a party by a proviso to Art III, § 2: "but the judicial power of the United States shall extend to no case where the cause of action shall have originated before the ratification of the Constitution, except in disputes between states about their territory, disputes between persons claiming lands under the grants of different states, and suits for debts due to the United States."[82]

The debate in the Virginia Convention regarding state suitability in federal courts for diversity cases illustrates well the confusion that reigned, even among those who supported the Constitution and were involved in its drafting, over whether the states retained their sovereign immunity under the Constitution. Although James Madison and John Marshall argued that the states did retain their immunity, other federalists, most notably Edmund Randolph, argued that citizens of other states and foreigners could sue the states in federal courts without regard to the nature of the claim or whether it was founded on state law or federal law. Moreover, both Madison and Randolph were at the Philadelphia drafting convention and each had a significant role in the drafting of Article 3. Whatever confusion existed in the federalist ranks, the amendment adopted by the Convention strongly indicates that at least the majority in Virginia believed that the states did not retain their sovereign immunity under the proposed Article 3. Moreover, amendment 14, by limiting the restriction of federal jurisdiction to those claims that originated before the Constitution was ratified, supports Professor Pfander's argument that the concern for preserving state sovereign immunity was only with respect to debts incurred fighting the Revolutionary War.

New York

In New York, the issue of whether the states retained their sovereign immunity under the proposed Constitution received attention both inside and outside the ratifying convention. Outside the convention, anti-federalist publications criticized Article 3 because it subjected states to suits by citizens of other states and foreigners, while *The Federalist Papers* seemed to claim that a state could not be sued by an individual without the state's consent. The actions of the delegates at New York's ratifying convention indicate that they were equally divided on this issue, making it very difficult to determine what powers the New York Convention believed Article 3 bestowed on the federal court system.

On the anti-federalist side there were two main publications in New York prior to the state's ratification of the Constitution, *The Letters of "Brutus"* and *The Observations of the Federal Farmer*. Both were widely published and read in New York during the debates over ratification. *The Letters of "Brutus"* were published in the newspaper *New York Journal and Weekly Register*.[83] *The Observations of the Federal Farmer* were printed as a whole series only by the newspaper *Poughkeepsie Country Journal*. However they were extremely popular in pamphlet form.[84] Both anti-federalist publications argued that dire consequences would arise from Article 3's apparently allowing citizens of other states and foreigners to sue the states in United States' courts.

Letter No. XIII, written on February 21, 1788, discussed § 2 of Article 3 of the proposed Constitution, giving special attention to the clause-granting jurisdiction in controversies between a state and citizens of other states:

> But, I conceive the clause, which extends the power of the [judiciary] to controversies between a state and citizens of another state, improper in itself, and will, in its exercise,

prove most pernicious and destructive. It is improper, because it subjects a state to answer in a court of law, to the suit of an individual. This is humiliating and degrading to a government and, what I believe the supreme authority of no state ever submitted to. The states are now subject to no such actions. All contracts entered into by individuals with states were made upon the faith and credit of the states; and the individuals never had in contemplation any compulsory mode of obliging the government to fulfill its engagements. The evil consequences that will flow from the exercise of this power will best appear by tracing it in its operation.[85]

The letter continues:

When a citizen of another state becomes possessed of one of these [state obligations], he may commence an action in the Supreme Court of the general government; and I cannot see any way in which he can be prevented from recovering. It is easy to see that when this once happens, the notes of the state will pass rapidly from the hands of citizens of the state to those of other states. And when the citizens of other states possess them, they may bring suits against the state for them, and by this means, judgments and executions may be obtained against the state for the whole amount of the state debt.[86]

The letter concludes by stating that, "if the power of the [judiciary] under this clause will extend the cases above stated, it will, if executed, produce the utmost confusion, and in its progress, will crush the states beneath its weight. And if it does not extend to these cases, I confess myself utterly at a loss to give it any meaning."[87]

In *Essay III*, of *The Observations of the Federal Farmer*, written on October 10, 1787, the author, among other things, identifies "...those powers, the exercise of which is not secured on safe and proper ground."[88] Among those powers was jurisdiction over controversies between a state and citizens of another state and foreigners:

How far it may be proper to admit a foreigner or the citizen of another state to bring actions against state governments, which have failed in performing so many promises made during the war, is doubtful: How far it may be proper so to humble a state, as to oblige it to answer to an individual in a court of law, is worthy of consideration: the states are now subject to no such actions; and this new jurisdiction will subject the states, and many defendants to actions, and processes, which were not in the contemplation of the parties, when the contract was made; all engagements existing between citizens of different states, citizens and foreigners, states and foreigners; and states and citizens of other states were made the parties contemplating the remedies then existing on the laws of the states—and the new remedy proposed to be given in the federal courts, can be founded on no principle whatever.[89]

The Federalist Papers, published by James Madison, John Jay, and Alexander Hamilton, under the pseudonym of "Publius," were designed to rebut the anti-federalist writings. *Federalist Nos. 78–83*, penned by Alexander Hamilton, were devoted to the judiciary. On the question of state suability, Hamilton managed to give conflicting arguments. In *Federalist No. 80*, he claimed that the jurisdiction of the federal courts should extend "...to all those [cases] which involve the PEACE of the CONFEDERACY...."[90] In defining those cases, Hamilton concluded that the United States will be "answerable" to any foreign powers for the actions of any of the states. As a result, the federal government should possess the power to prevent or fix any injury suffered by a foreign power at the hands of an individual state.[91] In order to allow the federal government this ability, Hamilton argued that all cases involving foreigners should be in the federal courts.[92] *Federalist No. 80* thus advocates that federal courts hear all cases between a state and foreign states and foreign citizens.

Federalist No. 80 also addresses the question of jurisdiction in cases between a state and citizens of another state. Referring to his discussion of jurisdiction over cases involving foreign powers and subjects, Hamilton stated, "[t]he power of determining causes between two States, between one State and the citizens of another, and between the citizens of different States, is perhaps not less essential to the peace of the Union than that which has been just examined."[93] In order to ensure this peace, the citizens of each state should be entitled to the same privileges and immunities as the citizens of all the states. The federal government could achieve this, according to Hamilton by permitting:

> The national judiciary . . . to preside in all cases in which one State or its citizens are opposed to another State or its citizens. To secure the full effect of so fundamental a provision against all evasion and subterfuge, it is necessary that its construction should be committed to that tribunal which, having no local attachments, will be likely to be impartial between the different States and their citizens and which, owing its official existence to the Union, will never be likely to feel any bias inauspicious to the principles on which it is founded.[94]

Thus, *Federalist No. 80* both acknowledges and praises Article 3's rejection of the states' sovereign immunity.

In *Federalist No. 81*, however, Hamilton takes the opposite position, that the Constitution does not abrogate the states' sovereign immunity. Here, Hamilton echoes the arguments James Madison and John Marshall made at the Virginia convention:

> Though it may rather be a digression from the immediate subject of this paper, I shall take occasion to mention here a supposition which has excited some alarm upon very mistaken grounds. It has been suggested that an assignment of the public securities of one State to the citizens of another would enable them to prosecute that State in the federal courts for the amount of those securities: a suggestion which the following considerations prove to be without foundation.

> It is inherent in the nature of sovereignty not to be amenable to the suit of an individual *without its consent*. This is the general sense and the general practice of mankind; and the government of every State in the Union now enjoys the exemption, as one of the attributes of sovereignty. Unless, therefore, there is a surrender of this immunity in the plan of the convention, it will remain with the States and the danger intimated must be merely ideal. The circumstances, which are necessary to produce an alienation of State sovereignty, were discussed in considering the article of taxation and need not be repeated here. A recurrence to the principles there established will satisfy us that there is no color to pretend that the State governments would, by the adoption of that plan, be divested of the privilege of paying their own debts in their own way, free from every constraint but that which flows from the obligations of good faith. The contracts between a nation and individuals are only binding on the conscience of the sovereign, and have no pretensions to a compulsive force. They confer no right of action independent of the sovereign will. To what purpose would it be to authorize suits against States for the debts they owe? How could recoveries be enforced?[95]

Not surprisingly, the conflicting language in *Federalist Nos. 80 and 81* have confused attempts to determine whether the New York Ratification Convention believed that Article 3 permitted citizens of one state or foreigners could sue another state in federal court.[96] The records of the Convention do not indicate that the questions of state sovereign immunity, and whether citizens of other states or foreigners could sue a state were formally debated. Yet, there is no doubt that both questions received some attention. On July 5, 1788, Samuel Jones submitted several resolutions to be adopted as amendments to the Constitution. The fourth amendment dealt with the issue of state sovereign immunity: "'*Resolved*, as the opinion of this committee, that nothing in the Constitution now under consideration contained, is to be construed to authorize any suit to be brought against any state, in any manner what ever.'"[97] There is no record indicating what happened to this proposed amendment. However, we do know that on July 26, the New York convention, by a vote of thirty to twenty-seven, ratified the Constitution.[98] Attached to the Constitution were several recommended amendments and a declaration of understanding. Among the various amendments was one that stated, "[t]hat the Judicial Power of the United States in cases in which a State may be a party, does not extend to criminal Prosecutions, *or to authorize any Suit by any Person against a State*."[99] Alfred Hill argues that the purpose of the amendment was explanatory only. Its only purpose was "to remove all doubt or controversies respecting the [issue]."[100] One can undoubtedly read the amendment in that way. Certainly the Tenth Amendment, as interpreted by the Court, simply reflects the general understanding that states retain the powers not granted to the federal government. United States v. Darby, (1941). On the other hand, those few words do not explain the vehemence with which *Brutus* and the *Federal Farmer* attacked Article 3's grant of jurisdiction to the federal courts when the state is a party. Nor does it explain Samuel Jones' earlier amendment, which certainly did not read as merely a confirmation of what was generally agreed upon. There is thus some room for reasonable people to differ about the Convention's consensus regarding whether the states' sovereign immunity survived Article 3.

North Carolina and Rhode Island

Two things set North Carolina and Rhode Island apart from the other states. First, they were the only two that chose not to send delegates to the Constitutional Convention in Philadelphia. Hence, neither had any say in what the text of the original document contained nor did they have any direct evidence as to what the text meant. Second, both waited until the last minute to consider ratifying the Constitution.

By the time the North Carolina Ratification Convention was held, eleven states had already ratified the Constitution, including Virginia and New York. The Constitution had, in other words, been ratified. But that did not in any way dissuade the anti-federalists from mounting a strong campaign of opposition to the Constitution. Anti-federalist sentiment was so strong that the Convention, by a large majority, "thought proper neither to ratify nor reject the Constitution...."[101] Judge Gibbons reports that a number of comments regarding Article 3 were made at the Ratification Convention.[102] However, the official records of the convention reported only one comment concerning the diversity clauses. On July 29, 1788, William Davie, a federalist, noted: "It has been equally ceded, by the strongest opposers to this government, that the federal courts should have cognizance of controversies between two or more states, between a state and the citizens of another state, and between the citizens of the same state claiming lands under the grant of different states. Its jurisdiction in these cases is necessary to secure impartiality in decisions, and preserve tranquility among the states."[103] There is no recorded response to Davie's comment, nor is it possible to discover which, if any, prior speeches Davie is referring to that "ceded" this.

Prior to the final decision of the Convention to neither ratify nor reject the Constitution, a proposal was made to attach to the Constitution a declaration of rights and twenty-six other amendments. Two of these amendments dealt with the issue of whether a citizen of one state or a foreigner could sue another state in federal court. One amendment, identical to the one proposed by the Virginia convention,[104] removed the federal courts' jurisdiction over cases between a state and citizens of another state and foreigners. It also removed federal jurisdiction over all matters whose cause of action arose before the Constitution. The second amendment dealt directly with the state's fear that the federal courts would be used by out-of-state creditors to collect the state's Revolutionary War debts:

That Congress shall not, directly or indirectly, either by themselves or though the judiciary, interfere with any one of the states in the redemption of paper money already emitted and now in circulation, or in liquidating and discharging the public securities of any one of the states, but each and every state shall have the exclusive right of making such laws and regulations for the above purposes as they shall think proper.[105]

Both amendments passed overwhelmingly, indicating that the North Carolina convention believed that Article 3, as drafted and submitted, abrogated North Carolina's sovereign immunity.[106]

Rhode Island did not hold its ratifying convention until 1790. The sparse records from this convention do not indicate that any discussion or debate took place concerning whether a citizen of one state or foreigner could sue another state in federal court. The convention did, however, recommend twenty-one amendments and a declaration of rights when it ratified the Constitution, one of which dealt explicitly with the issue of state sovereign immunity:

It is declared by the Convention, that the judicial power of the United States, in cases in which a state may be a party, does not extend to criminal prosecutions, or to authorize any suit by any person against a State; but to remove all doubts or controversies respecting the same, that it be especially expressed as a part of the constitution of the United States, that Congress shall not directly or indirectly, either by themselves or through the judiciary, interfere with any one of the states, in the redemption of paper money already emitted and now in circulation, or in liquidating or discharging the public securities of any one state: that each and every state shall have the exclusive right of making such laws and regulations for the before mentioned purpose, as they shall think proper.[107]

If the Rhode Island convention had agreed with the Madisonian interpretation of Article 3 as it was expressed at the Virginia convention (that citizens of other states or foreigners under the Constitution could not sue states in federal court), the first part of this amendment would have been unnecessary. Moreover, the second part of the amendment, taken from the twenty-fifth amendment proposed by the North Carolina convention, clearly indicates that the Rhode Island convention, like North Carolina and New York, believed Article 3, § 2, removed the states' sovereign immunity in suits over which the federal courts had jurisdiction.

Nevertheless, we can conclude very little regarding whether a majority of states, let alone a majority of delegates to the various state ratifying conventions, believed the Constitution allowed suits against the states by citizens of other states or foreigners. Perhaps the best and only accurate observation that can be made about the state ratification process, and what it illustrates regarding the Constitution's impact on state sovereign immunity, was made by Martha Field when she wrote that existing evidence on the ratification process, "supports, at least, a lack of consensus,"[108] but that "in weight of numbers, the anti-immunity comments clearly prevail."[109]

From the Convention to the Eleventh Amendment: The Judiciary Act of 1789, the Supreme Court, and the Eleventh Amendment

THE JUDICIARY ACT OF 1789

Article 3 of the Constitution creates only one court, the United States Supreme Court. The Constitution empowers Congress to establish and define the jurisdiction of all lower courts, those we now know as District Courts and Circuit Courts of Appeal (referred to in Article 3 as "inferior Courts").[110] Regarding the jurisdiction of the Supreme Court, Article 3 grants it the power to hear two categories of cases as an original matter (as if it were a trial court), what Article 3 describes as original jurisdiction. These are "Cases affecting Ambassadors, other Public Ministers and Counsels and *those in which a State shall be a Party*." [111] The Supreme Court's appellate jurisdiction (the power to review decisions of lower federal or state courts) is granted only, "with such Exceptions, and under such Regulations as the Congress shall make."[112]

Congress was thus given the primary responsibility of structuring the federal judiciary, including creating lower federal courts and defining their jurisdiction, as well as defining the appellate jurisdiction of the Supreme Court. The first Congress wasted no time in tackling this task. On April 7, 1789, the Senate appointed a committee to draft a judiciary bill. The committee consisted of people who had actively participated either in the Constitutional Convention or in the ratification conventions in their respective states, or both. Included among their numbers were Oliver Ellsworth of Connecticut, William Paterson of New Jersey, Caleb Strong of Massachusetts, and Richard Henry Lee of Virginia.[113] Indeed, the Massachusetts federalist, Caleb Strong, had the distinction of not only being an active participant in the Massachusetts ratification debates *and* a member of the committee that drafted the Judiciary Act, but was also instrumental in drafting the language of the Eleventh Amendment that was enacted to overturn the Supreme Court's first interpretation of Article 3. (Chisholm v. Georgia, 1793)

There is little question that those in the First Congress believed that the judicial power of the United States courts extended to cases in which a state was a defendant. An early draft of the Judiciary Act provided that the Supreme Court shall have original, but not exclusive jurisdiction over civil cases "between a State and its Citizens and...a State and the Citizens of other States or Foreigners...."[114] A bill with essentially the same language was reported to the Senate on June 12, 1789, and passed five days later, on June 17, by a vote of fourteen to six. As far as we know, there was no debate in the Senate on the portion of the bill that gave the Supreme Court original, nonexclusive jurisdiction over suits in which a state was one party and a citizen of another state or a foreigner was the other party.[115] Likewise, there is also no record of debate in the House of Representatives on this portion of the bill.[116] The final bill, which was signed into law by President Washington on September 24, 1789,[117] read much like the early Senate draft quoted by Caleb Strong to Robert Trent Paine: "[T]he Supreme Court shall have exclusive jurisdiction of all controversies of a civil nature, where a state is a party, except between a state and its citizens; and except also between a state and citizens of other states, or aliens, in which latter case it shall have original but not exclusive jurisdiction."[118] In other words, cases in which a state was one party and the other party was one of its citizens, a citizen of another state, or a citizen of a foreign country, could be brought either directly in the Supreme Court of the United States, in a lower federal court, or in a state court. However, like the Constitutional Convention and the ratification debates, the Judiciary Act of 1789 was not explicit about whether the authors of the Act understood its language to extend the jurisdiction of the United States courts to *all* cases in which a state was a party, or only those cases in which the state was a plaintiff or had consented to become a defendant.[119] The Supreme Court cleared up this confusion in 1793.

THE SUPREME COURT AND STATE SUABILITY

Between the adoption of the Judiciary Act of 1787 and January 8, 1798, the date on which the Eleventh Amendment became effective,[120] seven suits were instituted *against* states in the United States Supreme Court.[121] The facts of all seven cases are similar. First, all involved activities that occurred or debts that were contracted prior to the adoption of the Constitution. This fact is highly important to those who believe that the Eleventh Amendment was only a "declaratory" or "explanatory" amendment, which reaffirmed that the Constitution left to the states the authority to dispose of their pre-Constitution debts as they saw fit, subject only to the federal government's discretionary ability to assume those debts on behalf of the states.[122] Second, all were filed directly in the Supreme Court, invoking its original jurisdiction. Thus, all fell directly within the language of the Judiciary Act cited previously.[123] Finally, in all but the first case filed, Vanstophorst v. Maryland (1791), the state did not defend on the merits but rather objected to the Court's attempt to exercise jurisdiction over them.[124]

The most well known of all of these cases, and the one that prompted Congress to enact the Eleventh Amendment, is Chisholm v. Georgia (1793). Alexander Chisholm was the executor of the estate of Robert Farquhar, a South Carolina merchant who had sold clothing and blankets to the Georgia militia and for which he claimed never to have received payment.[125] A petition had been presented to the Georgia legislature in 1789 to pay the claim, but Georgia refused on the ground that payment had already been made to agents of Farquhar. The state argued that the appropriate remedy, therefore, was to sue the agents who had apparently absconded with the payment. Unfortunately, one of the agents (a man named Davis) had died insolvent and the other, while still alive, was also apparently insolvent.[126] Chisholm therefore chose to pursue his claim against the state of Georgia.

When the suit was actually instituted in the Supreme Court is a bit unclear, but summons was issued on February 8, 1792, commanding that the state of Georgia appear to answer the complaint. The summons was served on the Governor and the Attorney General on July 11.[127] The hearing on the case was convened on August 11, 1792, Chisholm being represented in the Supreme Court by attorney John Hallowell and Edmund Randolph, the Attorney General of the United States. Georgia chose not to file an appearance. Randolph requested that the Court issue a default judgment against Georgia if it did not either appear or show cause why it should not appear. The hearing was continued until February 4, 1793. When Georgia did not appear on that date, the Court set the matter down for argument the next day, February 5. Attorney General Randolph argued his motion for a default judgment for two and one-half hours with not a soul arguing on behalf of Georgia, even after the Court invited *any* attorney present to say something on the State's behalf. The Court announced its decision on February 19, 1793.[128]

The major issue before the Court, and that to which Attorney General Randolph devoted most of his argument was, "[c]an the State of *Georgia*, being one of the *United States of America,* be made a party-defendant *in any case*, in the Supreme Court of the United States, at the suit of a private citizen, even though he himself is, as his testator was, a citizen of *South Carolina*?"[129] Randolph's argument was founded on the text of the Constitution and on the Judiciary Act of 1789, both of which gave the Supreme Court jurisdiction over cases in which the state was a party. The issue that the Court had to consider was whether there was anything that might prevent the clear language of both the Constitution and the Judiciary Act from including cases in which a state was, against its will, a defendant.

Randolph made four points in support of his argument that the Court should ely on the plain language of Article 3 and the Judiciary Act. First, the Constitution places numerous prohibitions on states. They cannot, for example, enact bills of attainder and ex post facto laws, enter into treaties or alliances, or coin money. These restrictions on state authority could not be fully enforced if states could not be made defendants. Second, while the states are sovereign, they freely entered into a union that was defined by a Constitution that abrogated this sovereignty in certain particular cases. Further, the Constitution was derived from the people, the states being only, "assemblages of these individuals" (a profoundly federalist argument). There was thus, "nothing in the nature of sovereignties, combined as those of America are, to prevent the words of the Constitution...from receiving an easy and usual construction." Third, allowing an individual to sue a state other than the state of her residency in federal court is necessary to avoid disruption of domestic tranquility and international peace by providing a judicial remedy where none would exist otherwise.[130] Finally, in response to the claim that since the Court has not been given any power to enforce a judgment against a state when it is sued by an individual, jurisdiction should not be implied, Randolph argued that no method of enforcement was granted even when jurisdiction over a state was made explicit, such as in an action by one state against another.

Four of the five Justices agreed with Randolph's arguments regarding the Court's ability to exercise jurisdiction when a state is sued by a citizen of another state or of a foreign country. Of the four who wrote to affirm the Court's jurisdiction over states as defendants under the citizen-diversity clause, two relied solely on the text of Article 3. Justice John Blair noted that the judicial authority of the United States is "expressly extended" to controversies between a state and citizens of another state. And "[a] dispute between A and B is surely a dispute between B and A. Both cases . . . were intended . . . ." Moreover, Justice Blair argued, because the state must be a party defendant in controversies between two or more states, there is no reason in the language of the Constitution to conclude that the same should not be true when the other party is a citizen of another state or a foreign jurisdiction. Justice William Cushing reached the same conclusion for essentially the same reasons. In addition, Justice Cushing responded to the sovereignty argument, essentially agreeing with Attorney General Randolph's first argument: The Constitution places many restrictions on states that lessen their sovereignty in an attempt to establish some "fundamental uniform principles of public justice, throughout the whole *Union*."

Justice James Wilson and Chief Justice John Jay were more far-reaching in their opinions. Both mounted a full frontal attack on the argument that the states retained any sovereign immunity after they ratified the Constitution. The Chief Justice began his opinion by asking, "[I]n what sense *Georgia* is a sovereign state?" In forming the Constitution, "...the people exercised their own rights and their own proper sovereignty...," and while acting as sovereigns, the people established "...a Constitution by which it was their will, that the State Governments should be bound...." "[T]he sovereignty of the nation is in the people of the nation and the residuary sovereignty of each State in the people of each State." With regard to suability, Chief Justice Jay argued that because a state may be sued by another state, *suability* and *state sovereignty* are not incompatible. Thus, Georgia's objection is not to its appearance in the Supreme Court against its will, but that it is there at the behest of one or more citizens of a different state. However, because it is the people who, under our system of government, are sovereign, a suit against another state is actually a suit by all citizens of one state against all the citizens of the other. Hence, the distinction between one citizen of a state suing all of the citizens of another state and all of the citizens of one state suing all of the citizens of another is one of degree only and should make no legal difference.

Finally, the Chief Justice looked to the language and structure of the Constitution itself and determined that the language of Article 3 should be interpreted as granting federal courts jurisdiction over cases between states and citizens of other states and foreign countries. Article 3 was an attempt to right the wrongs of the judicial process under the Articles of Confederation. Prior to the Constitution, the citizens of each state were at the mercy of the justice system of other states, with no recourse to a neutral tribunal. Moreover the nation, while responsible to foreign governments for the acts of the several states, was unable to adjudicate disputes between those states and foreign governments except in the courts of the disputant state. "These were among the evils against which it was proper for the nation, that is, the people of all the *United States*, to provide a national judiciary...." Chief Justice Jay then turned the sovereignty argument on its head: "The exception contended for, would contradict and do violence to the great and leading principles of a free and equal national government, one of the objects of which is, to ensure justice to all; to the few against the many, as well as to the many against the few." Chief Justice Jay, however, stopped short of giving a ringing endorsement to Chisholm's claim. "I am clearly of the opinion, that a State is suable by citizens of another State; but...I am far from being prepared to say that an individual may sue a State on bills of credit issued before the Constitution was established, and which were issued and received on the faith of the State, and at a time when no ideas or expectations of judicial interposition were entertained or contemplated." The Chief Justice's reluctance to permit recovery for pre-Constitutional debts in federal courts, despite the language of Article 3, supports James Pfander's interpretation of the Eleventh Amendment as applying only to those claims. As noted previously, it also reflects the concerns that prompted a number of proposed amendments to Article 3 enacted by the Virginia, North Carolina, and Rhode Island ratifying conventions.

Justice James Wilson was, if anything, more emphatic and less measured than Chief Justice Jay regarding the states' lack of sovereign immunity after 1787.[131] Relying on what he termed, "principles of general jurisprudence," Wilson analogized the state to a corporation, an artificial entity that had the ability to acquire property in its own name, make rules for the benefit of its members, etc. But "for something to be a sovereign it must have subjects, but the Constitution only speaks in terms of citizens and only uses the term subjects to refer to members of foreign countries." In the United States, he concluded, states are not sovereign. They are merely the servants of the true sovereigns, the free man. The states, in other words, are the subjects of the people, and not the other way around. Relying on the structural principles underlying the Constitution, Justice Wilson concluded that the Constitution was intended *by the people* to bind the states by the judicial power of the United States, as much as by the legislative and executive power. "The declared objects of the Constitution show that the Constitution was intended to vest the Supreme Court with jurisdiction over the states, because such power in the judicial branch is essential for the achievement of such objectives."

Justice James Iredell, whose opinion was relied on ninety-seven years later by the majority in Hans v. Louisiana (1890), was the only Justice to conclude that the Supreme Court had no jurisdiction to impose monetary liability on the state of Georgia. But in doing so, he did not rely on constitutional grounds as did the other Justices, but instead he grounded his reasoning in the common law. Justice Iredell argued that the Judiciary Act of 1789 only allows the Court to issue writs (over-simplified, orders) necessary for the exercise of its jurisdiction that are "agreeable to the principles and usages of law." Since there are no such principles of the particular laws of the states that affect this case, "[t]he only principles of law...that can be regarded, are those common to all the States." The only common law principles existing in the states are English common law principles that apply to suits against the Crown and, according to these principles, a suit against the Crown could only be maintained through a petition of right; that is, with the Crown's consent. The Judiciary Act therefore permits suits against the states only with their consent. Justice Iredell mentioned the Constitution only in passing: "[s]o much, however, has been said on the Constitution, that it may not be improper to intimate that my present opinion is strongly against any construction of it, which will admit, under any circumstances, a compulsive suit against a State for the recovery of money. This opinion I hold, however...may be deemed in some measure extra-judicial."

While Chisholm v. Georgia sparked the Eleventh Amendment, it was not the only source of states' concern regarding their sovereign immunity. Virginia and Massachusetts enacted resolutions as a result of two cases that were similar to *Chisholm*; Grayson v. Virginia (1796) and Vassal v. Massachusetts (1793).[132] *Grayson* involved a land dispute between the state of Virginia, which had declared the disputed land public domain, and the Indiana Company (most of whose shareholders were residents of Pennsylvania), which claimed the same land under a grant from England. England, in turn, claimed the land under a 1768 treaty between England and several Indian tribes to cover the damages suffered by England as a result of an Indian raid.[133] When Virginia began selling the land, the Indiana Company petitioned the Virginia legislature to recognize its claim. The Indiana Company also sought redress from the Continental Congress. Failing in both efforts, seventy shareholders of the Indiana Company filed suit in the United States Supreme Court seeking the value of the land or, in the alternative, the value of the property destroyed by the Indians.[134] Shortly after the suit was commenced, the Virginia legislature, with no opposition, passed two resolutions: (1) that the Court could not exercise jurisdiction over the states in suits by individuals because such jurisdiction, "is incompatible with, and dangerous to the sovereignty and independence of the individual states....," and (2) instructing Virginia's United States Senators and Representatives to obtain constitutional amendments that would prohibit the federal courts from having jurisdiction in such cases.[135]

Vassal v. Massachusetts, decided just days after the Court affirmed its jurisdiction in Chisholm v. Georgia, was a challenge to the state's confiscation of the property of a British loyalist, Vassal, who had fled to England at the beginning of the revolution. When Governor John Hancock (*the* John Hancock) was served with a summons in the case, he called for a special session of the Massachusetts General Court (the legislature), which convened on September 18, 1793.[136] In his address, Governor Hancock denied that when Massachusetts adopted the Constitution it understood Article 3 § 2 to mean that a state could be held liable to answer, "to every resident in another State, or in a foreign kingdom. It is true, that States, kingdoms and Empires ought to do justice; but it is as true, that there are certain inherent principles in the Constitution of each, which can never be surrendered, without essentially changing the nature, or destroying the existence of the Government."[137] On September 27, the General Court passed a two-part resolution that more or less mirrored that enacted by Virginia. The first part called upon Massachusetts Senators and Representatives, "to obtain such amendments in the Constitution...as will remove any clause or article of the said Constitution which can be construed to imply or justify a decision that a State is compellable to answer in any suit by an individual or individuals in any Court of the United States."[138] The second part asserted that the exercise of judicial power by the federal government requiring a state to be a defendant at the suit of an individual was dangerous and contrary to the independence of the states and the principles of the federal government.[139]

New York raised similar objections to the Court's jurisdiction when it was sued by the widow of one John Holt for wages owed but never paid for Holt's services as state printer (Oswald v. New York, 1792, 1793). The state argued that as a "free, sovereign, and independent" state, it could not be forced against its will to appear before the Supreme Court.[140] New York's Governor, George Clinton, in a speech before a joint session of the New York legislature on January 8, 1794, underscored the threat to New York's sovereignty that *Oswald* posed:

Among many other important matters, which will occupy your deliberations, are certain resolutions of the Legislature of Massachusetts and Virginia, respecting the suability of a state: which are submitted to you at the request of the executives of those commonwealths. The decision of the Supreme Federal Court which gave rise to these resolves, involves so essentially the sovereignty of each state, that no observations on my part can be necessary to be speak your early attention to the subject matter of them.... To you, therefore, it will belong to pursue such measures as the occasion may require, consistent with the constitution of the United States, and best corresponding with our own sovereignty, and the general welfare of the Union.[141]

Interestingly, the New York State assembly defeated three resolutions proposed by the New York Senate: (1) directing the Attorney General to appear in such cases and argue the jurisdiction of the Court, but not the merits of the case; (2) instructing the Attorney General to make the best possible defense available on the merits; and (3) calling for an amendment to the Constitution barring cases by nonresident citizens or foreigners against states. However, it should be noted that the latter of these resolutions was apparently rejected because the United States Senate had, by this time, approved what was later ratified as the Eleventh Amendment.[142]

Does this tell us anything about whether those New York and Virginia delegates who debated and ratified the Constitution believed that the states waived their sovereign immunity? Intuitively the answer appears to be that sovereign immunity was not waived. Why else would New York and Virginia have reacted so in the way they did only a few years after its delegates voted for ratification? On the other hand, it is difficult to glean A's intent from how B reacted to a different stimulus at a different time. This is particularly true when individuals currently reacting are the Governor and the legislators (Governors John Hancock and George Clinton were unabashed anti-federalists), both of whom are dependent upon the electoral process and public opinion for the maintenance of their office. Electoral politics creates incentives that do not exist when individuals are given a singular task and no continuing responsibility once that task is completed.

CONGRESSIONAL REACTION

Congressional reaction to Chisholm v. Georgia was swift. On February 20, 1793, only two days after the Supreme Court's decision, a resolution was introduced in the Senate to amend the Constitution. The resolution prohibited the exercise of federal jurisdiction over any claim whatsoever asserted against one of the United States: "The Judicial power of the United States shall not extend to any suits in law or equity, commenced or prosecuted against one of the United States by citizens of another State, or by citizens or subjects of any foreign state."[143] Because the Congressional term expired, that resolution was never voted upon.[144]

The next Congress agreed to the Eleventh Amendment, but only after several amendments to its proposed form were rejected. These amendments may shed some light on how broadly or narrowly the enacting Congress intended the Eleventh Amendment to be interpreted. On January 2, 1794, a resolution to amend the Constitution was introduced in the Senate. This resolution reintroduced the February 20, 1793 amendment with one exception, the insertion of the words *"shall not be construed to"* extend, etc.: "The Judicial power of the United Sates shall not be construed to extend to any suit in law or equity, commenced, or prosecuted against on of the United States by citizens of another State, or by citizens or subjects of any foreign state."[145] Debate on this resolution began in earnest on January 14. Senator Gallatin proposed the first amendment to the resolution, making an exception to permit federal jurisdiction against states in "cases arising under the treaties made under the authority of the United States." This motion failed. A second amendment to limit the proposed amendment to those cases in which "the cause of action shall have arisen before the ratification of this amendment" also failed. The resolution as introduced was then passed by a vote of twenty-three to two.[146]

Debate on the Senate's resolution began in the House of Representatives on March 4, 1794. There was only one proposed amendment, prohibiting federal jurisdiction only in cases where the state had not, "previously made provision in their own Courts, whereby such suit may be prosecuted to effect." The amendment was rejected, seventy-seven to eight.[147] The House then voted ninety-one to nine to concur with the Senate resolution.[148]

All three proposed amendments were designed to be narrow exceptions to what eventually became the Eleventh Amendment. Their rejection certainly points to a Congress determined to recognize a broad sovereign immunity exception to Article 3. But it is somewhat problematic to base an interpretation of constitutional (or statutory) text on what the body proposing that text rejected by way of modifications. The fact of rejection tells us very little about the beliefs individual members of Congress harbored regarding the Eleventh Amendment. Various motives could have inspired individual votes: support for a broad exception to federal jurisdiction, objection to the particular exception, the desire for a broader exception, the belief that the exception was not needed because it was already implicit in the original resolution, or a host of political factors. Since there is no officially recorded debate on these amendments, one can only guess at why each was rejected. Some theories, however, have been suggested. Carlos Manuel Vázquez, a proponent of a broad sovereign immunity reading of the Eleventh Amendment, has argued that the House's rejection of the amendment suggests that the Eleventh Amendment was designed to do more than protect states from being forced to defend claims in federal court. Professor Vázquez maintains that it was meant to prohibit any federal attempt to even indirectly induce states to create causes of actions in their own courts.[149] On the other hand, James Pfander, a proponent of a narrower interpretation of the Eleventh Amendment, views the rejection of Senator Gallatin's amendment, which permitted claims under treaties to be heard in federal courts, as an indication that Congress merely wanted to abolish diversity jurisdiction where the state is a party. Further, Professor Pfander opines, the rejection by the Senate of the other amendment, which would have only foreclosed pre-Constitution claims, suggests that Congress recognized that states were suable in United States courts when the claim was based on federal law and that it desired to protect that avenue of redress in the future.[150] The congressional history of the adoption of the Eleventh Amendment thus leaves the breadth of sovereign immunity afforded the states by the Eleventh Amendment, and the extent to which, if at all, Congress has the legislative authority to abrogate this immunity, without any clear evidence one way or the other.

THE SUPREME COURT AGAIN—ONE MORE BIT OF HISTORICAL EVIDENCE

When President Adams proclaimed the Eleventh Amendment to have been ratified, four of the seven cases filed between 1789 and 1798 against states by individual creditors were still awaiting final judgment: Grayson v. Virginia, (1796) [also titled Hollingsworth v. Virginia (referred to here as Hollingsworth v. Virginia) and Indiana Company v. Virginia], Vassal v. Massachusetts (1793), Cutting v. South Carolina (1797) and Moultrie v. Georgia (1797).[151] Quite naturally, the question arose whether the Eleventh Amendment would be applied retroactively to those cases filed before and still pending at its adoption. In Hollingsworth v. Virginia, the Court unanimously held that the Eleventh Amendment required the dismissal of all four cases. The plaintiffs argued that to interpret the Eleventh Amendment retroactively would give it the quality of an ex post facto law, which violated the "spirit of the Constitution." The Court clearly did not agree. More pertinent to the interpretation of the Eleventh Amendment is one statement of United States Attorney General Charles Lee, who, when arguing that the Eleventh Amendment should be applied retroactively to pending cases, very simply stated that "[t]he amendment, in the present instance, is merely explanatory, in substance, as well as language." In other words, the Constitution always meant what the Eleventh Amendment now states—federal courts have no jurisdiction to hear cases filed against states by individuals. It does not therefore work an ex post deprivation of jurisdiction.

The extent to which the Court accepted Lee's explanation of the Eleventh Amendment is impossible to determine since the Court did not issue an opinion, only a decree denying its jurisdiction with respect to both past and future cases. However, Hollingsworth, unlike Chisholm, was not simply an ordinary creditor asserting a claim against Virginia for its failure to live up to its promise to pay its notes. Rather, his claim was based on a chain of title from the British Crown that was part of implementing the peace treaty with Britain. The claim was thus based on federal law, the Jay Treaty. An argument might be advanced that when the

Court issued the decree in *Hollingsworth* it held that the Eleventh Amendment was more than an exception to Article 3's diversity jurisdiction; it was an affirmation of a broader notion of state sovereign immunity, thus justifying the holding ninety years later in Hans v. Louisiana.[152]

NOTES

1. Carlos Manuel Vázquez, "What is Eleventh Amendment Immunity," 106 *Yale Law J.* (1997) 1683,1700–01.
2. Martin H. Redish, *Federal Jurisdiction: Tensions in the Allocation of Federal Judicial Power* (Charlottesville: Michie Co. 2d ed. 1990) 186.
3. *See for example,* Akhil Reed Amar, "Of Sovereignty and Federalism," *Yale Law J.* (1987) 1425, 1473–92; William A.Fletcher, "A Historical Interpretation of the Eleventh Amendment: A Narrow Construction of an Affirmative Grant Rather Than a Prohibition of Jurisdiction," 35 *Stanford Law Rev.* (1983) 1033; and Daniel J. Meltzer, "The Seminole Decision and State Sovereign Immunity," *Supreme Court Rev.* (1996).
4. Melvyn R. Durchslag, "Should Political Subdivisions be Accorded Eleventh Amendment Immunity," 43 *DePaul Law Rev.* (1994) 577, 588.
5. Louis L. Jaffe, "Suits Against Governments and Officers: Sovereign Immunity," *Harvard Law Rev.* (1963) 1, 2–3.
6. Jacobs, *Eleventh,* 5. *See also,* Jaffe, *Suits* 3–4; Gibbons, *Eleventh* 1889, 1896.
7. Jacobs, *Eleventh* 5.
8. Jaffe, *Suits* 5.
9. Jaffe, *Suits* 5.
10. Jacobs, *Eleventh* 6.
11. Gibbons, *Eleventh* 1895–96.
12. Gibbons, *Eleventh* 1896–97.
13. Gibbons, *Eleventh* 1897.
14. Gibbons, *Eleventh* 1897–98.
15. Gibbons, *Eleventh* 1898.
16. Jacobs, *Eleventh* 8, *citing* Ashby v. White 6 Mod. 45, 87 Eng. Rep. 808 (Q.B. 1702).
17. James E. Pfander, "History and State Suability: An 'Explanatory' Account of the Eleventh Amendment," 83 *Cornell Law Rev.* (1998) 1269 n.69.
18. Pfander, *History* 1283.
19. Pfander, *History* 1282–83.
20. Jaffe, *Suits* 19.
21. When Chisholm v. Georgia was decided in 1793, Massachusetts still owed approximately $2 million to pre–constitution creditors. Jaffe, *Suits* 1339 n.312.
22. Jaffe, *Suits* 1283.
23. Jaffe, *Suits* 1286–87.
24. Jaffe, *Suits* 1339.
25. Robert N. Clinton, "A Mandatory View of Federal Court Jurisdiction: A Guided Quest for the Original Understanding of Article III" 132 *University of Pennsylvania Law Rev.* (1984) 741, 758.

26. 1 James Madison, "The Debates in the Federal Convention of 1787 Which Framed the Constitution of the United States of America" (Gaillar Hunt and James Brown Scott eds., 1987) 17–21.

27. 2 Max Farrand, *The Records of the Federal Convention of 1787* (New Haven and London: Yale University Press, 1966) 20–23.

28. 2 Farrand, *Records* 21–22.

29. 2 Farrand, *Records* 22.

30. Jacobs, *Eleventh* 15–16.

31. Hunt and Scott, *Debates* 96.

32. 2 Farrand, *Records* 223–24.

33. 2 Farrand, *Records* 224.

34. 2 Farrand, *Records* 39.

35. 2 Farrand, *Records* 46.

36. Hunt and Scott, *Debates* 337. Another resolution submitted by Charles Pickney was also submitted at the same time. Hunt and Scott, *Debates* 337. Because that resolution seemed to have had no independent influence it is not reproduced here.

37. The entire document is at Hunt and Scott, *Debates* 137–50.

38. This addition was made by a marginal note in the handwriting of Rutledge.

39. Hunt and Scott, *Debates*146–47. Portions of the text in parentheses were crossed out in the original, those in brackets were additions in Rutledge's handwriting, and those in italics were changes made by Rutledge.

40. Hunt and Scott, *Debates* 172–73. Portions of the text in parentheses were crossed out in the original and those in brackets were additions made in Rutledge's handwriting.

41. Hunt and Scott, *Debates* 186.

42. Hunt and Scott, *Debates* 545.

43. 2 Farrand, *Records* 600–01.

44. Jacobs, *Eleventh* 27–28.

45. Paul Leicester Ford, *Pamphlets on the Constitution of the United States: Published During its Discussion by the People* (New York: DaCapo Press, 1968).

46. Robert Clinton believes that Coxe's views should be "discounted somewhat" because he did not attend either the Constitutional Convention or Pennsylvania's ratifying convention. Clinton, *Mandatory* 825.

47. Tench Coxe, *An Examination of the Constitution for the United States of America. By an American Citizen*, reprinted in Ford, *Pamphlets* 149.

48. 2 Jonathon Elliot, *The Debates in the Several State Conventions on the Adoption of the Federal Constitution as Recommended by the General Convention at Philadelphia in 1787* (Charlotteville: Mithie and Co., 1846) 491.

49. 2 Elliot, *Debates* 491–93.

50. John Bach McMaster and Frederick D. Stone, *Pennsylvania and the Federal Constitution, 1787–1788* (1970).

51. 2 Elliot, *Debates* 545–46.

52. 2 Elliot, *Debates* 181.

53. William V. Wells, *The Life and Public Services of Samuel Adams* (Boston: Little, Brown and Co., 1865) 300–31.

54. Samuel B. Harding, *The Contest over the Ratification of the Federal Constitution in the State of Massachusetts* (New York: Longmans, Green and Co., 1896) 40–41.

55. Charles R. King, *The Life and Correspondence of Rufus King* (New York: Putnam, 1894) 260.

56. Harding, *Contest* 40–41.

57. Although at the time they were published they were widely believed to have been written by James Winthrop, there appears to be some doubt as to whether he was in fact the actual author. Ford, *Pamphlets* 49–52.

58. Ford, *Pamphlets* 97.

59. Ford, *Pamphlets* 119.

60. What did pass was an amendment that imposed minimum monetary or amount in controversy requirements on diversity jurisdiction. Jacobs, *Eleventh* 30, n.8.

61. Jacobs, *Eleventh* 31–32.

62. 3 Elliot, *Debates* 318–319.

63. "All debts contracted and Engagements entered into, before the adoption of this Constitution, shall be as valid against the United States under the Constitution, as under the Confederation." U.S. Constitution, art. 6, clause 1. For an extended discussion of the federal government's assumption of state war debts, *see* Pfander, *History* 1268.

64. Pfander, *History* 477.

65. Pfander, *History* 518.

66. Pfander, *History* 521–22.

67. Pfander, *History* 526–27. Judge Gibbons includes an extended discussion of Mason's concerns, particularly the land claims of the Indiana Company under a grant from the terms of England. Gibbons, *Eleventh* 1903–05.

68. 3 Elliot, *Debates* 527.

69. 3 Elliot, *Debates* 530.

70. 3 Elliot, *Debates* 533.

71. 3 Elliot, *Debates* 533–34.

72. Gibbons, *Eleventh* 1906.

73. Martha A. Field, "The Eleventh Amendment and Other Sovereign Immunity Doctrines: Part One," 126 *University of Pennsylvania Law Rev.* (1977) 515, 534.

74. 3 Elliot, *Debates* 543.

75. 3 Elliot, *Debates* 549. The context of the quote does not help to determine if Pendleton is in fact referring to the clauses granting jurisdiction to the federal courts over controversies between a state and citizens of other states or foreigners. Gibbons believes that he is. Gibbons, *Eleventh* 1906.

76. 3 Elliot, *Debates* 555 (italics in original).

77. 3 Elliot, *Debates,* 555–56.

78. 3 Elliot, *Debates* 557.

79. Gibbons, *Eleventh* 1907; Clinton, *Mandatory* 847–49.

80. 3 Elliot, *Debates* 566–67 (italics in original).

81. 3 Elliot, *Debates* 573.

82. 3 Elliot, *Debates* 660–61 (emphasis added).

83. William Jeffrey, Jr., "The Letters of 'Brutus'—A Neglected Element in the Ratification Campaign of 1787–88," 40 *University of Cincinati Law Rev.* (1971) 643, 643–46. The author of the *Letters* is unknown.

84. Herbert J. Storing, *The Complete Anti-Federalist, Vol. 2* (Chicago: University of Chicago Press, 1981) 214. It is generally thought that Richard Henry Lee was the author

of the *Observations*, although Storing feels that "...the case for Lee's authorship is surely a good deal weaker than has usually been assumed." Storing, *Complete* 215–216.

85. "The Letters of 'Brutus,'" reprinted in Jeffrey, *Brutus* 754.

86. Jeffrey, *Brutus* 754–55. Jeffrey claims that this is the argument that Hamilton was responding to in *The Federalist No. 81*. Jeffrey, *Brutus* 755 n.62.

87. Jeffrey, *Brutus* 757.

88. *The Observations of the Federal Farmer*, reprinted in The Complete Anti-Federalist, 3 Storing, *Complete* 235.

89. 2 Storing, *Complete* 245.

90. *The Federalist No. 80*, at 494 (Alexander Hamilton) (Henry Cabot Lodge ed., 1902) (emphasis in original).

91. Lodge, *Federalist* 495.

92. Lodge, *Federalist* 495–96.

93. Lodge, *Federalist* 495–496.

94. Lodge, *Federalist* 497.

95. *The Federalist No. 81,* at 508–09 (Alexander Hamilton) (Henry Cabot Lodge ed., 1902).

96. *See, for example,* Gibbons, *Eleventh* 1911 (explaining *The Federalist No. 81* as arguing not that states could not be sued by citizens but that there would be no right of action to sue on): Field, *Eleventh* 534–35 (discussing how the two are not consistent); John E. Nowak, "The Scope of Congressional Power to Create Causes of Action Against State Governments and the History of the Eleventh and Fourteenth Amendments," *Columbia Law Rev.* (1975) 1413, 1429 (arguing that *The Federalist Nos. 80* and *81* are consistent "if Hamilton intended that only Congress should have the power to grant federal court jurisdiction over cases against states").

97. 2 Elliot, *Debates* 409 (italics in original).

98. 2 Elliot, *Debates* 413.

99. 2 *Documentary History of the Constitution of the United States of America, 1787–1870* (Washington: Department of State, 1894) 194 (emphasis added).

100. Alfred Hill. "In Defense of Our Law of Sovereign Immunity," 42 *Boston College Law Rev.* (2001) 485.

101. 4 Elliot, *Debates* 251.

102. Gibbons, *Eleventh* 1912–13 (citing statements made by James Iredell [p. 146], William Davie [p. 160] Archibald Maclaine [p. 173,] and Richard Spaight [p. 210] to show that the North Carolina convention believed that the state could be sued without its consent in federal court); Gibbons, *Eleventh* 1913 ("the convention discussed North Carolina's liability on the notes at length").

103. 4 Elliot, *Debates* 159.

104. 4 Elliot, *Debates* 246.

105. 4 Elliot, *Debates* 247.

106. Jacobs, *Eleventh* 38.

107. 2 *Documentary History* 190.

108. Field, *Eleventh* 534.

109. Field, *Eleventh* 531, 534.

110. U.S. Constitution art. 3, sec. 2, clause 2.

111. U.S. Constitution art. 3, sec. 2, clause 2 (emphasis added)

112. U.S. Constitution art. 3, sec. 2, clause 2 (emphasis added)

113. Julius Goebel, Jr., *History of the Supreme Court of the United States: Antecedents and Beginnings to 1801* (New York: Macmillian, 1971) 458. According to Goebel, Ellsworth, Paterson, and Strong, all lawyers, "were mainly responsible for the form and content of the Judiciary Bill."

114. Goebel, *History* 462 n.19, *quoting* a letter from Caleb Strong to Robert Trent Paine, Massachusetts Attorney General, May 24, 1787.

115. Goebel, *History* 494–503.

116. Goebel, *History* 503–6.

117. Goebel, *History* 507.

118. Orth, *Judicial* 27, *quoting* Act of Sept. 24, 1787, ch. 20, sec. 13, 1 stat. 73, 80.

119. Professor Orth is of the opinion that the former is the case. Orth, *Judicial* 27.

120. The Eleventh Amendment was ratified by the required twelve of the then existing fifteen states nearly three years earlier, on February 7, 1795. But President Adams did not issue his proclamation of ratification until January 8, 1798. Orth, *Judicial* 20. The latter date is also the one which the Supreme Court recognized the amendment to have been officially ratified. Hollingsworth v. Virginia, 3 Dall. 378 (1798). The reasons for the delay between the states' ratification and the President's proclamation of ratification are described in Orth, *Judicial* 20–21.

121. Grayson v. Virginia, 3 Dall. 320 (1796); Chisholm v. Georgia, 2 Dall. 419 (1793); Oswald v. New York, 2 Dall. 401 (1792), 2 Dall. 415 (1793); Vanstophorst v. Maryland, 2 Dall. 401 (1791); Vassal v. Massachusetts (unreported by Dallas); Cutting v. South Carolina (unreported by Dallas); and Moultric v. Georgia (unreported by Dallas).

122. Pfander, *History* 1257.

123. Chisholm originally brought suit against the state of Georgia in the Circuit Court for the District of Georgia under the name of Farquhar's Executor v. Georgia, seeking £100,000 for goods delivered to a garrison stationed near Savannah during the Revolutionary War. However, that case was dismissed. Doyle Mathis, "Chisholm v. Georgia: Background and Settlement," 54 *Journal of American History* (June, 1967) 19, 22. Mathis has implied that the Supreme Court case, Chisholm v. Georgia, was not a matter of original jurisdiction, but both Jacobs and Orth disagree. Jacobs, *Eleventh* 46–48 and Orth, *Judicial* 12–13. Jacobs and Orth appear to be correct. The relief sought in the Supreme Court differed from that sought in the Circuit Court. And Edmund Randolph, who argued the case in the Supreme Court supporting the Court's jurisdiction over the state of Georgia, never mentioned the proceedings in the Circuit Court.

124. Even though Maryland did not object to the Court's jurisdiction, the suit did prompt some commentary outside of Maryland. James Sullivan, *Observations upon the Government of the United States of America* (1791) (challenging the Court's jurisdiction) and Hortensius, *An Enquiry into the Constitutional Authority of the Supreme Federal Court over the Several States in Their Political Capacity* (1792) (defending the Court's exercise of jurisdiction) Jacobs, *Eleventh* 25. *See also* Doyle Mathis, "The Eleventh Amendment: Adoption and Interpretation," 2 *Georgia Law Rev.* (1968) 207.

125. There is, or was, some confusion as to exactly who Farquhar was. As reported by Charles Warren, Farquhar was a Georgia resident who left America prior to the Revolution and who took bonds from his two partners in settlement of the liquidation of his partnership. 1 Charles Warren, *The Supreme Court in United States History, 1789–1835*, 93 n.1

(Boston: Little, Brown, and Co., 1922). Doyle Mathis argues that Warren is incorrect on his facts; he is rather referring to Georgia v. Brailsford, 2 Dall. 402 (1792), 2 Dall. 415 (1793), 3 Dall. 1 (1794), in which Georgia intervened as a party in a private suit between Brailsford, a Colonial ex-patriot, and others, claiming that if Brailsford prevailed, Georgia was entitled to the judgment proceeds under Georgia's law that confiscated property of British loyalists. Mathis, *Background and Settlement* n.5. The historical record seems to support Mathis. Jacobs, *Eleventh,* 46–48; Orth, *Judicial* 12–13. I will therefore use his account of the facts.

126. Mathis, *Background* 22 and n.14.

127. Mathis, *Background* 23.

128. Mathis, *Background* 23–24.

129. The Court requested the Attorney General to address three additional questions: (1) "If the State of *Georgia* can be made a party defendant in certain cases, does an action of *assumpsit* lie against her" (2) "Is the service of the summons upon the Governor and Attorney General...a competent service" and (3) "[b]y what process ought the appearance of the State of *Georgia* be enforced." Chisholm v. Georgia, 2 Dall. at 420 (emphasis in original). These other three issues addressed by Randolph, as can be seen, were not *directly* germane to the debate over state suability and the resulting Eleventh Amendment. However the second, whether an action of assumpsit (a common law writ or cause of action used to enforce a promise) will lie against a state, was an integral part of Justice Iredell's opinion and will thus be mentioned briefly in the text.

130. Jacobs, *Eleventh* n.15. *See also Chisholm,* 2 Dall. 423–24.

131. Clyde Jacobs opined that Justice Wilson used Chisholm v. Georgia as an opportunity to articulate his nationalist philosophy as constitutional law. This prompted "many contemporary statesmen and politicians [to read] it as an exercise in judicial usurpation, which called for repudiation." Jacobs, *Eleventh* 52.

132. Although not appearing in the official reports, accounts of Vassal v. Massachusetts can be found in Jacobs, *Eleventh* 60–62, Clyde E. Jacobs, *"Prelude to Amendment: The States Before the Court," 12 American Journal of Legal History* (1968) 19, 33–34 (hereinafter "Prelude to Amendment,"), and Mathis, "The Eleventh Amendment," 225–26.

133. Jacobs, "Prelude to Amendment," 30; Mathis, "The Eleventh Amendment" 229.

134. Jacobs, "Prelude to Amendment," 30.

135. Mathis, "The Eleventh Amendment," 225–26. At the time of these resolutions, that Court had decided Chisholm v. Georgia in which it affirmed its authority to exercise jurisdiction over state defendants.

136. Mathis, "The Eleventh Amendment," 224.

137. Mathis, "The Eleventh Amendment," 224–25 (*citing* Resolves of the General Court of the Commonwealth of Massachusetts, 31–32 [1793]).

138. Mathis, "The Eleventh Amendment," 225.

139. Jacobs, *Eleventh* 62 (*citing* Herbert Allen, John Hancock 357–58 [1953]).

140. Mathis, "The Eleventh Amendment," 215.

141. Jacobs, *Eleventh* 175 n.19 (*citing Journal of the Assembly of the State of New York, Seventeenth Session* Jan.–Mar. 1794) 7.

142. Jacobs, *Eleventh* 46.

143. 3 *Annals of Congress* (1793) 651–52

144. 3 *Annals of Congress* (1793) 656.

145. 3 *Annals of Congress* (1794) 25.
146. 3 *Annals of Congress* (1793) 656.
147. 4 *Annals of Congress* (1794) 476.
148. 4 *Annals of Congress* (1794) 477.
149. Vázquez, *Eleventh* 1725–26.
150. Pfander, *History* 1362–63. For a review of the debate surrounding the other "amendment," the words "be construed to" *see* Pfander, *History* 1363–65. Technically, Senator Strong's addition of those words were not an amendment since they were added to a resolution of the previous Congress, which died with the end of that Congressional session. In terms of the interpretation of the Eleventh Amendment, however, the resolution introduced in the Fourth Congress can be treated as an amendment.
151. Of the other three, one was Chisholm v. Georgia. The first case filed, Vanstophorst v. Maryland (2 Dall. 401 [1791] was discontinued by consent of the parties. Mathis, "The Eleventh Amendment" 215. In the the third, Oswald v. New York, (2 Dall. [1792] 401, 2 Dall [1793] 415), the Court entered a default judgment against the state for $5,315. There is no record as to whether New York ever satisfied the judgment. Jacobs, *Eleventh* 46.
152. *See also*, William P. Marshall, "The Diversity Theory of the Eleventh Amendment: A Critical Evaluation," 102 *Harvard Law Rev.* 1372 (1989) (arguing against the diversity theory of the Eleventh Amendment and in favor of a broader affirmation of sovereign immunity).

PART II

ANALYSIS

The Evolution of the Eleventh Amendment from Diversity Jurisdiction to Sovereign Immunity

INTRODUCTION

As noted in the Introduction, the text of the Eleventh Amendment is unambiguous: "The Judicial power of the United States shall not be construed to extend to any suit in law or equity, commenced or prosecuted against one of the United States by citizens of another State, or by Citizens or Subjects of any Foreign State."[1] And as discussed in Part I, the Eleventh Amendment was the result of the Supreme Court's ruling in Chisholm v. Georgia that states were not immune from suit by citizens of other states and foreign countries. Moreover, the language of the Eleventh Amendment tracks exactly the facts of that case: a citizen of South Carolina suing the state of Georgia *eo nominee* (in its own name) in a United States Court. In addition, the language of the amendment uses precisely the same language used in Article 3 to describe the jurisdiction of the United States courts. The first seven words of the Eleventh Amendment mimic the opening phrase of Article 3, § 2, "The Judicial power shall extend to all cases in Law and Equity, arising under the Constitution, the Laws of the United States, and treaties made or which shall be made, under their authority; . . . to controversies . . . between a state and citizens of another state . . . ." The Eleventh Amendment simply inserts the words 'shall not be construed' into the opening phrase. Finally, of the nine general categories of cases within the jurisdiction of the federal courts, the Eleventh Amendment mentions only one that the judicial power of the United States "shall not be construed to extend to," those in which a state is a party defendant *and* the plaintiff is either a citizen of another state or a citizen or a subject of a foreign state. Current Eleventh Amendment doctrine, however, has far outstripped its plain language.

The cases which led, in one way or another, to this result will largely proceed chronologically. The case law in this area has not developed linearly. Cases once thought to be controlling have lost favor only to reappear again as controlling or persuasive authority. This will undoubtedly be a recurring theme in Eleventh Amendment jurisprudence. Consequently, a chronological presentation seems best suited to an attempt to clarify and, in some instances, to simplify what can be an enormously confusing area.

The road that led from the plain language of the Eleventh Amendment to the Court's eventual extension of it in Hans v. Louisiana took nearly 100 years to travel and was anything but straight. For most of the years between *Hollingsworth* and *Hans*, the Court, with a few exceptions discussed later, dealt with cases in which the controversy was between a state and citizens of a different state. However, in Hans v. Louisiana (1890) the plaintiff was a citizen of Louisiana *and* the claim was founded on a violation by the state of the Contract Clause of the Constitution: "No State shall . . . pass any . . . law impairing the obligation of Contracts . . . ."[2] The *Hans* Court decided to abandon both the history and the language of the Eleventh Amendment in favor of certain broader "postulates"[3] of state sovereignty underlying our constitutional structure. In doing so, it fashioned a constitutional doctrine of state sovereign immunity that has affected not only the power of the federal judiciary, but also the power of the United States Congress. Moreover, according to some, *Hans* seriously undercut the supremacy of federal law, and indeed, the rule of law itself. Hans v. Louisiana is thus *the* seminal Eleventh Amendment case, the case from which all significant Eleventh Amendment doctrine now flows, and to which both supporters and critics of Eleventh Amendment jurisprudence look to begin their discussion. It will, therefore, be the focal point of much of Part II.

In the intervening years between 1793, the year the Eleventh Amendment was ratified, and 1890, the year *Hans* was decided; the Court was not on holiday from the Eleventh Amendment. Quite the contrary. History teaches that the diversity clauses of Article 3, both those relating to claims involving citizens of different states and those relating to citizens of one state and another state, were born of a fear that out-of-state citizens could not get a "fair" adjudication in state courts of claims brought against interests that the state had an incentive to protect, whether its own or those of its citizens. The diversity clauses opened a neutral forum, the federal judicial system, in which to adjudicate these claims. The Eleventh Amendment closed those courts to the citizen/state line of cases. One might expect, then, that resourceful lawyers would look for ways back into the neutral federal forum despite the proscriptions of the Eleventh Amendment. Two obvious avenues were left open by the language. First, if the plaintiff could sue someone other than the state, someone against whom a claimant could obtain a judgment that would accomplish precisely or nearly precisely what the plaintiff could accomplish if a judgment were issued against the state itself, the Eleventh

Amendment would be little more than a nuisance. Second, the plaintiff could get back into federal courts if he could assert one of the remaining eight Article 3 bases for federal jurisdiction that was not described in the Eleventh Amendment's prohibitions. Hans v. Louisiana was such a case.

Before discussing *Hans* and the second tactic to avoid the Eleventh Amendment, it is important to briefly discuss the first avoidance mechanism: suing the appropriate state officer rather than the state itself. First, these cases are important because they form part of the historical corpus of Eleventh Amendment cases that are currently relied upon by the Supreme Court in fashioning its present-day Eleventh Amendment doctrine. Second, these cases are occasionally significant, if not determinative, of disputes today. Finally, and most importantly, these mostly nineteenth century cases, whatever their contemporary currency, speak to the Court's ongoing attempt to find some balance to the conflict between the supremacy of federal law and the preservation of the states rightful place in our governing structure. In that sense, these cases, certainly as a whole if not individually, are as important to understanding how the Court has perceived its role in the never-ending federalism battle as are the landmark federalism cases of McCulloch v. Maryland (1819)[4], Martin v. Hunter's Lessee (1816)[5], Cohens v. Virginia (1821), Hans v. Louisiana (1890), and Ex parte Young (1908).[6]

SUITS AGAINST STATE OFFICERS—WHO IS THE REAL PARTY IN INTEREST?

It was sixteen years after the Eleventh Amendment was ratified that the United States Supreme Court was asked to decide when a suit in which the state is not a named party defendant will, nevertheless, be considered to have been, "commenced or prosecuted against one of the United States." In United States v. Peters (1809) the Court faced the question of whether a federal judge, Richard Peters, could be required to execute a judgment previously rendered by him. The judgment required the estate of the late Treasurer of Pennsylvania to pay over money to a third individual, which was in the late Treasurer's personal estate, but which the state claimed was in fact state money. Pennsylvania took the position that since the Treasurer received the funds in his official capacity, although deposited into his personal account, they belonged to the State. The State argued that because it had a claim on the funds the plaintiff was seeking, the Eleventh Amendment precluded Judge Peters from entering a judgment that the funds be paid to a private individual. There was, in other words, no difference between the plaintiff's request and requiring the state itself to pay the amount awarded to the plaintiff.[7]

The Court rejected the state's Eleventh Amendment argument. Read most narrowly, the Court held that the Eleventh Amendment could not be asserted as a defense in a case between two individuals. That rule seems simple enough.

Looking solely at the text, the Eleventh Amendment only prohibits the state itself from being forced to defend a claim brought by a particular class of plaintiffs. Very simply, Pennsylvania was not a party to the suit in *Peters*. But Chief Justice Marshall, in announcing the judgment of the Court, used language that left open the possibility that there could be cases in which the state's interest in the lawsuit is enough to allow it to invoke the Eleventh Amendment even if not actually a party to the suit. "If these proceeds had been the actual property of Pennsylvania, however wrongfully acquired, the disclosure of that fact would have presented a case on which it is unnecessary to give an opinion; but it can certainly never be alleged that a mere suggestion of title in a state to property, in possession of an individual must arrest the proceedings of the court...."

Three years later, Osborne v. Bank of the United States (1824) presented the case that the Chief Justice had alluded to in *Peters*. However, this time Chief Justice Marshall was unequivocal in rejecting the Eleventh Amendment defense, holding that the Eleventh Amendment only applied to those cases in which a state was a defendant *on the record*. While it is true that *Osborne*'s holding on the Eleventh Amendment was modified somewhat by Chief Justice Marshall, and eventually all but abandoned as the nineteenth century drew to a close, its significance should not be underestimated. It was only five years before the decision in *Osborne* that the United States Supreme Court in McCulloch v. Maryland upheld the right of Congress to establish the Second Bank of the United States and, in doing so, held that the Supremacy Clause ("This Constitution, and the laws of the United States . . . made in pursuance thereof . . . shall be the Supreme Law of the Land . . . .")[8] prohibited Maryland from taxing the bank. In *Osborne*, the Court faced a very similar situation as that in *McCulloch*, with one exception. In *McCulloch*, the state sued the cashier of the United States Bank to recover the taxes. In *Osborne*, the bank sued the state auditor. The Eleventh Amendment was thus not at issue in *McCulloch* but was ostensibly at issue in *Osborne*.

In 1817, the Bank of the United States opened two branches in Ohio. At the time, Ohio taxed state banks on their dividends but did not tax banks not chartered by the state. That changed two years later, due in large part to a financial panic that put severe financial strains on both the state and the state chartered banks. Two weeks before the decision in *McCulloch*, the Ohio legislature enacted a statute that taxed each of the two federally-chartered banks $50,000 (state banks were taxed only $10,000). Ralph Osborne was the state auditor who was responsible for levying and collecting the tax. To make a long story short,[9] Osborne, through one of his agents, collected $120,000 from the Chillicothe branch of the Bank of the United States. Ninety-eight thousand dollars was deposited in an account of Osborne's in his capacity as tax collector, $2,000 was kept by Osborne's agent for his fee, and the balance was returned to the bank.

The difficulty (and the reason why Osborne was a party to the suit filed by the bank) was that the money was collected and deposited in violation of an injunction issued by the United States Circuit Court (actually several of them) restraining the state treasurer, the state auditor, and other state employees from disposing of the funds collected. This dispute went on for two years until, in 1821, the bank and the state agreed that the treasurer should restore the $98,000, plus interest, to the bank, pending an appeal to the United States Supreme Court. However, the treasurer refused to return the money. The funds were then seized by the federal circuit court pursuant to the agreement and given back to the bank. The whole matter was appealed to the Supreme Court.

Osborne raised a number of objections to the bank's claim for an injunction, ranging from the necessity of the state being made a party defendant in the original action to the impropriety of an injunction as opposed to an action for trespass (a common law action to challenge one's possession or occupation of property) to test the legality of Osborne's possession of the funds obtained from the tax. The Eleventh Amendment challenge to the circuit court's jurisdiction was based on the same claim raised in *Peters*—because the state had an interest in the funds, the suit by the bank was in effect a suit against the state. However, *Osborne* was a far more difficult case to deny the applicability of the Eleventh Amendment than was *Peters*. First, the state officers in *Osborne* were commanded to do what they did by a state statute. They were thus acting in their official, not their individual, capacities. And second, it was conceded that the funds being held were the state's funds. Unlike *Peters*, the Court could not say that this was a "mere suggestion of title." The question in *Osborne* was therefore whether a state officer can be restrained *by a federal court* from performing his *official* duties as defined by state law.

The Court, speaking through Chief Justice Marshall, had no difficulty in answering in the affirmative:

> It may, we think, be laid down as a rule which admits of no exception, that, in all cases where jurisdiction depends on the party, it is the party named in the record. Consequently, the 11th Amendment, which restrains the jurisdiction granted by the constitution over suits against states, is of necessity, limited to those in which a state is a party on the record. The amendment has its full effect, if the constitution be construed as it would have been construed, had the jurisdiction of the court never have been extended to suits brought against a state, by citizens of another state, or by aliens.

By holding that the Eleventh Amendment is a bar to federal judicial power only when the state is a formal party, the Court made two important points. First, the Eleventh Amendment is not a constitutional grant of state sovereign immunity. It only restricts federal jurisdiction in diversity cases, cases in which federal jurisdiction is based on the character of the parties. Second, when the choice is to either preserve the supremacy of federal law (in this case, the act creating the Second Bank of the United States) through the use of a federal forum *or* to preserve a state's sovereign interest in its taxing authority and the funds derived therefrom, federal supremacy and, thus, federal jurisdiction trumps.

The first of *Osborne*'s points, that the Eleventh Amendment does not generally insulate the state's treasury from all claims of whatever nature, was slightly modified by the Marshall Court in Governor of Georgia v. Madrazo (1828). In that case the Court held that, "where the chief magistrate of a state is sued, not by his name, but by the style of office, and the claim made upon him is entirely in his official character, we think the state itself may be considered as a party on the record." The formalistic interpretation of the Eleventh Amendment requiring that the state be a party of record, as modified by *Madrazo* to include suits against the governor of a state *in the name of the governor*, remained the law for nearly sixty years.

However, hints of dissatisfaction with this interpretation appeared eleven years earlier in a dissenting opinion in Davis v. Gray (1872). *Davis* was a suit by the court appointed receiver of a bankrupt railroad against the governor of Texas (Davis) and other officials to recover land that was ceded to the State of Texas. The land was yielded under a state constitutional provision that reclaimed land that was given to railroads when certain conditions were not met. Although Davis was the governor of Texas, since he was sued in his own name and not as "Governor of Texas" the case was distinguishable from *Madrazo*. Moreover, the state permitted similar suits to be filed in state court. The Supreme Court held that the Eleventh Amendment does not deprive any person of a right or remedy in federal court that can be asserted in a state court of the same jurisdiction. Rather, where the state opens its courts to a particular claim, an individual has a choice of forums.[10]

On the broader question of state sovereignty, the Court noted that this case implicated the constitutional prohibition on impairing the obligation of contracts, the Contracts Clause: "(W)hen a state becomes a party to a contract...the same rules of law are applied to her as to private persons under like circumstances. When she or her representatives are properly brought into the forum of litigation, neither she nor they can assert any right or immunity as incident to her political sovereignty." Like *Osborne*, then, no accommodation to state sovereignty will be made when the supremacy of federal law is at stake, even if state courts are available to hear those federal claims. Indeed, according to the *Davis* Court, the availability of state courts as an alternative forum is one justification for the availability of a federal forum since the state court is not likely to be neutral. The decision, however, was not unanimous. Justice Davis (no relation to the Texas governor), joined by the Chief Justice, argued that the suit was essentially one against the state of Texas because it sought to enjoin the disposition of property clearly belonging to the state, and in which the individual defendants had no personal interest.[11]

The nominal party rule was revisited ten years later in a case in which the Eleventh Amendment was not at issue because the defendants were federal officers. It is important nevertheless because, like the states, the federal government is protected from individual lawsuits by sovereign immunity. Indeed, the Court has, properly or improperly, often analogized the states' Eleventh Amendment immunity to the sovereign immunity of the federal government (Seminole Tribe of Florida v. Florida [1996]). United States v. Lee (1882) was a suit by the heirs of General Robert E. Lee to recover possession of General Lee's plantation (now known as Arlington National Cemetery) "purchased" by the United States Government at a tax sale in 1864. The Court held that while the United States enjoys sovereign immunity, its officers do not. Seeing as its duty the protection of individual property rights against the claims of the government, the Court held that the principle, "when an individual is sued in regard to property which he holds as officer or agent of the United States, his possession cannot be disturbed when that fact is brought to the attention of the court, has been overruled and denied in every case where it has been necessary to decide it." This time, however, the nominal party rule, applied in *Osborne* and *Davis* as a device to ensure the supremacy of federal law, could only muster a bare majority of five votes. Justice Gray, who was appointed to the Court after the decision in *Davis*, dissented. Because the sovereign cannot possess property except through its agents, he argued, this was a suit against the United States just as certainly as if the United States had been a party on the record. Justice Gray's opinion is far more than a reassertion and application of the common law doctrine of sovereign immunity. He described it as "a fundamental axiom of public law, 'essential to the common defense and general welfare.'"

The nominal party rule was all but abandoned in Louisiana ex rel v. Jumel (1882), and finally laid to rest one year later in New Hampshire v. Louisiana (1883). The abandonment of the nominal party rule significantly altered the balance that the Court in *Osborne* and its progeny had previously struck between the federal courts' responsibility to ensure the supremacy of federal law and protecting state sovereignty. But first a short history of those cases that fall between *Osborne* and *Jumel* in which the Court gradually replaced the formalistic holding of *Osborne* with a more functional "real party in interest" rule. These cases involved debt-ridden southern states whose economies had been destroyed by the Civil War, and which, as did their counterparts during the Revolutionary War, issued bonds as a means of paying for needed government services and infrastructure.[12] One of those states, Louisiana, enacted the Funding Act of 1874 which authorized the state to issue bonds to existing bondholders at 60 percent of their face value with the promise of state court enforcement of its obligations and a new tax that would be levied specifically to pay for the new bonds. A constitutional amendment was ratified a short time later declaring that the new bonds issued were a contractual obligation of the state. Unfortunately, politics got in the way of the state's good intentions. Soon after the constitutional amendment, the state enacted a law permitting one company that was not eligible to exchange existing bonds for the 60 percent bonds, to exchange its bonds for new bonds, dollar for dollar.[13] This, of course, prompted a lawsuit by an individual who had exchanged his bonds for the discounted value. A unanimous Supreme Court in Board of Liquidation v. McComb (1876) upheld an injunction prohibiting state officers from making the new bond exchange on the grounds that the dollar-for-dollar exchange offered by the Louisiana legislature violated the Contract Clause of the United States Constitution. Regarding the Eleventh Amendment, the Court held that this was a suit against state officers and not the state itself. Since the statute under which the officers claimed authority violated the federal Constitution, the officers' attempted actions were without authority of law. The actions were, thus tortuous (constituted a civil wrong) and, under these circumstances, an injunction prohibiting the exchange was an appropriate remedy. Since the officers themselves were guilty of the tortuous acts they, and not the state, were the "real parties in interest."

However, just seven years later, an attempt by creditors of Louisiana to collect on the reduced-price bonds in reliance on *McComb* failed. In Louisiana ex rel. Elliot v. Jumel (1882) the plaintiff bondholder sued Louisiana's state auditor to compel him to use tax funds in the state treasury to pay the interest and principal owed on the bonds. While conceding that the Funding Act of 1874, which enacted a special tax to retire the bonds, created a contractual obligation binding on the state, the Court held that the Eleventh Amendment precluded the plaintiff from seeking relief in federal court. The suit, while nominally against the auditor, was in reality against the state since the auditor's decision not to dip into the state treasury was not a ministerial but rather a political or discretionary decision. For the Court to require him to use state tax funds would require it to assume the executive authority of the state. This it could not do. As to *McComb*, the Court said that in that case the officers were simply trustees of bonds on behalf of certain creditors who, by statute, were entitled to payment. Their responsibilities were thus purely ministerial and not discretionary. And *Osborne* was distinguished on the ground that unlike this case, in *Osborne* the funds had not yet reached the state treasury.

Evidence that these distinctions, while technically defensible, represented a significant shift in the Court's thinking about the appropriate balance between the supremacy of federal law and state sovereignty is found in the dissents of Justices Field and Harlan. First Justice Field:

When a State enters into the markets of the world as a borrower for sale, she, for the time, lays aside her sovereignty and becomes responsible as a civil corporation, and although suits against her even then may not be allowed, her officers can be compelled to do what she then contracts that they shall do. If contracts are not observed no property will in the end be respected; and all history shows that rights of persons are unsafe when property is insecure.

Justice Harlan was even more explicit: "[T]he opinion of the Court is in conflict with the spirit and tenor of our former decisions, subversive of long-established doctrines, and dangerous to the national supremacy as defined and limited by the Constitution."

Shortly after *Jumel*, the Supreme Court in New Hampshire v. Louisiana, (1883) again looked beyond the nominal parties to hold a suit was barred by the Eleventh Amendment. The states of New Hampshire and New York both enacted laws that permitted citizens holding bonds of Louisiana to assign them to the state, thus allowing the state to sue Louisiana on their behalf. Despite the fact that the Eleventh Amendment does not bar one state from suing another, the Court held that since the citizens of New Hampshire would be precluded by the Eleventh Amendment from suing Louisiana in their own name, they cannot use the name of the state to accomplish the same *personal* end. "Real party in interest" thus became the essential Eleventh Amendment inquiry, whether it was to determine if the named state officer was effectively the defendant state or to determine whether the plaintiff state was nothing more than a surrogate for its individual citizens.

Having decided that cases brought against state officers would be looked at "functionally" rather than "formalistically," the Court's decisions in the cases that followed *Jumel* and New Hampshire v. Louisiana broke down into two categories. In one category were the cases that sought relief from acts of state officers pursuant to an unconstitutional statute. These cases were held to be against the officer personally and not against the state, even if the remedy was to prevent the officers from acting pursuant to that statute. (*The Virginia Coupon Cases*, 1885). On the other hand, cases that sought to compel state officers to perform acts on behalf of the state, even though the failure to do so might arguably violate the United States Constitution, were held to be suits against the state and thus barred by the Eleventh Amendment (Pennoyer v. McConnaughy, 1891).

Both *The Virginia Coupon Cases* and *Pennoyer* arose out of a several decade attempt by Virginia to reduce its antebellum debt, which by 1871 had reached over $47 million.[14] In that year, Virginia enacted the Funding Act of 1871 which permitted bondholders to exchange their previous bonds for "consols" (short for consolidated bonds) which carried a 6 percent interest rate, payable upon the periodic presentation of coupons attached to the bonds. However, in a new twist, these coupons could also be used by the holder to pay any taxes or other obligations owed by the holder to the state. The ability to use the coupons in lieu of taxes was a major inducement to Virginia's creditors to exchange their existing bonds for the consols. Unfortunately, accepting the coupons in lieu of taxes did little for Virginia's cash-strapped treasury, resulting, a year later, in the repeal of the provision of the Funding Act permitting the use of consols coupons as legal tender for tax obligations. After the Virginia Court of Appeals declared that repealer to be a violation of the Contract Clause,[15] Virginia enacted a series of laws designed to depreciate the value of the coupons as substitutes for tax payments. The seven Virginia Coupon Cases arose out of those efforts by Virginia and the countermoves by the coupon holders.

One strategy used by coupon holders was to tender the coupons to the tax collector knowing the tender would be refused and the property taxed. The coupon holders would then refuse to pay the taxes, forcing the tax collector to levy on the individual's property. The taxpayer would then sue the tax collector for the value of the property taken or for the return of the property. In *The Virginia Coupon Cases*, the Court, in an opinion by Justice Matthews, determined that suits against state officers for the value of property seized or for return of the property itself could be brought in federal court despite the Eleventh Amendment. Since the attempt to repeal the "coupon in lieu taxes" provision of the Funding Act of 1871 was unconstitutional (a violation of the Contract Clause), the tax collector was obligated by state law to accept the coupons when tendered. His failure to do so and his later seizing of the plaintiffs' property were, thus, actions taken in his private capacity and were tortious. The suits were therefore not suits against the state, but against the state officer personally.

One year later, however, the Court in Hagood v. Southern (1886), an opinion also penned by Justice Matthews, dismissed a claim against a state officer because the state was the real party in interest and, as such, the Eleventh Amendment precluded the federal courts from exercising jurisdiction. South Carolina, like Virginia, had issued bonds in settlement of its previous financial obligations. And, like Virginia, part of the inducement for accepting these new bonds was that the bond scrip could be exchanged for taxes owed by the bondholder. Finally (also like Virginia), South Carolina later repudiated its obligation to accept the bond scrip in lieu of taxes. The Supreme Court held that while the repudiation was a violation of the Contract Clause, the Eleventh Amendment prohibited the federal courts from issuing the remedy sought by the plaintiffs—compelling the state tax collector to accept the bonds in lieu of taxes. "A judgment against [the state's official representatives], in their official and representative capacity, commanding them to perform official functions on behalf of the State according to the dictates and decrees of the court, is, if anything can be, a judicial proceeding against the State itself."

The only difference between the Virginia and South Carolina cases was the remedy. In the latter, the Court was asked to compel a state officer to perform his official duties. In the former, the officer was held to account for *his* decision to perform his state duties. One might argue, as did Justice Matthews, that the latter compelling a state officer to perform his obligations under state law is a greater threat to and interference with state sovereignty. Later cases have, at least on their face, supported that distinction (Larson v. Domestic & Foreign Commerce Corp., 1949). And while the distinction might appear thin, it does have a basis in the Eleventh Amendment. Compelling an officer to pay for the damages caused by that officer's unlawful action has no impact on the state's treasury, the central concern of the Eleventh Amendment. Even if the state reimburses its employees for the damages they may incur while performing the state's business, that is an obligation the state has voluntarily undertaken. It has, in other words, consented to an invasion of its treasury. On the other hand, when the Court orders the state treasurer to accept the coupons in lieu of taxes, the impact on the state's treasury is evident, immediate, and nonconsensual.

Finally, a year after *Hagood*, the Court was again faced with another case stemming from Virginia's repudiation of its promise to accept consol coupons in lieu of taxes. In an attempt to avoid the ruling in *The Virginia Coupon Cases*, in 1887 Virginia enacted a statute requiring that anyone tendering coupons in lieu of taxes must pay the taxes in money subject to a refund after a determination, in a lawsuit to be filed by the state, that the coupons tendered were not counterfeit. In a suit initiated by foreign citizens who held Virginia consol coupons, a federal circuit court enjoined the Virginia Attorney General from bringing suit to test the validity of the coupons tendered. When he filed suit nonetheless (obeying the Virginia statute rather than the United States Circuit Court), he was held in contempt. The Attorney General's appeal of that contempt citation reached the United States Supreme Court in *In re Ayers*, (1887). Once again, Justice Matthews wrote the Court's opinion. As in *Hagood,* the Court held that the Eleventh Amendment precluded the circuit court's exercise of jurisdiction in the original suit to enjoin the Attorney General from filing the action required by the Virginia statute. While the state was not a party to the action, Ayers was sued, not in his individual capacity, but solely in his capacity as Attorney General. And the impact on the Virginia treasury was as real as it was in *Hagood*. The suit was thus a suit against the state and barred by the Eleventh Amendment. As the Court noted:

> To secure the manifest purposes of the constitutional exemption guaranteed by the 11th Amendment requires that it should be interpreted, not literally and too narrowly, but fairly and with such breadth and largeness as effectually to accomplish the substance of its purpose. In this spirit it must be held to cover, not only suits brought against a State by name, but those also against its officers, agents, and representatives, where the State, though not named as such, is nevertheless, the only real party against which alone in fact the relief is asked, and against which the judgment or decree effectively operates.

If anything was left of the nominal party rule of *Osborne* after *Jumel* and New Hampshire v. Louisiana, it died with *In re Ayers*. What then of the supremacy of federal law that the nominal party rule was designed to ensure? The Court declared that the continued possibility of suits against state officers in their private capacities was enough:

> Nor need it be apprehended that the construction of the 11th Amendment...will in anywise embarrass or obstruct the execution of the laws of the United States.... The government of the United States, in the enforcement of its laws, deals with all persons within its territorial jurisdiction, as individuals owing obedience to its authority. The penalties of disobedience may be visited upon them, without regard to the character in which they assume to act, or the nature of the exemption they may want to plead in justification. If, therefore, an individual, acting under the assumed authority of a State, as one of its officers, and under color of its laws, comes into conflict with the superior authority of...the United States, he is stripped of his representative character, and subjected in his person to the consequences of his individual conduct. The State has no power to impart to him any immunity from responsibility to the supreme authority of the United States.

HANS V. LOUISIANA—FROM TEXT TO UNDERLYING POSTULATES

As noted previously, Hans v. Louisiana (1890) is clearly the seminal Eleventh Amendment decision. All modern Eleventh Amendment jurisprudence traces its roots to *Hans*. And those who either support that jurisprudence or criticize it must ultimately either trace their defense or critique to *Hans*. In order to understand *Hans*, however, it is necessary to explore two lines of cases that preceded this seminal case. The first has its foundation in another of the great Marshall-era cases, Cohens v. Virginia. The other was the subject of the previous subsection, the bond cases and particularly *The Virginia Coupon Cases*. The latter are revisited here, not for their doctrinal significance (the subject of the previous discussion) but for the markedly contrasting view of the balance between federal and state power that characterized the earlier decades of the ninteenth Century.

Cohens v. Virginia

Cohens v. Virginia (1821) held that the Eleventh Amendment did not prohibit an individual from pursuing a writ of error (an order by an appellate court requiring that a lower court deliver the record of proceedings to it) against a state in the United States Supreme Court. The Cohen brothers were residents of Virginia, or so it was assumed.[16] They were prosecuted criminally for selling lottery tickets in Virginia in violation of Virginia law. Their defense was based on an act of Congress that allowed the District of Columbia to permit lottery sales, and a District of Columbia ordinance that did just that. The Cohen brothers argued that this congressional act permitted them to sell lottery tickets not only in the District of Columbia but anywhere they chose. The Virginia court rejected that defense and convicted the Cohens. Their conviction was upheld by the Virginia Court of Appeals (the highest court in the state) and they appealed to the United States Supreme Court.

The state argued that the Supreme Court could not exercise appellate jurisdiction over the state's conviction of the Cohens. The essence of Virginia's argument was that the so-called "arising under" jurisdiction conferred by Article III (the judicial power of the United States shall extend to all cases *arising under* the Constitution [and] laws of the United States . . . .") was contingent upon there being an appropriate party, one who is denominated in Article 3, § 2, to bring the case. Since a dispute between a citizen and the state of his residence was not enumerated in Article 3, there was no proper party and, thus, no case upon which the Supreme Court could exercise its authority. In short, Virginia argued that the character of the parties modified the grants of jurisdiction based on the nature of the claim. The Eleventh Amendment was argued only because it was thought to bolster Virginia's interpretation of Article 3. The state argued that if Article 3 were interpreted to grant jurisdiction to federal courts in any case in which a claim or defense was based on federal law, it would, given the Eleventh Amendment, create the anomalous situation that individuals could sue their state of residency in federal court when federal law was claimed to have been violated, while residents of other states or foreign states would be prevented from doing so.[17]

Chief Justice Marshall, for a unanimous Court, rejected Virginia's argument that the character of the parties modified any grant of jurisdiction based on the subject matter of the case. Speaking to Article 3, unamended by the Eleventh Amendment, Chief Justice Marshall made it perfectly clear that the necessity of maintaining the supremacy of federal law required that the courts of the United States be available to interpret federal law whatever the character of the parties:

> [It] has been pressed with great force...that the judicial power of every well-constituted government must be coextensive with the legislative, and must be capable of deciding every judicial question which grows out of the constitution and laws.
>
> If any proposition may be considered as a political axiom, this, we think, may be so considered. In reasoning upon it as an abstract question, there would...exist no contrariety of opinion respecting it. Every argument proving the necessity of the department [the judiciary], proves also the propriety of giving this extent to it. We do not mean to say that the jurisdiction of the courts of the Union should be construed to be coextensive with the legislative, merely because it is fit that it should be so, but we mean to say that this fitness furnishes an argument in construing the constitution which ought never to be overlooked, and which is most especially entitled to consideration, when we are inquiring whether the words of the instrument which purport to establish this principle, which shall be contracted for the purpose of destroying it.
>
> The mischievous consequences of the construction contended for on the part of Virginia...would prostrate...the government and its laws at the feet of every State in the Union.

The Court did, however, concede the possibility that some claims against a state may not be asserted by citizens of that state in federal courts even though the claim may have arisen as a result of a state's acting in violation of federal law, either constitutional or statutory. For example, Chief Justice Marshall opined that if a state confiscates land in violation of a treaty, the claim must be asserted against the current occupant of the land, not the state. However, the Court did not equivocate on the necessity of providing a federal forum for the interpretation of federal law. Rather, the Court distinguished between a claim founded on the common law and one founded on the Constitution or statutes. "Were a state to lay a duty on exports (a violation of Article I, § 10 of the Constitution), to collect the money and place it in her treasury," there would be some doubt about whether any individual could sue the state to recover. Even though the state may have acted in violation of the United States Constitution, an individual who pays money to the state under an unconstitutional state law is in the same position as one who pays money to anyone, state or individual, under the mistaken belief that he is obligated to do so. The claim in either case is, as it was in Chisholm v. Georgia, based on common law *assumpsit* (a common law action to recover damages for breech of a contractual promise), not on the illegality which precipitated the mistake in the first instance. And federal courts have no jurisdiction over contract claims between a state and its citizens under Article 3. This is different, the Court said, than a claim brought against an individual by a state that asserts an unconstitutional statute as authority for its action. In the latter case, if individuals were unable to assert a claim in any United States court, there would be no judicial mechanism by which the states could be held to obey federal law.

The *Cohens* Court was, in a technical sense, correct. A suit by an individual to recover money wrongfully or mistakenly paid would be based on a common law theory for money had and received, or somewhat less accurately, for unjust enrichment. The reason why the state has a plaintiff's money, as long as it is wrongful, matters little to a plaintiff's right to recover. On the other hand, Chief Justice Marshall's distinction does leave to the state courts the determination of whether money in the hands of the state was legally acquired or not. If he meant to suggest that a state court's determination that it lawfully acquired the property or money, even if based on an interpretation of federal law, is not subject to federal appellate review, federal supremacy and the uniformity of federal law would be threatened. *Cohens* thus sent mixed messages to future courts on how to balance state sovereignty against the need to maintain the supremacy of federal law.

The *Cohens* Court's equivocation on whether *all* cases in which federal law is implicated fall within Article 3's arising under jurisdiction was only exacerbated by the Court's ambiguity with respect to the scope of the Eleventh Amendment. The Court began its Eleventh Amendment analysis with a recitation of the concern that the states had during ratification that they might be held accountable in federal courts for their pre-Constitution debts, a fear that was realized in

Chisholm v. Georgia. The Court went on to note that "its [the Eleventh Amendment] motive was not to maintain the sovereignty of a state from the degradation supposed to attend a compulsory appearance before the tribunal of the nation [because the amendment] does not comprehend controversies between two or more States, or between a State and a foreign state." What then was the purpose of the Eleventh Amendment? According to the Chief Justice, to do exactly and *only* what its words purport to do—to prevent those most likely to be the states' creditors from using the courts of the United States to collect their debts. The Court saw no inconsistency with this rather limited interpretation of the Eleventh Amendment and the principle of state sovereignty: "[a] general interest might...be felt in leaving to a State the full power of consulting its convenience in the adjustment of its debts, or of other claims upon it; but no interest could be felt in so changing the relations between the whole and its parts, as to strip the government of the means of protecting, by the instrumentality of its courts, the constitution and laws from active violation."

That being said, the Court then decided that the reason why the Eleventh Amendment did not bar the Cohens' appeal was that a writ of error to a higher court to review the judgment of a lower court was not a suit in law or equity, which rendered much of what was said about how the Eleventh Amendment balances the supremacy of federal law against state sovereignty simple *dictum* (purported statements of law not necessary to the decision). Only as an alternative holding did the Court return to its earlier federal supremacy theme:

> But should we in this be mistaken, the error does not affect the case now before the court. If this writ of error be a suit in the sense of the 11th amendment, it is not a suit commenced or prosecuted "by a citizen of another State, or by a citizen of any foreign state." It is not then within the amendment, but is governed entirely by the constitution as originally framed, and we have already seen that, in its origin, the judicial power was extended to all cases arising under the constitution or laws of the United States, without respect to parties.

What then did *Cohens* hold, other than a writ of error to the Supreme Court is not a suit within the meaning of the Eleventh Amendment? Did it hold that the Eleventh Amendment proscribes federal jurisdiction when a citizen sues his/her state of residence claiming a violation of federal law? Professor Jacobs is not quite sure.[18] The leading diversity theorists are quite convinced that the answer is no.[19] Because I read Chief Justice Marshall's distinction between cases founded on federal law and those in which the state obtains possession of money or property illegally more narrowly than Professor Jacobs, my own sense is that the Eleventh Amendment, in the eyes of *Cohens*, does not prohibit the exercise of federal jurisdiction when a citizen sues his/her state of residence. However, my confidence in that reading is not overwhelming. On the other hand, those who read Chief Justice Marshall's distinction more broadly to mean that the Eleventh Amendment prohibits all *affirmative* claims against the state for money damages, necessarily conclude that *Cohens* holds that the Eleventh Amendment indeed prohibits one from suing his/her state of residence in federal court even if the claim is based on federal law.[20]

Is the Eleventh Amendment, in Chief Justice Marshall's view, applicable at all to diverse citizenship cases, even those in which the claim is one arising under federal law? It is hard to tell. Like many significant Marshall Court opinions, both the arguments raised by counsel and the Court's response to those arguments, were broader than the final holding. Moreover, because the constitutional issues raised in the formative years of the Republic were largely matters of first impression for the judiciary, the Court's language is not free from ambiguity.

Professor Jacobs is reasonably certain that it is. He believes that the *Cohens* decision states that the Eleventh Amendment prohibits a citizen of one state from suing another state even if the claim is that the defendant state is actively violating federal law.[21] On this broader issue, those who believe that the Eleventh Amendment only applies to jurisdiction founded upon diversity of citizenship are split. Judge Gibbons and, with somewhat less certitude, Professor (now Judge) Fletcher, are clear that the Eleventh Amendment only applies in cases where the jurisdictional claim is based *only* on diversity of citizenship.[22] Professor Vicki Jackson, however, is more measured in her claims of how broadly *Cohens* can be read, describing Chief Justice Marshall's opinion of the relationship between the Eleventh Amendment and federal questioned jurisdiction as "somewhat opaque."[23] I cast my vote with Jackson. However, there is language in the *Cohens* opinion to support both positions. One must therefore look elsewhere to determine the scope of the Eleventh Amendment's proscriptions.

The Virginia Coupon Cases Revisited

As noted previously, *The Virginia Coupon Cases* were suits against officers of the state of Virginia, not against the state itself. Consequently, the Court's majority had no occasion to answer either question posited in the previous subsection regarding the implications of the *Cohens* decision. The only question directly before the Court was whether the suits against Virginia's officers were, in effect, suits against the state. The Court held they were not. The opinion in *The Virginia Coupon Cases* was not, however, unanimous. It is the dissent by Justice Bradley, the author of Hans v. Louisiana, joined by Chief Justice Waite and Justices Gray and Miller that dealt with the questions that Chief Justice Marshall's ambiguous opinion in *Cohens* left unanswered. In doing so, Justice Bradley foretold the Court's decision six years later in Hans v. Louisiana.

Arguing that the Eleventh Amendment must be interpreted broadly to effectuate its evident purposes, Justice Bradley had this to say:

> [T]he Eleventh Amendment is not intended as a mere formula of words, to be slurred over by subtle methods of interpretation, so as to give it a literal compliance, without regarding its substantial meaning and purpose. It is a grave and solemn condition, exacted by sovereign states, for the purpose of preserving and vindicating their sovereign right to deal with their creditors and others propounding claims against them, according to their own views of what may be required by public faith and the necessities of the body politic. We have no right...to fritter away the substance of this solemn stipulation by any neat and skillful manipulation of its words. We are bound to give it its full and substantial meaning and effect.

There is little doubt that Justice Bradley and his three colleagues believed that if an accommodation must be made between preserving a state's sovereign right to set its own fiscal priorities and the federal government's ability to ensure the supremacy of federal law, the weightier thumb must be placed on the supremacy of federal law. However ambiguous, Chief Justice Marshall's opinion in *Cohens* might be with respect to facts not before him at the time, there is little doubt that his unanimous opinion is fundamentally at odds with Justice Bradley's dissent. The *Cohens* Court clearly weighed in on the side of federal supremacy.

In one of *The Virginia Coupon Cases*, Poindexter v. Greenhow (1885), the plaintiff was a resident of Virginia. However, because the issue was the identity of interest between the state and its officers and the Court decided that the claim was against the officer individually, the majority had no occasion to mention that fact. However, Justice Bradley's dissent did:

> The Eleventh Amendment, it is true, does not prohibit the extension of the federal judicial authority to suits prosecuted against a State by its own citizens. But the evident reason for this is, that the judicial power was not granted to the United States by the original Constitution in such cases: hence, as it was not granted, it was not deemed necessary to prohibit it. It was evidently supposed that the control of all litigation against a State by its own citizens was in its own power, amongst that mass of rights which was reserved to the States and the people. It would be very strange to say that, although a State cannot...be sued by a citizen of another State since the adoption of the Eleventh Amendment, yet, in a case arising under the Constitution and laws of the United States, it may be sued by its own citizens. This would be to deprive the State, with regard to its own citizens, of its *sovereign right* of exemption from suit.
>
> We do not remember that it is anywhere contended that the state can be sued by its own citizens, against its own law, merely because the Eleventh Amendment does not in terms extend to that case.

Justice Bradley simply rejects the rationale of *Cohens* in favor of that upon which the state of Virginia in *Cohens* based its arguments. Moreover, with respect to the interpretive methodology of the Eleventh Amendment and the question of whether Article 3, as an original matter, permits suits in federal courts by citizens against their states of residency, Justice Bradley introduced a theme that has come to be the Rehnquist Court's rationale for prohibiting Congressional abrogation of a state's Eleventh Amendment immunity: general principles governing the constitutional relationship between the Union and the States, sometimes described in the literature as principles of structural federalism. These principles, most often thought to inhere in the spirit of the Tenth Amendment, gird the Eleventh Amendment as well (Alden v. Maine, 1999).

Finally, *In re Ayers*, the appeal of the contempt citation issued against the Virginia Attorney General, cut from *Cohens* whatever legs to its rationale were left standing. First, contrary to *Cohens'* holding that the Eleventh Amendment had nothing to do with the dignity of the state, the *Ayers* Court stated:

> The very object and purpose of the 11th Amendment were to prevent the indignity of subjecting a State to the coercive process of judicial tribunals at the instance of private parties. It was thought to be neither becoming nor convenient that the several States of the Union, invested with that large residuum of sovereignty which had not been delegated to the United States, should be summoned as defendants to answer the complaints of private persons...or that the course of their public policy and the administration of their public affairs should be subject to and controlled by the mandates of judicial tribunals without their consent, and in favor of individual interests.

Second, *Ayers* repeated the state autonomy rationale previously introduced in Justice Bradley's *Virginia Coupon Cases* dissent, and made it the basis of its holding that the order issued by the lower court violated the Eleventh Amendment. The stage was set for *Hans*.

Hans v. Louisiana

In Hans v. Louisiana (1890) Justice Bradley's dissenting opinion in *The Virginia Coupon Cases* became law. On its facts, *Hans* presented a new jurisdictional question. The plantiffs in *Jumel* and *Hagood* asserted claims based on federal law (the Contract Clause of the United States Constitution), but they were citizens of other states or foreign countries and were therefore barred from asserting their claims in federal court by the language of the Eleventh Amendment itself. Hans filed a claim in federal circuit court that was identical to that filed by *Jumel*. Based on Louisiana's Funding Act of 1874 declaring that the consolidated bonds issued by Louisiana were, "declared to create a valid contract between the state and...every holder of said bonds," and permitting the coupons on those bonds to be used to pay state taxes, Hans claimed that the failure of Louisiana to live up to the promises in the statute violated the Contracts Clause. The difference between the cases was that Hans was a citizen of Louisiana while Jumel was not. Consequently, Hans did not belong to one of the classes of plaintiffs barred from suing the state in federal court by the language of the Eleventh Amendment.

Hans' claim was, in effect, one for specific performance (a common law equitable action requiring a party to perform according to the terms of a contract) by the state of its promise in the Funding Act, a claim that the Court in *Jumel* and *Hagood* held was barred by the Eleventh Amendment.

The plaintiff's argument in *Hans* was directly from Chief Justice Marshall's clear holding in Cohens v. Virginia: Article 3 jurisdiction based upon the nature of the claim is separate and distinct from jurisdiction based upon the character of the parties. *Hans*' claim was that Louisiana violated the Contract Clause by refusing to pay on the tendered coupons of its consolidated bonds. Justice Bradley's opinion in *Hans* did not, not directly at least, deny that the two heads of jurisdiction (the character of the parties and the nature of the claim) were distinct. However, it did not have to because the Court held that Article 3, as an original matter, never conferred jurisdiction on the courts of the United States when the state was an involuntary defendant: "The truth is, that the cognizance of suits and actions unknown to the law, and forbidden by the law, was not contemplated by the Constitution when establishing the judicial power of the United States."

The Court supported its assertion in three ways. First, it cited Alexander Hamilton's *Federalist No. 81* and the statements of James Madison and John Marshall in the Virginia Ratification Convention as supporting the proposition that the Constitution could not be read to deprive the states of their sovereign immunity. *Chisholm*'s mistake was to read the *letter* of the Constitution rather than looking "at the subject . . . in the light of history and experience and the established order of things . . . ." Second, the Court looked at the established order of things in the same way as did Justice Iredell in *Chisholm*. At the time of the founding, (1) states were not subject to suit without their consent, and (2) there was a presumption "that no anomalous and unheard of proceedings were intended to be raised up by the Constitution . . . ."[24] Third, the Court looked at the Eleventh Amendment in light of that background, experience, and constitutional presumption, and concluded, counter-factually, that the Eleventh Amendment could not be reasonably interpreted to leave open the possibility that a state could be sued in federal court by its own citizens. Speculating on what might have occurred if the Eleventh Amendment debate in Congress had taken a different turn, the Court stated: "Suppose that Congress, when proposing the Eleventh Amendment, had appended to it a proviso that nothing therein contained should prevent a State from being sued by its own citizens in cases arising under the Constitution or laws of the United States: can we imagine that it would have been adopted by the States? The supposition that it would be is almost an absurdity on its face."

What of *Cohens*' alternative holding that the Eleventh Amendment did only what its language said: removed federal jurisdiction based on the character of the parties? Justice Bradley dismissed that as "unnecessary to the decision, and in that sense *extra judicial*." His only concession to the concern voiced in *Cohens* that the supremacy of federal law must be preserved was to say that "[H]e (Chief

Justice Marshall) showed that this power (appellate review of state court decisions) was absolutely necessary in order to enable the judiciary of the United States to take cognizance of all cases arising under the Constitution and laws of the United States." *Hans* thus limited *Cohens*' Eleventh Amendment analysis to the facts of that case, Supreme Court appellate review of state court decisions.

Some Concluding Comments

Much of the commentary has been critical of the *Hans* decision. Detailed discussion of this criticism will be postponed to later sections where the various extensions of, and exceptions to, *Hans* are explored. Suffice it to say at this juncture that *Hans* is criticized on two levels. First, and most significantly, *Hans* has been criticized as being inconsistent with two principles essential to the maintenance of the rule of law, (1) that legal remedies must be available to vindicate legal wrongs, and (2) that judicial and legislative power must be coextensive. Consequently, if Congress possesses the authority to create a legal right, the federal courts must have power to enforce that right.[25] The first principle, taken from Marbury v. Madison (1803), is essential to ensure that what we have created is a "government of laws and not of men." The second, taken from Alexander Hamilton's *Federalist No. 80*, is essential to prevent unchecked legislative power. Moreover, to give Congress the power to make law while denying a forum by which that law can be enforced would be to diminish substantially the authority of the national government. Enforcement of federal law would be dependent upon states, as it was under the Articles of Confederation. Second, *Hans* has been criticized for misreading history, substituting the counter-factual "profound shock" theory for a careful reading of history, one that many scholars argue demonstrates that Chisholm v. Georgia correctly understood the original grant of authority of Article 3.[26]

Most who read history differently than did the *Hans* Court subscribe to the diversity theory of the Eleventh Amendment—that it was intended only to divest federal courts of jurisdiction in those cases.[27] However, that interpretation is far from universal.[28] Moreover, even among those who subscribe to the diversity theory of the Eleventh Amendment have divergent views both with respect to its original purposes,[29] and whether the immunity that it preserves is a constitutional immunity or one based only in the common law.[30]

The constitutional immunity theory of *Hans* is not, however, without its supporters. To begin with, *Hans* was a unanimous decision. Even Justice Harlan, who dissented in *Jumel* because of his disagreement with the Court's tilting the federal/state balance in favor of the states, wrote a brief concurring opinion which left little doubt that, whether as an original matter (the majority's position) or because of the Eleventh Amendment (what appears to be Justice Harlan's position), the Constitution prohibits suits in federal courts against the state whatever the nature of the claim. Moreover, as pointed out in the previous subsection, there is some historical support for a general fear that Article 3 would open states' treasuries to courts over which they had no control. Indeed it was John Marshall, along with James Madison, who attempted to assure the Virginia Ratification Convention that it was never intended that Article 3 would have this effect. This history coupled with the anomaly that noncitizens would be relegated to state courts to assert their federal rights while citizens could make use of the federal courts to assert those very same rights, have prompted some scholars to conclude that *Hans* was correctly decided.[31]

It may well be that the critics are correct: That *Hans'* holding that the Eleventh Amendment grants states a general constitutional sovereign immunity is so devoid of support, historical or otherwise,[32] that it ought to be reconsidered despite *stare decisis* (the doctrine that admonishes courts to decide cases in accordance with precedent).[33] Indeed, the Supreme Court came within one vote of doing so, certainly once (Welch v. Texas Department of Highways and Public Transportation, 1987) and, if one reads between the lines, maybe twice (Pennsylvania v. Union Gas Company, 1989). More will be said about this below. For the moment, however, the focus must be elsewhere. If it is true that "the devil is in the details," the "stuff" of the Eleventh Amendment is in how the Court, since *Hans*, has interpreted the scope of the states' sovereign immunity in the often disparate contexts in which that defense has been asserted. That is the focal point of much that follows. By way of conclusion and critique, the analysis will briefly return to the overriding structural concern of the Eleventh Amendment, accommodating the often conflicting *constitutional* requirements of the supremacy and uniformity of federal law with assuring that the states maintain an essential role in our bifurcated system of governance.

Ex parte Young— Suing State Officers Redux

INTRODUCTION

The Court has grafted upon its constitutional state sovereign immunity doctrine five major exceptions. The first, discussed earlier, is that states are subject to the appellate jurisdiction of the United States Supreme Court. That discussion will not be repeated here. The extent to which this exception adequately ensures the supremacy of federal law will, however, be revisited when the discussion turns to Congress' power to abrogate the states' Eleventh Amendment immunity. Three exceptions to the Eleventh Amendment, for political subdivisions of the state, for states that waive their sovereign immunity, and for private actions commenced in the courts of other states, will be discussed below. The present focus will be on what many consider to be the most significant exception to a state's Eleventh Amendment immunity, an individual's ability to sue state officers in United States courts to prevent them from implementing state policies that conflict with federal law. The seminal case is Ex parte Young (1907).

Ex parte Young

Ex parte Young, decided seventeen years after Hans v. Louisiana, held that the Eleventh Amendment did not prohibit an individual from suing a state officer in federal court to enjoin him/her from enforcing a statute alleged to be unconstitutional under the Fourteenth Amendment. Ratified in 1868, the Fourteenth Amendment provides in part that "[n]o state shall make or enforce any law which shall abridge the privileges or immunity of citizens of the United States; nor shall any state deprive any person of life, liberty, or property, without due process of law; nor deny any person within its jurisdiction the equal protection of the laws." *Ex parte Young* was one of a number of cases, beginning in the last decade of the nineteenth century, in which the United States Supreme Court was called upon to rule on the constitutionality of states' efforts to regulate the rates interstate railroads charged to in-state shippers.[34] Because *Hans* precluded private actions against a state in federal court, plaintiffs sued those state officers charged with administering the prescribed rates. Unlike previous actions against state officers, however, these claims generally asked the federal court to enjoin the officers from complying with their statutory mandates rather than requesting money damages either from the officers or the state itself. The actions against state officers thus resembled *In re Ayers*, discussed previously, which held because the state was the real party in interest in a suit to enjoin the state's Attorney General from suing to enforce a state statute, the action was barred by the Eleventh Amendment.

The *In re Ayers* Eleventh Amendment defense was first raised only four years after *Hans* in Regan v. Farmers' Loan & Trust Company (1894). But unlike *Ayers*, *Regan* was not a case that posed a threat to the state's treasury, the historical concern of the Eleventh Amendment. The *Regan* Court relied on this distinction in deciding that the state was not the real party in interest. Unlike the previous bond cases, the state of Texas in *Regan* stood to lose nothing from its inability to enforce its prescribed rates other than its general interest in "the well being of its citizens [and] the just and equal enforcement of all of its laws." This interest was insufficient to invoke the proscription of the Eleventh Amendment.

This reasoning was basic to the Court's decision in *Ex parte Young*. Edward Young was the Attorney General of Minnesota, and, as such, was charged with enforcing the laws of that state, including the state's railroad rate legislation. In addition to fixing rates in the state of Minnesota, the legislation provided that violations of passenger rates were a felony and would subject officers and employees of the railroad to imprisonment for up to five years and a $5,000 fine. Violations of the prescribed freight rates were only misdemeanors, but each day's violation was a separate offense. Not wanting to put employees of the railroad in jeopardy, shareholders of several railroads sued in United States district court to enjoin the Railroad and Warehouse Commission from implementing the proposed rates and Attorney General Young from enforcing the rates. The plaintiffs claimed the rates were excessively low and therefore violated the due process clause of the Fourteenth Amendment. The district court issued the requested injunctions. Young, nevertheless, commenced a *mandamus action* (a common law action to compel a public or corporate officer to perform his/her statutory duties) in state court against the railroads to require their compliance with the rates set by the state. For this, Attorney General Young was held in contempt of court by the district court. He then filed a writ of *habeas corpus* (an order directing a state or federal officer to justify one's imprisonment) challenging the district court's contempt citation. *Ex parte Young* was decided as an appeal from the denial of that writ.

Speaking for the Court, Mr. Justice Pekham tipped the obligatory hat to the earlier *In re Ayers* line of cases and bowed graciously to the Eleventh Amendment: "we must give to the Eleventh Amendment all the effect it naturally would have, without cutting it down or rendering its meaning any more narrow than the language, fairly interpreted, would warrant." The Court then proceeded to claim the authority to enjoin state officers from enforcing unconstitutional state statutes:

> The answer to all of this is the same as made in every case where an official claims to be acting under the authority of the state. The act to be enforced is alleged to be unconstitutional, and if it be so, the use of the name of the state to enforce an unconstitutional act to the injury of complainants is a proceeding without the authority of and one which does not affect the state in its sovereign or governmental capacity. It is simply an illegal act upon the part of a state official in attempting by the use of the name of the state to enforce a legislative enactment which is void because unconstitutional. If the act which the state Attorney General seeks to enforce be a violation of the Federal Constitution, the officer proceeding under such enactment comes into conflict with the superior authority of that Constitution, and he is in that case stripped of his official or representative character and is subjected in his person to the consequences of his individual conduct. The State has no power to impart to him any immunity from responsibility to the supreme authority of the United States.

Responding to the argument that there is a difference between a state officer being held accountable for damages resulting to tangible property or from a direct trespass and enjoining a state officer from performing his public duty, the Court made the following observations:

> A bill to prevent the commencement of suits to enforce an unconstitutional act...is no new invention.... In the case of the interference with property the person enjoined is assuming to act in his capacity as an official of the State, and justification for his interference is claimed by reason of his position as a state official. Such official cannot so justify when acting under an unconstitutional enactment of the legislature. So, where the state official, instead of directly interfering with tangible property, is about to commence suits, which have for their object the enforcement of an act which violates the Federal Constitution, to the great and irreparable injury of the complainants, he is seeking the same justification from the authority of the state as in other cases. The sovereignty of the State is, in reality, no more involved in one case than in the other.

Surprisingly, Justice Harlan who had dissented so vigorously in *Ayers*, mounted the same spirited dissent for the opposite result in *Young*.

> The principle, if firmly established, would work a radical change in our governmental system. It would inaugurate a new era in the American judicial system and in the relations of the National and state governments. It would enable the subordinate Federal courts to supervise and control the official action of the States as if they were "dependencies" or

provinces. It would place the States of the Union in a condition never dreamed of when the Constitution was adopted or when the Eleventh Amendment was made a part of the Supreme Law of the Land.... Too little consequence has been attached to the fact that the courts of the states are under an obligation equally strong with that resting upon the courts of the Union to respect and enforce the provisions of the Federal Constitution.... [A] decent respect for the States requires us to assume...that the state courts will enforce every right secured by the Constitution. If they fail to do so, the party...can come by writ of error...to this tribunal for redress....

Ex parte Young was not well received by the states.[35] Just seventeen years earlier in Hans v. Louisiana the Court declared that the Eleventh Amendment recognized a general constitutional sovereign immunity for the states. But *Ex parte Young* opened the door to the possibility that federal judges would, as Justice Miller opined in 1873, become "perpetual censor(s) upon all legislation of the States," (*The Slaughter House Cases*, 1873). Moreover, *Young* rested on a legal fiction that created an inconsistency between the Eleventh and Fourteenth Amendments.

The Legal Fiction

On its face, *Young* did little more than choose between two conflicting lines of cases. The *In re Ayers* line held that a state officer who has only an official interest in the outcome of a particular lawsuit is, for purposes of that lawsuit, the state. The *Regan* line held that a state officer can have no official interest in enforcing an unconstitutional statute. Certainly, the latter was more conducive to the enforcement of the Fourteenth Amendment during a period of time when the Court appeared preoccupied with reigning in state regulation of private business activity. But the Court's preference for enforcement of the Fourteenth Amendment was not simply a "political" decision; it had some basis in law. First, in terms of the Eleventh Amendment, there is indeed something to the distinction between a suit requesting a federal court to hold the state to its contractual obligations and one that seeks to enjoin the application of a statute in order to relieve an individual from allegedly unconstitutional regulatory burdens. While it is not improper to characterize the protections of the Contract Clause as being equally important to the individual as are the rights secured by the Due Process and Equal Protection clauses of the Fourteenth Amendment, the Eleventh Amendment, at a minimum, was ratified specifically in order to protect states from out-of-state plaintiffs using the federal courts to enforce states' contractual obligations. *Hans* merely extended that minimum. Consequently, a state and the officials responsible for implementing that state's policies regarding its contractual indebtedness are difficult to separate, making the states' real party in interest assertions likely to succeed in the Contract Clause setting.

Second, the Fourteenth Amendment was ratified after the Eleventh Amendment, giving rise to the venerable argument of construction that explicit inconsistencies between an earlier and a later enacted provision should be resolved in favor of the latter. But if the inconsistencies are not explicit, the two seemingly inconsistent provisions should be read to make them compatible. In one sense, an inconsistency exists between the Eleventh and Fourteenth Amendments. In the name of federalism, the Eleventh Amendment, as interpreted by *Hans*, enabled the states to choose whether they would be judicially accountable to individuals for their actions. The Fourteenth Amendment, by providing an explicit prohibition on state action, removed that choice. On the other hand, it is possible to read the Eleventh and Fourteenth amendments as compatible. And that is arguably what the Court did in *Ex parte Young*. First, by permitting actions to enjoin state officers from enforcing unconstitutional legislation and regulations, the Court blunted any indignity to the states from requiring them to appear *eo nominee* in a federal court. Second, by limiting the private claim to injunctions, which affected the state only prospectively, the Court did not open the door to private claims on the state's treasury, the original purpose of the Eleventh Amendment.

Third, and Justice Harlan's dissent to the contrary notwithstanding, enforcing the Fourteenth Amendment against state officers, preventing them from performing their official duties, may impinge less on state autonomy than enforcing the Contract Clause to require a state or its officials to own up to the state's contractual obligations. While both the Fourteenth Amendment and the Contract Clause deprive the states of a certain power to act with respect to individuals, the remedial impact of the mid-to-late nineteenth century bond litigation under the Contract Clause was to hold the state to the performance of an affirmative, contractual obligation. Either that, or a state officer would be held to a contractual liability that he did not assume, and whose responsibility for the contract was, in any event, not contemplated by either party to that contract. Holding an officer liable would therefore be a windfall to the other contractual party. On the other hand, the exercise of jurisdiction by a federal court in a Fourteenth Amendment case such as *Ex parte Young* required the state to undertake no affirmative obligation. Nor did it impose on state officers any federally mandated affirmative duty. It merely prohibited the implementation of a state law that was void because it violated the federal Constitution. The principle that a law inconsistent with the United States Constitution is void and unenforceable dates back at least to Marbury v. Madison (1803) and Martin v. Hunter's Lessee (1816) and probably before.

Finally, as Clyde Jacobs argues, the Contract Clause and the Fourteenth Amendment secure very different individual interests. The Contract Clause secures only vested rights, that is, previously undertaken contractual obligations awaiting only performance by the obligee. The Fourteenth Amendment, on the other hand, protects a broader notion of economic liberty, the right of the parties to set the terms and conditions of their own undertakings (Lochner v. New York,

1905). At least it did when *Ex parte Young* was decided. *Ex parte Young* thus represented, "a jurisdictional adjustment expediting and expanding federal judicial protection of certain substantive rights, which . . . had become ascendant in the Court's scheme of values."[36]

As noted previously, treating the Eleventh Amendment differently in Fourteenth Amendment cases than in Contract Clause cases was made possible only by creating a legal fiction that resulted in a doctrinal anomaly: That state officers who propose to implement an unconstitutional state policy are not acting for the state, but only for themselves. To put the anomaly in terms more congenial to the analysis of nineteenth-century Eleventh Amendment Cases, the real party in interest in the enforcement of an unconstitutional state policy is not the state, for the state cannot act *ultra vires* (beyond its legal authority). Rather, the real party in interest is the individual officer in his individual capacity.

Merely stating the theory removes all necessity for explaining why it is a fiction—it is preposterous. But for the state policy and the officer's legal obligation to enforce that policy, no action against the officer would lie. To use the Court's own method of determining the state's pecuniary interest in the officer's actions, Attorney General Young had far less interest, pecuniary or otherwise, in what rates are charged in-state users of interstate railroads than did the state of Minnesota. Indeed, he had no personal interest at all. The doctrinal anomaly that flows from the legal fiction is that the word "state" means different things for purposes of the Eleventh Amendment depending upon whether the claim is to prohibit a state from acting contrary to the Contract Clause or to prevent a state from acting contrary to the proscriptions of the Fourteenth Amendment.

Neither the fiction nor its resulting doctrinal anomaly is, for that reason alone, a basis for criticism.[37] The common law is rife with legal fictions.[38] And the Court has virtually painted the Constitution with doctrinal anomalies. Indeed, one might argue that the fiction created by *Ex parte Young* and the resulting doctrinal anomaly are the least of the internal inconsistencies with current Eleventh Amendment jurisprudence. Arguably *Ex parte* Young is a, albeit not the only, sensible way of reconciling the Eleventh and Fourteenth Amendments and, more generally, preserving the Constitution as the "supreme law of the land." The difficulty is that the fiction of *Ex parte Young* created a logical weakness in Eleventh Amendment jurisprudence that is subject to being exploited by later Justices and courts more sympathetic to states rights than the exertion of federal authority and the supremacy of federal laws. That has occurred, albeit only at the margins. Recent Supreme Court cases have carved out three, and according to some, four, exceptions to *Ex Parte Young*'s holding that state officers can be prevented from enforcing policies that are found to be inconsistent with federal law.

Edelman v. Jordan: The Prospective/Retrospective Distinction[39]

Edelman v. Jordan (1974) was a suit filed by a recipient of federal assistance for the Aged, Blind, and Disabled against the Director of the Illinois Department of Public Aid. The suit sought an injunction prohibiting him from continuing to violate certain federal regulations regarding the time within which payments had to be made and for an order requiring him to pay monies owed for that period of time when the state was not complying with the federal regulations. The state argued that while *Ex parte Young* permitted the injunctive order, it did not permit a federal court to order a state official to pay monetary damages that must come from the state's treasury rather than from the official's personal assets. Put simply, the Eleventh Amendment requires a court to focus on the likely source of the payment rather than on the party against whom the order to pay is issued. The plaintiff's argument, which was accepted by the court of appeals, focused neither on the source of payment nor on the party against whom the order was issued but rather on the nature of the claim. Because the nature of the relief sought was *equitable restitution* (an equitable remedy to restore something taken from the owner) rather than damages for *breech of contract* (a legal remedy under the common law), the plaintiff argued that this case more closely resembled the relief sought in *Ex parte Young* than the relief sought in Hans v. Louisiana.

The Court held that the nature of the action is not what determines the applicability of the Eleventh Amendment. Nor is it that the order will necessarily have an impact on the state's treasury. Rather, "the difference between the type of relief barred by the Eleventh Amendment and that permitted under *Ex parte Young*, rests on whether the relief, *in its effect*, can properly be characterized as retrospective:

> It [the district court's decree] requires payment of state funds, not a necessary consequence of compliance in the future with a substantive federal-question determination, but as a form of compensation to those whose applications were processed on the slower time schedule at a time when petitioner was under no court-imposed obligation to conform to a different standard. While the Court of Appeals described this retroactive monetary relief as a form of "equitable restitution," it is in practical effect indistinguishable in many aspects from an award of damages against the State. It will to a virtual certainty be paid from state funds, and not from the pockets of the individual state officials....It is measured in terms of a monetary loss resulting from a past breach of a legal duty on the part of the defendant state officials.

The rule of *Edelman* seems simple enough—*Ex parte Young* permits actions against state officers except when the relief sought (1) will impose a monetary burden on the state treasury, *and* (2) the nature of remedy causing that burden is retrospective, compensation for a *past* breach of a legal duty. As it turned out, however, the rule is not nearly this simple. *Edelman* left unresolved two rather obvious questions: (1) how does a court determine whether relief is retrospective or prospective, and (2) is all retrospective relief sought against state officials barred by the Eleventh Amendment or only that retrospective relief which resembles an award of damages against the state and which will, with "virtual certainty," be paid from the state's treasury?

The second question was recently answered—any relief designed to remedy a past violation of federal law is retrospective, regardless of whether a state's treasury is affected (Breard v. Greene, 1998). But *Breard* was not decided until 1998. Between 1974 and 1998, the Court decided several cases in which it had to grapple with the questions left open in *Edelman*. *Breard* is the only case in this line in which the state's treasury was not in the least bit implicated by the plaintiff's assertions. In all the other cases decided between *Edelman* and *Breard*, the plaintiffs' claims, at least indirectly, had an impact upon the state's treasury. Looking backward from *Breard*, these cases are more important for what they say about the distinction between prospective and retrospective claims than for whatever implications one can derive regarding whether a claim on the state's treasury is a necessary condition for invoking the Eleventh Amendment defense.[40] But this was not always the case. As such, the analysis that follows will reference both issues.

Three years after *Edelman*, the Court decided Milliken v. Bradley (II) (1977). *Milliken* was a suit to desegregate the Detroit public schools brought against Detroit school officials and the Governor of Michigan, George Milliken. It was a complicated suit that reached the Supreme Court on two occasions, only the second of which raised Eleventh Amendment concerns.[41] After the Supreme Court in *Milliken (I)*, remanded (that is, returned) the case to the trial court, that court ordered the implementation of thirteen remedial and compensatory programs, the costs of these programs to be shared equally between the Detroit School District and the state of Michigan. The state appealed to the Supreme Court arguing that the order requiring it to fund half the cost of the new programs violated the Eleventh Amendment.

The Court rejected the state's argument despite the fact that (1) the money to comply with the order would come from the state treasury not Governor Milliken's personal assets, and (2) the reason for finding the state liable for those costs was its past breach of its constitutional obligation to maintain a unitary (that is, desegregated) school system. The Court distinguished *Edelman* on two distinct grounds: (1) the plaintiffs were not the personal beneficiaries of whatever monetary liability the order imposed on the state, and (2) the order was prospective because it was designed to remedy a continuing violation of the plaintiffs' right to a unitary school system. Neither ground, however, provides a satisfactory distinction between *Edelman* and *Milliken*. The first, while true, would seem to make little difference if the purpose of the Eleventh Amendment is to protect the state's treasury from any demands other than those of the state's legislature. The second can just as easily be said of *Edelman*; that is, the order in that case merely compensated the plaintiffs for the state's continuing violation of failing to pay the plaintiffs what it owed them under federal law. *Milliken* did make clear, however, that even an order that imposed a direct requirement that monies be distributed from the state's treasury pursuant to an order of a federal court is not a sufficient condition to deny the *Ex parte Young* exception to the Eleventh Amendment. The order must also be retrospective. The order in *Milliken* was not retrospective because it corrected the continuing effects of maintaining a dual segregated school system.

Milliken (II)'s distinction between retrospective and prospective relief was reaffirmed eight years later in Green v. Mansour (1985), albeit only in dictum. *Green* was a suit against several Michigan Department of Public Aid officials requesting a declaratory judgment that they had violated federal law in distributing AFDC benefits. The plaintiffs also requested that their class be given notice that they could take advantage of state administrative remedies to be compensated for their lost benefits.[42] The plaintiffs also sought an injunction to prevent the state officials from continuing to violate federal law. After the suit was filed, Congress amended the relevant statute in a way that made the injunctive claim moot. The district court then dismissed the plaintiff's declaratory and notice relief claims on the grounds that they violated the Eleventh Amendment. The court of appeals affirmed this decision, as did the Supreme Court. According to the Court, the only value of declaratory relief was that it would be *res judicata* (binding upon the state) in a subsequent state court proceeding for the recovery of monetary damages. That would, in effect, be a "partial 'end run' around...Edelman v. Jordan." That is, the effect would be the same as a federal court directly holding the state liable in damages to the plaintiff.

However, the Court did not stop with reaffirming the *Edelman* rule that one cannot sue state officers in federal court for the equivalent of monetary damages when it is clear that it is not the officers but the state that will satisfy the award. The Court also discussed the prospective/retrospective distinction. In doing so, it essentially redefined and narrowed *Ex parte Young* so that it was applicable only in cases where the court is called upon to remedy an "ongoing" or "current" violation of federal law.

> Both prospective and retrospective relief implicate Eleventh Amendment concerns, but the availability of prospective relief of the sort awarded in *Ex parte Young* gives life to the Supremacy Clause. Remedies designed to end a continuing violation of federal law are necessary to vindicate the federal interest in assuring the supremacy of the law. But compensatory interests are insufficient to overcome the dictates of the Eleventh Amendment.

The result of *Green*, as Professor Carlos Manuel Vázquez quite properly notes, is that the only inquiry in an *Ex parte Young* suit is *when* the violation occurred.[43]

What may have been dictum in *Green* became the holding one year later in Papasan v. Allain (1986). *Papasan* was a very complicated case involving certain conditions regarding the setting aside of land for public education that were imposed by Congress when Mississippi entered the Union. The conditions, however, did not cover certain land in the northern twenty-three counties that, at the time, belonged to the Chickasaw Nation. In 1832 these lands were ceded to the United States, and in 1836 the ceded land was given by the United States to Mississippi on the condition that it be held in trust for public education in northern counties in which the land was located. Then, in 1856, with Congress' permission, the state sold the trust land and loaned the proceeds to the state's railroads that, in turn, were destroyed in the Civil War, leaving nothing of the initial grant for equal education in the northern counties. The plaintiffs asserted two claims, each with its own request for relief. The first claim was that the defendant state officials had violated their fiduciary obligation with respect to the plaintiffs' education. They should therefore be required to set aside an amount of money (or an amount of land of equivalent value to the original lands) to be held in perpetual trust for the benefit of the plaintiffs' education. The second claim was that the state was in violation of the equal protection clause of the Fourteenth Amendment because it provided more money for education in the southern counties than in the northern ones. The remedy requested for this claim was an injunction to prohibit that disparity.

The Court dismissed the first claim holding that the Eleventh Amendment prohibited it. It upheld the second claim, however, saying that it fell within the *Ex parte Young* exception that state officers could be sued to prevent their violation of federal law. The difference between the two claims that justified this different treatment was that the first asked for retrospective relief while the latter was prospective. The Court held that only those claims that seek to end a *continuing violation* of federal law are prospective. Those claims that either seek compensation for past wrongs, apparently even if the plaintiffs are not personally benefitted by that compensation, or which are designed to deter future violations by imposing a penalty for past transgressions, are retrospective and thus not within the *Young* exception. The Court concluded that the breach of trust claim was retrospective because, while ongoing, it was nevertheless a "liability for past breach of trust"—the sale of the trust land in order to benefit the railroads. On the other hand, the equal protection claim asserted a current and ongoing violation of federal law: the disparity in funding between the northern and southern counties. The Court was apparently not troubled by the financial implications of either of the two claims, thus reaffirming *Green*'s dictum that the only pertinent question in deciding whether the *Ex parte Young* exception can be asserted is *when* the allegedly illegal act occurred.

If at this point the reader is confused, that is to be expected. The breach of trust claim could easily be described as an ongoing violation—continuing to maintain an inadequate education fund for the northern counties. That conclusion would certainly be consistent with Milliken v. Bradley (II). Therefore, if the claim in *Milliken (II)* was prospective, then so is the breach of trust claim in *Papasan.* About the best one can say about *Papasan* is that the decision regarding the breach of trust assertion may only be a symbolic gesture to state sovereignty since the equal protection holding obligated the state to equalize state educational funding despite the Court's Eleventh Amendment ruling on the trust claim. But this may not follow. The state could comply with the prospective order in *Papasan* by cutting funds to the southern school districts and redistributing those funds to the northern districts. The breach of trust theory on the other hand, would require significant additional appropriations. While the Court may have been concerned with this, the order in *Milliken (II)* also required significant additional state appropriations. This concern therefore does not justify the result in *Papasan* unless the Court is indeed prepared to overrule Milliken v. Bradley (II). It did not give any indication of that however.

Breard v. Greene (1998), the latest Supreme Court foray into the prospective/retrospective relief distinction, closes the circle by cementing the distinction between retrospective and prospective relief. Angel Breard, a citizen of Paraguay, was convicted in Virginia of attempted rape and capital murder and sentenced to death. After exhausting all state appellate remedies, Breard filed a writ of habeas corpus in United States district court alleging, *inter alia*, and for the first time, that the state violated his rights under the Vienna Convention by failing to inform him that he had a right to contact the Paraguayan Consulate upon his arrest. In addition, Paraguay filed a separate action, against the Governor of Virginia for a declaratory judgment (a special judicial proceeding to declare the legal rights of the parties without an enforcement order) and an injunction to stop Breard's execution, also alleging a violation of the Vienna Convention. The latter action was dismissed by the court of appeals in part on the basis of the Eleventh Amendment. The Supreme Court, in a *per curiam opinion* (an opinion of the Court with no particular Justice denominated as the author), held that the *Milliken (II)* exception for continuing violations did not apply because: "(t)he failure to notify the Paraguayan Consul occurred long ago and has no continuing effect. The causal link present in *Milliken* is absent in this case."

As noted previously, *Breard* was not a case that imposed any burden on the state's treasury. Its ruling therefore dispelled all doubt that such an impact is a necessary condition for invoking the Eleventh Amendment. Its ruling on the prospective/retrospective distinction is somewhat more difficult to assess. Certainly it accepts the distinction drawn in *Green* between compensating for past violations of federal law, preventing continuing violations, and remedying current effects of those past violations. It may not have said any more than that however. Indeed, given its statements regarding the lack of nexus between the past violation of federal law (the failure to notify the defendant of his rights under the

Vienna Convention) and the outcome of the trial that imposed the death penalty, the opinion could be read as a judgment on the merits of the plaintiff's claim rather than a step, one way or the other, in the Court's continuing effort to distinguish between prospective and retrospective relief. If that is true, the law, as it currently stands, is firm that all retrospective relief is prohibited by the Eleventh Amendment and not subject to the *Ex parte Young* exception. However, what retrospective relief is and precisely how it is to be distinguished from prospective relief is still very much a work in progress. Given the nature of that question, and, as *Breard* illustrates, the ease with which it can be conflated with the merits of the claim, the distinction may never be anything but a work in progress.

The *Pennhurst* Exception for State Law Claims

Pennhurst State School and Hospital v. Halderman (1984) interpreted the Eleventh Amendment to prohibit an injunction by a federal court against state officials even though the relief sought was clearly prospective within the meaning of Edelman v. Jordan. *Pennhurst* was a suit by a resident of a state hospital for the mentally retarded against a variety of state institutions and state and county officials alleging that the conditions at the hospital fell below those mandated by the federal constitution, a number of federal statutes, and a Pennsylvania statute. The district court dismissed the federal claims on their merits but issued an injunction against the state and county[44] officials based on their violation of the Pennsylvania statute. The district court justified its action under the well-recognized doctrine that federal courts have jurisdiction to rule on questions of state law when they are appended to the federal claims that provide the court's jurisdictional base. Put more simply, the Court, for reasons of judicial economy, has held that when a claimed violation of state law arises out of the same transaction(s) and/or set of facts as the federal claim, federal courts have the power to adjudicate that state law claim.

The Supreme Court's Eleventh Amendment holding in *Pennhurst*, stated in its simplest doctrinal fashion, seems narrow and rather unexceptional—*Ex parte Young* permits federal courts to enjoin state officers from violating federal law but does not extend this privilege when the injunction is for a violation of state law. *Pennhurst*'s reasoning, however, reaches far more broadly. First, *Pennhurst* apparently rejected the authority-stripping legal fiction rationale of *Ex parte Young*—that state officers who act without constitutional authority cannot be said to be acting in their official capacity and thus lose their immunity from private civil actions.[45] However, the Court was not clear how far down the road it goes in rejecting the *Ex parte Young*'s legal fiction rationale. At one point, it quoted the district court, saying, "the individual defendants 'acted in the utmost good faith...*within the sphere of their official responsibilities.*'" Had that been the Court's rationale it could have disposed of the appeal in one paragraph, noting only that the officials were acting lawfully and fully within the scope of their state granted authority. The "real party in interest" would have thus been the state, and the Eleventh Amendment would have barred the action.

But the Court chose instead to undercut *Ex parte Young* by explicitly recognizing that it reached the result it did only by creating a fiction. Moreover, according to the Court, it was a fiction "that has been narrowly construed": *Ex parte Young*'s "'well recognized [doctrinal] irony' has been accepted as necessary to permit the federal courts to vindicate federal rights." Absent that necessity, state sovereign immunity must be respected by the federal courts because of the "vital role...the doctrine of sovereign immunity [plays] in our federal system." Certainly the *Pennhurst* Court was correct both about the fictional quality of *Ex parte Young* and the reason why that fiction was appropriate. To my knowledge no one has ever questioned either conclusion. But by explicitly shifting the rationale of the *Ex parte Young* exception from the state officer's lack of legal authority to the need to make compromises in state sovereignty that are *necessary* to ensure the supremacy of federal law, the *Pennhurst* Court adopted a far more pliable test. The test is now one dependent upon any given Court's view of how necessary it is to the sanctity of federal law that a federal court exercise jurisdiction over a state officer. Finally, by viewing Eleventh Amendment sovereign immunity as just one piece in a larger federalism puzzle, *Pennhurst*, maybe without realizing it, laid the foundation for the Court's current limitations on Congress' authority to abrogate a state's sovereign immunity pursuant to its substantive legislative powers.[46]

Maintaining Sovereignty Over Property—Idaho v. Coeur d'Alene Tribe of Idaho

Idaho v. Coeur d'Alene Tribe of Idaho (1997) arose because of a dispute between the Coeur d'Alene Tribe of Idaho and the state of Idaho. The two parties disagreed about who was entitled to possess and exercise sovereignty over certain banks and submerged lands under and abutting Lake Coeur d' Alene and its tributaries, including the headwaters of the Spokane River. The Tribe claimed ownership and control over the land under an executive order issued by President Grant in 1873, and later confirmed by congressional legislation enacted in 1891. The Tribe, contending that a number of state laws interfered with its claimed sovereignty over the land, filed suit requesting an order declaring its exclusive right to occupy and enjoy the land. The suit also sought to enjoin the state officers from continuing to interfere with the Tribe's right to occupy and enjoy the land. The state responded with arguments both on the merits of its claim of ownership of and sovereignty over the land, and on the grounds that the Tribe's suit was, in essence, a suit against the state and therefore barred by the Eleventh Amendment. In a 5–4 opinion, much of which was only subscribed to by the author, Justice Kennedy, and Chief Justice Rehnquist, the Court agreed with the state and held that the action was not subject to the *Ex parte Young* exception. The Eleventh Amendment, therefore, foreclosed it.

The Court's opinion begins in an unexceptional fashion by reiterating that the Eleventh Amendment, "enacts a sovereign immunity from suit, rather than a nonwaivable limit on the federal judiciary's subject matter jurisdiction." As the Court had previously held in Blatchford v. Native Village of Noatak (1991), sovereign immunity insulates states from suit not only by individuals, but also from suits by other sovereigns, including Indian tribes. It is the Court's reasoning regarding the application of *Ex parte Young*, however, that raises questions about the extent to which *Ex parte Young* has been further narrowed. Relying on the assertion in *Pennhurst* that *Ex parte Young* created a fiction in order to maintain a proper balance between a state's immunity and the supremacy of federal law, the Court stated that, "(t)o interpret *Young* to permit a federal court action to proceed in every case where prospective declaratory and injunctive relief is sought against an officer named in his individual capacity, would be to adhere to an empty formalism...." The Court then held that the Tribe's action, "was *close to* the functional equivalent of quiet title (an action to establish the plaintiff's title to land) in that substantially all benefits of ownership and control would shift from the State to the Tribe."

At first blush, the notion that actions "close to" quiet title do not fall within the *Ex parte Young* exception is rather unremarkable. In an action to quiet title, a court is called upon to determine who, among two or more claimants, has legal title to the property in dispute. Where the state is one of the claimants, it, and not the officers who possess the property, is the real party in interest. If the Court rejected a state officer's argument in a quiet title case that she is in lawful possession of the property because the state's title is valid, it would be a judgment against the state in much the same way that the monetary relief requested in Edelman v. Jordan was a judgment against the state and not the individual actually sued. Moreover, the Court had previously determined that quiet title actions in which the state was one of the claimants were suits against the state (Florida Department of State v. Treasure Salvors Inc., 1982).

The difficulty with the Court's statement is that this case was not, as the Court itself recognized, an action to quiet title. It was only *close to* such an action. As Justice Souter pointed out in his dissent, the *Coeur d'Alene* decision is actually contrary to the holding in *Treasure Salvors* because that case, albeit in a plurality opinion, affirmed a federal court's power to levy on property held by the state under a claim of ownership in order to determine possessory rights. *Coeur d'Alene* almost certainly casts doubt on that holding. In addition, *Coeur d'Alene* is arguably inconsistent with a much earlier case, United States v. Lee (1882).

As described previously, *Lee* was a case in ejectment (an action to determine which of various contending parties has the right to possess property) by the heirs of Robert E. Lee against federal officers occupying Lee's estate, under a deed acquired at a tax sale. Lee's heirs contested the validity of the tax sale because the federal government refused to accept a third party's attempt to tender the back taxes (they went unpaid because General Lee was otherwise engaged leading the Army of Virginia in the Civil War). The government moved to dismiss, claiming that the suit was effectively a suit against the United States because the defendant officers held the property, not in their personal capacity but in trust for the citizens of the United States. The action was, in other words, *close to* an action to quiet title. The Court rejected the government's claim and held that since the suit was against the officers and not the government, it could not assert sovereign immunity as a defense.[47]

Justice Kennedy's opinion for the Court in *Coeur d'Alene* did not even mention *Lee*. Justice O'Connor, in her concurring opinion, distinguished *Lee* because the claim there challenged only the defendants' right to possession, not the validity of the United States' title. Thus, the United States was not bound by any judgment that might be issued against its officers regarding their continuing right to possess the property as a military cemetery and fort. Justice O'Connor, however, was wrong. As Justice Gray's dissent in *Lee* pointed out, the ejectment action in that case in fact affected title. Admittedly, *Lee* has been limited by subsequent cases to situations in which the officer holds the disputed property in violation of the federal constitution (Malone v. Bowdoin, 1962; Larson v. Domestic and Foreign Commerce Corp., 1949). But this should not distinguish it because the Tribe's allegation in *Coeur d'Alene* was that the state claimed sovereignty in violation of federal law, the 1873 Executive Order and the 1891 congressional statute. Further, *Ex parte Young* had not been limited to claims against state officers who acted in violation of the federal constitution as opposed to federal statutes (Edelman v. Jordan, 1974). Whether, in the name of maintaining a more acceptable balance between state sovereignty and federal supremacy, *Coeur d'Alene* will be the first step in limiting *Ex parte Young* to violations of the federal constitution only, remains to be seen.[48]

Possibly more ominous for the *Ex parte Young* exception, however, is that part of Justice Kennedy's opinion, joined by four other Justices, that appears to carve out an exception from *Ex parte Young* for matters that go to the heart of a state's sovereignty. In this case, the Court was referring specifically to the state's interest in submerged lands: "lands underlying navigable waters have historically been considered 'sovereign lands.' State ownership of them has been 'considered an essential attribute of sovereignty.'" But, as Justice Souter argued in his dissent, if the reason it is impossible in *Coeur d'Alene* to separate the state from its officers is that the state's vital sovereignty interests are at stake, there is no particular reason why one ought to distinguish the state's interest in land under navigable waterways from any number of other state interests and activities that are equally crucial to the state and its right of independent governance. As he noted, "a government's assumption of title to property is no different from its assumption of any state authority that it may ultimately turn out not to have." There are, in other words, no logical limits to the majority's analysis.

While Justice Souter's arguments do raise concerns about the breadth of *Coeur d'Alene*, it may be difficult for the Court to extend its reasoning much beyond *Coeur d'Alene*'s facts. First, the plaintiff Tribe, unlike the individual plaintiffs in *Lee* or even *Treasure Salvors*, is, like the state, a sovereign. A ruling against the state therefore would deprive it of any future right to legislate with respect to the contested property. Once the Tribe is declared to have ownership, unlike an individual asserting the same claims of ownership, the land is effectively removed from the state's borders. It is questionable whether *Ex parte Young* should be read to produce that result. Second, the *Coeur d'Alene* Court may have been expressing a judgment about the merits of the state's defense, that to divest it of its regulatory prerogatives with respect to the submerged lands would violate the equal footing doctrine which provides that states must be admitted to the Union under equal footing with all other states, that is with legislative sovereignty over all lands within its boundaries when admitted to statehood. Even Justice Souter seems to concede that if President Grant's 1873 Executive Order did not vest the Tribe with title before Idaho was admitted to the Union in 1890, any attempt to deprive the state of sovereignty over the land thereafter, through the 1891 congressional legislation, for example, would violate the equal footing doctrine. It thus remains to be seen how big a dent *Coeur d'Alene* puts in the *Ex parte Young* exception.

Coeur d'Alene, however, cannot be left there, for if Justice Kennedy and Chief Justice Rehnquist had their way, *Ex parte Young* could only be invoked (1) where there is no state remedy that would satisfy the plaintiff's claim, *and* (2) "if the suit would 'upset the balance of federal and state interests that if the [Eleventh Amendment] embodies.'" Whether the latter condition is met would, in Justice Kennedy's view, be determined by a case-by-case balancing of federal and state interests. Justice Kennedy's opinion regarding these issues is not a majority; it is indeed a dissent. Seven members of the Court, the concurring Justices O'Connor, Scalia, Thomas, and the four dissenters, rejected both the assertion that state courts, when available, could displace federal courts as the primary federal law enforcement mechanism and that federal courts should be available (even in the absence of a state forum) only when, on balance, the particular case presents a serious threat to federal interests. However, Justice Kennedy's views were not formulated on a whim and from whole cloth. Indeed, Vicki Jackson predicted that the Court's opinion one year earlier in Seminole Tribe of Florida v. Florida (1996) would lead to Justice Kennedy's view that *Ex parte Young* should be available only when the state courts are not.[49] In addition, once the Court moves the Eleventh Amendment beyond the strict confines of encapsulating state sovereign immunity to an essential element in calibrating the federal/state balance, as it did in *Pennhurst* and later in *Seminole Tribe* and *Coeur d'Alene*, the ad hoc balancing suggested by Justice Kennedy, if not *the* logical next step, is certainly *a* reasonable possibility.

The "Plain Statement" Requirement For Asserting *Ex parte Young*

Seminole Tribe of Florida v. Florida (1996) was a suit filed under the Indian Gaming Regulatory Act[50] by the Seminole Tribe against the state of Florida and its Governor, Lawton Childs, to require the defendants to negotiate with the Tribe regarding the use of Tribe land for gaming activities. The Court dismissed the claim against the state on the authority of the Eleventh Amendment. This is the most significant aspect of *Seminole Tribe* and will be discussed extensively below. Of present concern is that the Tribe claimed that even if the Eleventh Amendment barred the suit against the state, *Ex parte Young* would permit the district court to issue an injunction against the Governor requiring him to negotiate in good faith. The Court rejected that argument, holding that the Indian Gaming Act provided a detailed set of procedures regarding the negotiations between states and Native American Tribes that did not include an *Ex parte Young* action. Given the detailed remedies provided by Congress in the event that agreement could not be reached, the Court said that it would not assume that Congress intended to permit an additional injunctive remedy against state officers. Where a detailed set of remedies are not provided, however, the *Ex parte Young* remedy is available (Verizon Maryland, Inc. v. Public Service Commission of Maryland, 2002).

At this point, it is hard to know whether *Seminole Tribe* has created yet another exception to *Ex parte Young*. Read most narrowly, the opinion is little more than an application of the venerable rule of statutory construction that by detailing a specific set of (in this case) remedial procedures in the event that the state did not negotiate in good faith, Congress impliedly meant to exclude all other remedies, including the ability to sue a state officer for prospective relief. On the other hand, there is no reason to think that Congress should have known it would be required to specifically provide for the *Ex parte Young* remedy. Edelman v. Jordan imposed no such requirement. Nor did the Court's previous holdings regarding Congress' need to be explicit about its desire to abrogate a state's Eleventh Amendment immunity (Atascadero State Hospital v. Scanlon, 1985). *Ex parte Young* was a judicially created exception to the Eleventh Amendment designed to ensure the availability of a federal forum to maintain the supremacy and uniformity of federal law. Prior to *Seminole Tribe*, it was never thought that Congress had any part in determining its applicability. Nor did the Court ever suggest that Congress' failure to provide for an *Ex parte Young* remedy would be taken as evidence that Congress meant to exclude it. As Vicki Jackson argues, the Court in *Seminole*

Tribe confuses the substantive cause of action created by Congress with a jurisdictional immunity recognized by the Eleventh Amendment. *Ex parte Young* has something to do with the latter. It has nothing to do with the former.[51]

It may well be that *Seminole Tribe*'s refusal to permit a prospective claim against the Governor of Florida will be limited to cases like *Seminole Tribe*, in which Congress has established a detailed set of *extra-judicial* procedures to resolve disputes between states and other sovereign entities such as Indian Tribes. If so, it would not apply to individual claims against state officers to prevent continuing violations of, for example, the Fair Labor Standards Act (Alden v. Maine, 1999), the Age Discrimination in Employment Act (Kimel v. Florida, 2000), or the Americans with Disabilities Act (Garrett v. Trustees of the University of Alabama, 2001). On the other hand, coming as it did in a case in which the Court significantly altered the balance between federal power and state immunity, that conclusion is anything but certain. *Seminole Tribe* could well be read more broadly by courts to require that Congress explicitly provide for an individual's ability to sue state officers in order to ensure a measure of political accountability when federal law displaces state policies. As Justice Powell argued in his dissenting opinion in Hutto v. Finney (1978), "(a)bsent such authorization, grounded in statutory language sufficiently clear to alert every voting member of Congress of the constitutional implications of particular legislation, we undermine the values of federalism served by the Eleventh Amendment...."

SUMMARY

Ex parte Young established a reasonably clear rule—individuals can sue state officers to prevent them from continuing to violate the plaintiff's federally protected rights. Later cases, however, have significantly muddied the waters both by restricting what it means to prevent a continuing violation and by purporting to impose conditions on a plaintiff's ability to sue a state officer even when the action is only to operate in the future.

The test for determining whether one can sue a state officer to prevent a violation of federal law no longer has much to do with the nature of the cause of action (injunction or money damages, legal or equitable relief) or even whether the claim affects the state's treasury or not. Rather, the question is whether the claimed relief is prospective or retrospective.

Moreover, even when the action is clearly prospective, issues of the centrality of the state's interest to its sovereignty and remedial options that might be available other than a claim in federal court against a state officer *may*, under certain circumstances yet undefined, prevent an individual from using *Ex parte Young* as a way of avoiding the restrictions imposed by the Eleventh Amendment. This does not suggest that *Ex parte Young* has a limited shelf life. The essential core of *Ex parte Young*—the federal court's ability to enjoin a state officer from violating the United States Constitution—remains alive and well. Justice Kennedy's inability to garner more than one other Justice's support for his "federal court as a court of last resort" position in *Coeur d'Alene* testifies to this optimistic view. On the other hand, *Pennhurst*'s piercing of the fiction in *Ex parte Young* in favor of what appears to be a more open-ended balancing of federal and state interests, coupled with the *Coeur d'Alene* majority's recognition that interests essential to a state's sovereignty are an exception to *Ex parte Young* certainly opens the door for future courts to impose further limits on the federal courts' ability to maintain the supremacy and uniformity of federal laws when to do so might affect interests closer to the core of a state's sovereignty.

The Exception for Local Political Subdivisions

LINCOLN COUNTY V. LUNING

On the same day the United States Supreme Court decided Hans v. Louisiana, it decided in Lincoln County v. Luning (1890) that a state's Eleventh Amendment sovereign immunity did not extend to its political subdivisions. Individuals could therefore sue cities, counties, school boards, etc., in federal courts for whatever relief was appropriate, including money damages that might be paid from the local treasury.[52] The broad immunity granted to the state with respect to its contractual obligations was thus unavailable to its statutorily created agents.

The facts of *Lincoln County* were indistinguishable from those of *Hans* except for the status of the defendant. Luning held coupon bonds issued by Lincoln County, Nevada. The county defaulted on the coupons and Luning brought suit against the county in the Circuit Court of the United States. The county defended on two grounds. First, "because the county is an integral part of the State" the Eleventh Amendment barred suit against it in federal circuit court. Second, Nevada statutes provided exclusive jurisdiction in state courts. That was sufficient to bar suits in federal courts independent of the Eleventh Amendment. In a terse, four page opinion, the Court devoted only three paragraphs to the Eleventh Amendment. Citing Osborne v. Bank of the United States (1824), the Court held that the Eleventh Amendment applied only when the state itself is a party. The assertion that the state was the real party of interest whenever one of its political agents is a defendant failed to persuade the Court. While it may be true that a county is "territorially a part of the State, yet politically it is also a corporation created by and with such powers as are given to it by the State." In other words, the Supreme Court held that Lincoln County was indistinguishable from any other corporation created by the state, and thus, was not entitled to claim the state's Eleventh Amendment sovereign immunity. Parenthetically, it did not help

Lincoln County's argument that the Nevada constitution declared that all corporations, including municipal corporations, were liable on their contracts.

Lincoln County's second argument—that the Nevada statute which limited jurisdiction over counties to a certain named state court deprived the federal circuit court of jurisdiction—fared no better. Twenty-two years earlier, the Court in Cowels v. Mercer County (1868), without mentioning the Eleventh Amendment, held that a United States circuit court could decide a claim brought by out-of-state bond holders against the issuing Illinois county because the Illinois statute conferring jurisdiction on a particular state court did not explicitly *refer to* the jurisdiction of the national courts. Consequently, it should not be interpreted to prohibit what Article 3 permitted, diversity jurisdiction. This, according to the *Lincoln County* Court, was all that needed to be said about the relationship between a state statute and a political subdivision's sovereign immunity in federal courts. *Lincoln County* reserved judgment, however, on whether the state, if it were to do so explicitly, could confer Eleventh Amendment immunity on its political subdivisions by expressly limiting jurisdiction over its counties only to state courts.[53]

It took some time for the Court to answer this question, largely because state statutes creating municipal corporations followed the same pattern of establishing municipalities as corporations, giving them all the powers of private corporations, and permitting them to be sued for obligations incurred as a result of exercising those powers. It did decide the issue, however, in Mt. Healthy City Board of Education v. Doyle (1977). Doyle was a teacher employed by the Mt. Healthy Board of Education who did not have his contract renewed for a variety of reasons, including his giving a local radio station a copy of a memo written by the principal regarding the school's dress code. Claiming a violation of his First Amendment rights, Doyle sued the school board in United States district court for reinstatement and damages. The school board argued that as a state agency created to perform state functions it was immune from suit under the Eleventh Amendment. The district court, however, rejected that argument, not because of *Lincoln County*, but on the ground that the state had, by statute, waived school boards' sovereign immunity. On appeal, the Supreme Court did not decide whether the state had waived the immunity of its school boards,[54] deciding instead to tackle the question, "whether such an entity had any Eleventh Amendment immunity in the first place...." The Court held that a school board had no such immunity.[55] Only the state and those agencies that were, under state law, arms of the state can claim the protections of the Eleventh Amendment. And school boards in Ohio are not arms of the state. The question of political subdivision immunity, therefore, turns not on what the state may decide, one way or the other, about the sovereign immunity of its political subdivisions but rather on whether the entity claiming sovereign immunity is "an arm of the state" or an independent entity.

INDEPENDENT ENTITY OR ARM OF THE STATE?

The state's argument in *Mt. Healthy* was that local school boards should be covered under the state's sovereign immunity. The argument was based on a combination of several factors ranging from state financing of local school boards to the degree to which the state controlled such matters as standards for graduation, curriculum, required school days, and the like. These factors, the Court held, were insufficient to place local school boards under the protective umbrella of the state's Eleventh Amendment sovereign immunity. The Court first noted that under Ohio law, the term "state" did not include political subdivisions. The state and its political subdivisions were thus two distinct entities. Moreover, like counties and cities, the state grants "school boards extensive powers to issue bonds...and to levy taxes. On balance then a local school board...is more like a county or city than...an arm of the state," which has no such independent taxing and bonding authority.

What was a clear rule after *Mt. Healthy*, that political subdivisions are not covered under the state's Eleventh Amendment immunity, became somewhat ambiguous again after Pennhurst State School and Hospital v. Halderman (1984). As noted in the previous section, *Pennhurst* was a suit contesting conditions at the Pennhurst State School and Hospital. The plaintiffs sought both injunctive and monetary relief. The defendants included not only the state defendants,[56] but also various county officials from the five counties proximate to the school. The plaintiffs argued that even though the Eleventh Amendment might bar relief against the school, the Pennsylvania Department of Public Welfare and the state officers, it would not bar the claims against the county officials. The Court, however, dismissed the claims against the county officials as well, despite *Lincoln County* and *Mt. Healthy*. The Court's reasoning appeared to rest on how damages would be allocated. In a statement reminiscent of *In re Ayers*, the Court suggested that if, because of the state's funding of the School, the damages would be payable from the state's funds, the Eleventh Amendment might well be a bar: "Given that the actions of the county commissioners and mental-health administrators are dependent on funding from the state, it may be that relief granted against these county officials...effectively runs against the state." This real-party-in-interest reasoning was based upon two earlier decisions, albeit ones in which the facts were not directly on point. The first was Edelman v. Jordan (1974), in which the Court held that a monetary judgment against a *state officer* payable out of state funds was a suit against the state. The second was Lake County Estates Inc. v. Tahoe Regional Planning Agency (1979), which was a suit against a distinct political subdivision created by an interstate compact between California and Nevada. The Court opined that the Eleventh Amendment might bar monetary relief against local officials when such "liability...would have...the same practical consequences as a judgment against the state itself," presumably even if it was not obvious that the state treasury would be tapped.

The request for injunctive relief could not, however, be disposed of in the same manner. Since injunctive relief against *state* officers is permissible under *Ex parte Young* (assuming it is truly prospective), there is little reason to deny injunction relief against *political subdivision* officers. The Court did not deny that under *ordinary circumstances* both the county itself and its officers could be subject to prospective relief. That being said, however, the Court did seem troubled by the idea of a federal court issuing an injunction against local political subdivisions and their officers with respect to a program in which the state was an equal partner in both funding and administration. As explained previously, *Ex parte Young* was not available to overcome the Eleventh Amendment proscription because there was no longer a valid federal claim upon which the injunction could be founded, and thus, the injunction was not necessary to ensure the supremacy of federal law. And since an injunction against the county or its officials would be meaningless without an injunction against the state officers charged with administering the school, the political subdivision and its officers may end up cloaked with the sovereign immunity of the state. Admittedly, the facts of *Pennhurst* are rather unique and not likely to be often repeated. On the other hand, *Pennhurst* does open some opportunities for the expansion of Eleventh Amendment immunity to a state's political subdivisions when engaged in a true programmatic partnership with the state.

Another area of potential ambiguity is with respect to entities created by interstate compact.[57] In Hess v. Port Authority Trans-Hudson Corp. (1994) the Court held that the Port Authority, a creature of an interstate compact between the states of New York and New Jersey, could not assert sovereign immunity under the Eleventh Amendment in a suit by an individual for damages under the Federal Employees Liability Act (FELA). The Court thus treated the entity, not as an arm of the state, but as a local political subdivision. The Court did not, however, say that an entity created by interstate compact is more akin to a local political subdivision than to an arm of the state. Rather, the Court held that "(o)ne of the most important goals of the immunity of the Eleventh Amendment is to shield state treasuries." Since neither the treasuries of New York nor New Jersey were at risk from the FELA action, Eleventh Amendment immunity did not attach.

The most obvious question left open by *Hess* is what if the compact itself made the states liable for the financial obligations of the entity created? Would that allow Eleventh Amendment immunity to attach because the compact entity would then resemble an arm of the state? If the answer to that question is yes, its impact cannot be isolated to interstate compact entities. The logic would extend to any local political subdivision with respect to which the state has significant fiscal entanglement. The dictum in *Pennhurst* regarding jointly administered programs also points in that direction. Logically then, *Lincoln County* is currently good law only to the extent that the state is not ultimately responsible for the obligations of its local political subdivisions. While this may be true in most states for municipal corporations (for example, cities, villages, etc.) it is not so clear with respect to other local entities, such as the school board in *Mt. Healthy*.

THE FUTURE OF *LINCOLN COUNTY*

Surprisingly, there is a dearth of scholarship discussing the distinction drawn by the Court between the Eleventh Amendment immunity of the state and the lack of immunity of its political subdivisions. What has been written, however, is overwhelmingly critical of that distinction.[58] The critics are certainly correct that the *Lincoln County* doctrine has its fair share of anomalies not the least of which is how our conception of municipal corporations (cities) has changed over the past century.[59] Municipal corporations are no longer simply corporate entities that perform limited functions specifically delegated by the state. Many, if not most, have state constitutional authority to govern their territory in much the same way that states do. Indeed, municipal corporations are the first, most numerous, and most significant point of contact between citizen and government. Moreover, as the focus of the sovereign immunity debate shifts from state immunity per se to congressional authority to create causes of action against states and their political subdivisions, the less important the Eleventh Amendment should become to the analysis.[60] General federalism principles recognize no distinction between a state and its political subdivisions when the question concerns the right of Congress to implement its legislative agenda in opposition to the policy judgments of the states. Both are protected by the general principles of federalism embodied in the Tenth Amendment (National League of Cities v. Usery, 1976) and by whatever affirmative limitations that amendment imposes on federal attempts to enlist state and local officers to implement federal law (United States v. Printz, 1997). Moreover, the word "State," as it is used in the Fourteenth Amendment, includes not only the state but all levels of local governments (for example, Brown v. Board of Education of Topeka, 1954; City of Cleburne v. Cleburne Living Center, 1985). What reason then is there to maintain the *Lincoln County/Mt. Healthy* distinction between the state and its local political subdivisions?

It is tempting to respond that in an area so fraught with anomalies, the distinction between states and political subdivisions is relatively minor and indeed may be more well founded than, say, the fiction about legal authority created by *Ex parte Young*. After all, sovereignty is the touchstone of Eleventh Amendment immunity. And historically, local political subdivisions were not sovereign. In 1790, when the Eleventh Amendment was ratified, municipal corporations were largely indistinguishable from private corporations. Both were specially chartered by the state to perform certain tasks that were described in their charters. That one performed public tasks (the provision of public services) while the other enhanced private goals (earning money for their investors) was unimportant to those granting the charters. Since both were equally creatures of the state, neither possessed any attributes of sovereignty. Indeed, one major anti-federalist objection to the Constitution was that it might, "reduce the states to the status of municipal corporations."[61]

Undoubtedly, the relationship today between states and their political subdivisions bears little resemblance to 1790 or even 1890. Many political subdivisions have, over the years, assumed many of the governance responsibilities previously exercised only by the states. The Progressive Era saw many state legislatures responding to pressures for local control by delegating significant governing authority to local governments, albeit subject to state supervisory authority. In other states, constitutions were amended to give municipalities home rule, which provided municipalities with powers to initiate legislation without state authority and insulated them to some degree from state oversight.[62] However, despite all of these changes, the Eleventh Amendment seems uniquely unable to escape its history, or at least the Court's interpretation (or misinterpretation) of that history. In addition, despite their transformation over the past 200 years, local political subdivisions possess few of the trappings of sovereignty vis à vis the states that the states possess vis à vis the federal government.[63] As such, even with the modernization and expansion of the powers of local political subdivisions, notions of sovereignty and dignity, notions relied upon by the modern Court in defining the scope of the Eleventh Amendment, do not fit these local bodies easily.

In addition, there are structural reasons for not extending immunity to political subdivisions that are far more important than the historical ones. A number of the so-called anomalies in Eleventh Amendment jurisprudence, most particularly the *Ex parte Young* exception, the so-called plan waivers for suits by the United States (discussed below), and the appellate jurisdiction of the United States Supreme Court in cases in which the state is a party exist to ensure the supremacy of federal law. As the Court in Alden v. Maine (1999) recognized, the ability to sue a state's political subdivisions in federal court is an important element in maintaining that supremacy.

Finally, the ability to sue local political subdivisions in federal court has become important to the enforcement of both the Fourteenth Amendment and federal civil rights laws. Equating states with their political subdivisions, and extending the same Eleventh Amendment protections to both, would be a blow to those efforts.[64] As a result, the exception based on the difference between states and their subdivisions, while it may not contribute to doctrinal coherence, may be as necessary as the ability to sue a state officer in federal court for prospective relief. The exception may be necessary to the overall balance between maintaining the states as sovereign governing units and ensuring that federal law, particularly federal civil rights law, is respected by those governmental bodies most responsible for regulating an individual's day-to-day activities.

Waiver of Eleventh Amendment Sovereign Immunity

WAIVER BY CONSENT

The Eleventh Amendment doctrine of sovereign immunity prohibits private suits against states *without their consent.* While that statement seems simple enough, application has proved more difficult than might be imagined. This stems, in part, from an anomaly in the doctrine itself. The Eleventh Amendment speaks in terms of the subject matter jurisdiction of the federal courts: "The Judicial power of the United States shall not be construed to extend to...." And it has been consistently held that a party cannot invoke a jurisdiction that the Court does not constitutionally possess (for example, Minnesota v. Hitchcock, 1902). The concept of waiver or consent is thus not ordinarily applicable to questions of subject matter jurisdiction. If a federal court has no power under the Constitution to adjudicate a particular dispute, the parties, by their mutual consent, cannot confer that power on it. To allow jurisdiction by mutual consent would be inconsistent with the principle that the Constitution is a law superior to all others (Marbury v. Madison, 1803).

The Eleventh Amendment, however, is an exception. Despite the Eleventh Amendment's apparent prohibition on the exercise of subject matter jurisdiction when an individual sues a state, the Court in Clark v. Barnard (1883) held that a state's voluntary appearance in federal court constitutes its consent to be sued. Thus, the Court is allowed to adjudicate the claim. Put another way, a state's consent can operate to confer subject matter jurisdiction when it otherwise does not exist. Clyde Jacobs' explanation for this curiosity is that the Eleventh Amendment was enacted to preserve the states' sovereign immunity as understood in 1787 rather than to "modify the delegations of judicial power to the federal courts under Article 3...."[65] Be that as it may, an anomaly or not, the doctrine is clear that a state's consent to suit in federal court waives its Eleventh Amendment sovereign immunity defense.

Waivers of sovereign immunity, even by voluntary appearances, are not, however, easily implied. In Missouri v. Fiske (1933) the Court declined to extend the *Clark* holding to a case in which the state had intervened (voluntarily joined) in a private lawsuit. The Court reasoned that since the state had limited the character and purpose of its intervention in its petition, no general consent to be sued could be implied. Ordinarily, however, voluntary appearance in federal court waives a state's sovereign immunity even if the state's lawyer has no statutory authority to waive immunity (Lapides v. Board of Regents of the Univ. System of Georgia, 2002). Indeed, sovereign immunity can be raised for the first time on appeal since, "the Eleventh Amendment defense sufficiently partakes of the nature of a jurisdictional bar so that it need not be raised in the trial court." Edelman v. Jordan (1974). The result is that sovereign immunity is sufficiently *unlike* a bar to subject matter jurisdiction that the parties can consent to its exercise but is sufficiently *akin* to a jurisdictional bar to permit it to be raised at any point in the litigation.

It is often the case that states will, by statute, consent to suit with respect to certain claims. These statutes, however, are strictly construed against waiver in *federal court*. Statutory waivers of immunity for suits in state courts or even general waivers with respect to suits in "any court of competent jurisdiction" will not be interpreted to waive immunity to suits in federal court unless the statute is explicit in its waiver in that jurisdiction (Kennecott Copper v. State Tax Commission, 1946; Ford Motor Company v. Dept. of Treasury, 1945; Great Northern Life Ins. Co. v. Read, 1944). In addition, a state appears able to alter the statutory terms and conditions under which it waives its sovereign immunity in federal court even after it has been sued (Beers v. Arkansas, 1857).

Questions of statutory waivers of state sovereign immunity have arisen with respect to federal as well as state statutes. Whether Congress can abrogate a state's Eleventh Amendment sovereign immunity pursuant to its powers under Article 1, § 8, and under what circumstances, will be discussed later. For present purposes, federal waivers of state sovereign immunity will focus on the limited context of Congress' powers under the compact clause, the clause which prohibits states from entering into compacts with each other without congressional consent.[66] In Petty v. Tennessee-Missouri Bridge Commission (1959) a suit was filed under the Jones Act[67] against the Commission, an agency created pursuant to a congressionally approved interstate compact between Tennessee and Missouri. The compact provided, in general language, that the Commission could sue and be sued. This was held sufficient to imply a waiver of sovereign immunity in federal court. The Court reached the same result in Port Authority Trans-Hudson Corporation v. Feeney (1990), also a Jones Act claim against an entity established pursuant to an interstate compact, this one between New York and New Jersey. The Court's reasoning in *Feeney*, however, did not track that of *Petty*. Rather, it more closely resembled the reasoning of *Kennecott Copper* and *Ford Motor Com-*

pany in analyzing whether general statutory waivers of sovereign immunity implied a waiver in federal court. In the intervening period between *Petty* and *Feeney* the Court, in Atascadero State Hospital v. Scanlon (1985), held that congressional attempts to abrogate a state's sovereign immunity in federal court must be explicit. Relying on that case, *Feeney* held that there was an explicit waiver of immunity because the compact between New York and New Jersey expressly consented to suit in "any judicial district established...by the United States." But the reasoning in *Feeney* makes doubtful whether the Court would find the general sue and be sued language that constituted congressional abrogation in *Petty* to be sufficient today.

Waiver of Eleventh Amendment sovereign immunity has also been implied when a state engages in certain activities regulated by the federal government where such regulation creates a private right of action. In Parden v. Terminal Railway of Alabama (1964), the Court, in a 5–4 opinion, sustained an action brought under the Federal Employees Liability Act (FELA)[68] by a railroad worker injured while working for a railroad owned by the state of Alabama. Justice Brennan, writing for the majority, used two distinct lines of reasoning to sustain the action. First, he stated generally that the states had waived their sovereign immunity with regard to Congress' Article 1 powers simply by joining the Union, an argument that is more fully explored in the following subsection. Second, Justice Brennan noted that the state had begun the business of operating a railroad nearly twenty years after Congress had enacted the FELA. By deciding to operate a railroad knowing that Congress had conditioned entering that activity on the acceptance of FELA liability, the state had waived its sovereign immunity. Writing for the four dissenters, Justice White did not doubt that Congress, pursuant to its right to regulate commerce, could abrogate a state's Eleventh Amendment sovereign immunity. He argued, however, that it must do so explicitly. Sovereign immunity should not be held to have been waived simply because the state undertook an activity in which private persons were subject to suit in federal court.

Nine years later, in a suit brought against their employer by employees of the Missouri Department of Public Health and Welfare, the Court came close to overruling *Parden*, at least on its facts, by deciding that if Congress desires to abrogate a state's sovereign immunity it must make that intent clear[69] (Employees of Dept. of Public Health & Welfare of Missouri v. Dept. of Public Health & Welfare, 1973). Ultimately, however, the Court in *Employees* did not rest its decision on whether Congress intended to abrogate a state's sovereign immunity. Rather, it distinguished *Parden* on the grounds that, unlike operating a railroad, the activity of employing workers performing governmental functions was not voluntary. While *Parden* survived *Employees* with only dictum against it, it was not so lucky in Welsh v. Texas Department of Highways and Public Transportation (1987). *Welsh*, like *Petty* and *Feeney*, was a suit under the Jones Act. In addition, because the Jones Act merely extended the FELA remedies to seamen, *Welsh* was essentially indistinguishable from *Parden*. Where the question is waiver of a state's sovereign immunity by federal statute, the Court held that Congress must make its intent clear. *Welsh* thus overruled *Parden*'s doctrine of implied waivers.

Welsh, however, did not rule on the other aspect of *Parden*, the question of whether a state, *by its action* of voluntarily participating in an activity that is governed by federal regulation that provides a judicial remedy for violations, constructively waives its sovereign immunity. This issue was addressed, although not conclusively decided, one year after *Employees* in Edelman v. Jordan (1974). As is more fully explained below, *Edelman* was a suit by individuals receiving public assistance under the jointly operated program for the aged, blind, and disabled[70] who claimed that the manner in which Illinois computed their benefits violated federal law. The court of appeals held that by participating in a federal program that conditioned the receipt of federal money on compliance with federal statutes and regulations, the state had waived its Eleventh Amendment immunity. The Court rejected this holding in one sentence: "(t)he mere fact that a State participates in a program through which the Federal Government provides assistance...is not sufficient to establish consent...to be sued in the federal courts." The Court repeated this holding seven years later in Florida Department of Health and Rehabilitative Services v. Florida Nursing Home Association (1981). Even though *Edelman* and *Florida Nursing Home Association* would seem to have decided the constructive waiver issue, they did not. Both were cases that resembled *Employees*, in that the state was engaging in activities that were governmental in nature. Their sin, as it were, was they accepted federal funds to assist their efforts. In *Parden*, on the other hand, the constructive waiver was based on the state's engaging in an activity regulated by the federal government on the same basis as those in the private sector. Why then should the state government not be required to play by the same rules as the private parties?

The answer came in 1999 when in College Savings Bank v. Florida Prepaid Postsecondary Education Expense Board (1999), *Parden* and its doctrine of constructive waiver was finally laid to rest once and for all. This was a suit against Florida for violating the Lanham Act[71] by making false statements regarding its tuition savings plan. Because the Lanham Act was clear on the point that states were subject to the jurisdiction of the federal courts, the only question regarding waiver was whether Florida, by participating in an activity conducted in common with private parties, constructively waived its Eleventh Amendment immunity. Overruling what remained of *Parden*, the Court held that the state did not waive its sovereign immunity by participating in interstate commerce for profit in the same way as private parties. It reasoned that state sovereign immunity was a constitutional privilege that cannot be constructively waived under any circumstances. If the state is to be held to have waived its sovereign immunity, it must do so in unequivocal and express terms. As the Court explained, "[t]he constructive waiver experiment of *Parden* was ill conceived, and (we) see no merit in attempting to salvage any remnant of it." Thus, whether one looks at the acts of Congress or the acts of the state—the waiver of sovereign immunity must be explicit and unequivocal.

PLAN WAIVERS

"Plan waivers" are those conditions that the states acceded to by ratifying the constitution and joining the Union. "Essentially, it [a plan waiver] posits that the participation of the state in the constitutional compact inherently required the states to submit to the constitutional limits imposed by that compact, including the limits imposed by the federal government pursuant to its delegated powers. Federal court jurisdiction would then be necessary to enforce those restrictions."[72] While Hans v. Louisiana (1890) held that Article 3's conference of federal judicial power in cases arising under federal law did not constitute such a waiver,[73] the Court has never doubted that the "plan of the convention" and certain constitutional amendments, most prominently the Fourteenth, in fact constitute so-called plan waivers (Alden v. Maine, 1999). The Court, however, has recently begun to narrow plan waivers by insisting that an assertion that the states had surrendered their sovereign immunity must be supported by 'compelling evidence' that the States were required to surrender [their immunity] pursuant to the constitutional design" (Alden v. Maine).

The most venerable of the plan waivers, first recognized by the Supreme Court in Cohens v. Virginia (1821), is that the Supreme Court has appellate jurisdiction to review decisions of state courts regarding matters of federal law when the state is a party, even if the state did not consent to the Supreme Court's exercise of jurisdiction. As explained previously, agreement on this principle is not unanimous.[74] Arguably *Cohens* stopped just short of holding that the plan of the convention demanded that unconsenting states be subject to the Supreme Court's appellate jurisdiction. At the expense of repeating what was said earlier, the argument has two strands. First, part of the Court's reasoning in *Cohens* was that a writ of error was not a suit against the state and thus not within the strict language of the Eleventh Amendment. As such, the holding in *Cohens* does not have any bearing at all on Eleventh Amendment sovereign immunity. Second, Chief Justice Marshall, albeit by way of dictum, distinguished between writs of error that might result in an affirmative claim against the state and those in which the writ of error operated only defensively, prohibiting the state from acting against an individual. Only the second would be considered to be within the Court's appellate jurisdiction. As a result, *Cohens* was not barred by the Eleventh Amendment because it involved a review of a criminal proceeding *against* individuals by the state. Supreme Court review of a state court decision in a case like Hans v. Louisiana, an affirmative claim by an individual against a state might, nevertheless, be barred by the Eleventh Amendment.

Chief Justice Marshall's purported distinction, however, is not germane to the structural concerns of ensuring the supremacy and uniformity of federal law that are the justifications for plan waivers. Chief Justice Marshall makes clear in other portions of his *Cohens* opinion that the integrity of the nation itself depends upon the Court's appellate review of state court interpretations of federal law. Appellate jurisdiction, the Chief Justice said, was demanded in Article 3 for no less a reason than "the preservation of the constitution and laws of the United States, so far as they can be preserved by judicial authority." This conclusion, he stated, "is founded, not on the words of the Constitution, but on its spirit, a spirit extracted, not from the words of the instrument, but from a view of the nature of our Union, and of the great fundamental principles on which the fabric stands." On the other hand, as William Marshall argues, the distinction is relevant to the narrow view of the original purpose of the Eleventh Amendment, protecting the states' treasury from private claimants.

Until recently, the Court seemed firm that maintaining the supremacy and uniformity of federal law counseled against interpreting the Eleventh Amendment so as to diminish the Court's appellate jurisdiction, even against unconsenting states (for example, McKesson Corp. v. Dept. of Alcoholic Beverages & Tobacco, 1990). The first inkling of a change came in Seminole Tribe of Florida v. Florida (1996). In a footnote, the majority interpreted *Cohens* to mean only that the Court "is empowered to review a question of federal law arising from a state court decision *where a state has consented to suit*."[75] This statement is particularly troubling since, in discussing the exceptions to the Eleventh Amendment that ensure the supremacy of federal law three years later, the Court in Alden v. Maine[76] does not mention the appellate jurisdiction of the Supreme Court. What this portends is unclear. Certainly Congress' inability to subject a state to damages for violations of statutes enacted pursuant to Article 1 means that the issue of a state's consent to suit for violation of a federal statute will rarely arise. If a state is sued either in federal or state court for a violation of federal law it is likely that a sovereign immunity defense will be interposed. If not, the state will be deemed to have consented to the suit. If the state does claim sovereign immunity, the trial court will have to determine whether the state consented to the suit either by express waiver or by the plan of the Constitution. If consent is found, the state can appeal to the Supreme Court, in which case, it will have waived its sovereign immunity with respect to the appeal. If the state wins the consent issue in the lower court and the plaintiff appeals, it is hard to believe that the *Seminole Tribe* dictum can be taken to mean that the Supreme Court is deprived of the ability to determine its own jurisdiction under the Eleventh Amendment. To so hold would overrule *Cohens* in toto, including its ruling that a writ of error is not a suit against the state. There is no evidence that the Court is prepared to take such a drastic step. As a result, the question of whether the states have, by entering the Union, consented to the Supreme Court's appellate jurisdiction in cases arising under federal law may never be an issue.[77]

Rules governing other so-called plan waivers are somewhat less opaque. The Court in *Alden* mentions two other claims that have been waived by the states simply by becoming part of the Union: suits brought against a state by other states and suits brought against a state by the federal government. In South Dakota v. North Carolina (1904), the Court permitted a suit by South Dakota to recover on bonds held by the state that were assigned to it by its resident holders. The Court used real party in interest reasoning to hold that since South Dakota was both suing in its own name and seeking to recover on a debt that it was owed, North Carolina's Eleventh Amendment defense was unavailing. This is to be contrasted with New Hampshire v. Louisiana (1883), decided twenty-one years before, in which New Hampshire and New York took assignments of Louisiana bonds from their residents, but, unlike South Dakota, required those residents to finance, and in some cases permitted them to participate in, the litigation. These peculiarities prompted the Court to conclude, again using real party in interest reasoning, that "the State and the attorney-general are only nominal actors in the proceeding," the real parties being the individual assignors." As a result, "(t)o qualify for the [plan] waiver, the plaintiff must assert at least a sovereign, proprietary, or quasi-sovereign interest."[78] Since neither New Hampshire nor New York could demonstrate that kind of interest, the Eleventh Amendment protected Louisiana.

Finally and most recently, the Court in Kansas v. Colorado (2001) held that the Eleventh Amendment did not preclude Kansas from suing Colorado for damages resulting from the latter's diversion of water in violation of an interstate compact even though (1) the measure of damages to Kansas farmers from the diversion was used, at least in part, to measure damages to the state, and (2) the Kansas farmers would recover some money from the damage award. As long as the state is not merely a "nominal party," the Eleventh Amendment is not a bar. Whether the state is a nominal party or has an independent stake in the outcome seemed to be determined by three factors. First, the state had an interest independent of its citizens in preventing upstream diversions of the Arkansas River, as evidenced by Kansas' earlier attempts to prevent such diversions. Second, Kansas both financed the litigation and controlled the post judgment disposition of the damages to individuals to compensate them for their losses. Finally, the losses to individual farmers were not the only factor used to measure damages. The suit, in other words, was not simply a fig leaf to avoid the proscriptions of the Eleventh Amendment.

Suits against states by the United States have long been recognized as not encompassed by the Eleventh Amendment. In United States v. Texas (1892), the United States, invoking the original jurisdiction of the Supreme Court, sued to quiet title to certain land held by the state. (An action to *quiet title* seeks a declaration with regard to which of several claimants has legal title to real property.)

Texas raised several defenses to the Court's jurisdiction, including that it was immune to suit without its consent. Responding to the immunity assertion, the Court made it plain that the state could claim no immunity from suit by the United States: "The permanence of the Union might be endangered if to some tribunal was not entrusted the power to determine them [inter-sovereign disputes] according to the recognized principles of law." And in Principality of Monaco v. Mississippi (1934) the Court made it plain that federal jurisdiction for claims arising between a state and the federal government is not based on the text of Article 3, but rather "is inherent in the constitutional plan." This was reiterated most recently in Alden v. Maine (1999).

The open question is not whether the states can assert a general sovereign immunity claim in an action by the United States or one of its officers; they cannot. Rather, the question is whether the plan waiver is complete or is the real party in interest reasoning of New Hampshire v. Louisiana and Kansas v. Colorado is applicable as well to a suit against a state by the United States. Jonathan Siegel has argued that the United States always has a sovereign interest in the integrity of its regulatory scheme and thus, even under a real party in interest analysis, the constitutional plan should be deemed to have waived the states' immunity.[79] There are three difficulties with Professor Siegel's argument. First, his argument does not quite fit the rationale for a plan waiver where the United States is the plaintiff—that a federal forum is needed to resolve inter-sovereign disputes in order to provide an alternative to the possibility of "extra-legal measures" (Alden v. Maine, 1999). Assuming that extra legal actions loom as a real possibility in today's world, the fear of the Framers was that absent a neutral forum, the federal government might be tempted to ensure its sovereign interests by the use of force. Individuals who are real parties in interest in suits by the United States are not likely to resort to force of arms to require the state to meet its contractual obligations. Were this not so the Court would have found a way to abandon state sovereign immunity long ago, even if contrary to the text of the Eleventh Amendment. The probability of "extra-legal measures" does not increase simply because the United States is the plaintiff if all or most of the tangible benefits flow to individuals *in their individual capacity*. Second, Professor Siegel's argument would effectively negate the Court's current position, explored in depth in the following section, that Congress cannot abrogate a state's sovereign immunity under its Article 1 powers. Congress could avoid the holdings of *Seminole Tribe* and *Alden* simply by authorizing the United States to sue any time an individual would be precluded from doing so by the Eleventh Amendment, a reverse *qui tam* action if you will. (A *qui tam* action is one in which a private party is permitted to sue on behalf and for the benefit of the United States.) Finally, given the symmetry the Court has required between the sovereignty of the Federal Government and that of the states, it would be surprising to see a difference in the application of the real party in interest standard depending upon whether the plaintiff is a sister state or the United States. Consequently, it would not be surprising if the Court, were it ever confronted directly with the issue, would decide that suits by the United States that are intended to directly benefit private individuals in their individual capacity are barred by the Eleventh Amendment.[80]

Not covered by what Evan Caminker calls the state plan waiver are suits by foreign states (Principality of Monaco v. Mississippi, 1934) and Indian tribes (Blatchford v. Indian Village of Noatak, 1991). The Court used similar reasoning in both cases. First, the Court held that foreign states and Indian tribes lie "outside the structure of the Union." As a result, it is difficult to argue that the plan of the Union requires a waiver of a state's constitutional sovereign immunity in cases brought by these entities. Second, if an exception were carved from the Eleventh Amendment for suits by foreign states or Indian tribes, there would be no reciprocity of immunity. Both foreign states and Indian tribes would be immune from suits by states, but states would not be so immune. The Constitutional Convention, the Court reasoned, understood that each state relinquished its sovereign immunity with respect to suits by other states, understanding that if it could be sued, it could also sue. Since the Convention could not and did not waive the sovereign immunity of either foreign states nor Indian tribes there was no bargained for exchange. Unfortunately, this reasoning presupposes that the results of the Convention and the process of reaching those results resembled negotiating a private contract. If no "consideration" can be found for any particular waiver of states' "rights," the waiver does not exist. This private contractual model of the Constitutional Convention is, at best, contestable, if not simply wrong. Moreover, the argument rests on the problematic "compact theory" that the nation was formed as a compact between sovereign states rather than by "we the people."

SUMMARY

If the rules regarding waivers appear confused and incoherent, that is because they are. The concept of waiver is itself incompatible with a constitutional provision that purports to remove subject matter jurisdiction from the federal courts. Any rules that build upon that anomaly simply compound the confusion. Not only can states consent to the jurisdiction of the federal courts but in some cases this consent or lack thereof is deemed irrelevant. And the Court has been anything but clear about why the states will be held to have consented to the Supreme Court's appellate jurisdiction under Article 3 simply by joining the Union but will not be held to account to Congress' plenary authority under Article 1 to regulate commerce. Neither are self-executing; both require congressional legislation. Yet, legislation with respect to the former is consistent with the Eleventh Amendment while legislation with respect to the latter is not.

The answer seems to be that only where waiver is *necessary* to ensure the supremacy of federal law will it be implied. Therefore, if an action against state officers to prevent their continuing violation of federal law under *Ex parte Young* will provide that assurance, plan waivers based upon Congress' commerce powers will be rejected. Uniformity and supremacy of federal law, at least according to the Court, does not require that individuals be compensated for past wrongs. Mandated future compliance is apparently sufficient.

Congressional Abrogation of State Sovereign Immunity

ARTICLE I, FEDERAL JURISDICTION AND THE ELEVENTH AMENDMENT

Introduction

As previously mentioned, the story of the Eleventh Amendment does not end with questions about an individual's inability to sue a state in federal court. It also extends to the power of Congress to abrogate a state's Eleventh Amendment sovereign immunity pursuant to its legislative powers under Article 1, § 8 and § 5 of the Fourteenth Amendment. This is perhaps the most difficult and certainly the most controversial aspect of Eleventh Amendment jurisprudence.

Article 1, § 8 delineates the vast bulk of congressional legislative powers. Congress is granted authority not only to enact substantive regulations in matters such as interstate commerce, the armed forces, and bankruptcy, but in addition, the authority to choose the means by which its substantive regulations shall be implemented. The final clause of Art I, § 8, gives Congress the power, "to make all Laws which shall be necessary and proper for carrying into Execution the foregoing Powers, and all other Powers vested by this Constitution in the Government of the United States, or in any Department or Officer thereof."[81] In the seminal case of McCulloch v. Maryland (1819), Chief Justice John Marshall described Congress' "necessary and proper" powers in the broadest terms: a "sound construction of the Constitution must allow to the national legislature that discretion with respect to the means by which the powers which it confers are to be carried into execution . . . ." For example, Chief Justice Marshall opined, Congress' power to establish post offices[82] clearly encompasses the power to criminally punish those who would steal United States mail, even though the criminal law was then, and still is now, regarded as primarily a state prerogative (United States v. Lopez, 1996). And, despite the lack of explicit authority in the first seventeen clauses of Article 1, § 8, *McCulloch* itself held that both the constitutional structure itself and the Necessary and Proper Clause permitted Congress to establish the Second Bank of the United States as an instrumentality of the United States, thereby depriving the state of Maryland of its otherwise sovereign right to tax business enterprises operating within its boundaries. Allowing Maryland to tax the Bank, according to the Court, would permit it to destroy what Congress had created.[83]

The question posed by the intersection between Article 1, § 8, and the sovereign immunity principles embodied in the Eleventh Amendment is whether Congress, in furtherance of its substantive regulatory authority, has the same power to create private causes of action against states as it does against private parties. For example, does Congress have the authority to prescribe safety standards that must be followed by state-owned railroads and enforce those standards by giving injured state workers the right to sue in federal or state court for damages if the state does not meet those standards? May Congress, pursuant to its powers to promote innovation,[84] create a damage action in favor of private individuals whose patents or trademarks have been infringed by competing state business enterprises?

The Court's Pre-1996 Opinions

The question of whether Article 1, § 8, of the Constitution granted Congress the authority to abrogate state sovereign immunity as a means of implementing its substantive regulatory powers did not arise until after the New Deal.[85] Hans v. Louisiana never mentioned congressional power to abrogate state sovereign immunity even though there was a federal statute that, in a general way, conferred jurisdiction on federal circuit courts to hear claims founded on the federal constitution and laws.[86] It was never argued that this statute abrogated Louisiana's sovereign immunity. The only question in *Hans* was whether the Eleventh Amendment limited the exercise of federal *judicial* power. The effect on congressional legislative authority was only collateral. If Article 3 limited federal judicial power, Congress could not, by legislation, expand judicial authority beyond those limits (Marbury v. Madison, 1803).

The Court would not directly rule on Congress' power to abrogate a state's Eleventh Amendment immunity until 1976, and even then the question did not concern Congress' Article 1 powers but its § 5, Fourteenth Amendment authority (Fitzpatrick v. Bitzer, 1976).[87] Indeed it is probably fair to say that until Seminole Tribe of Florida v. Florida (1996), the Supreme Court assumed that Congress did possess the power to abrogate state sovereign immunity as a means of enforcing its legislative authorities under Article 1, § 8. As will be discussed in the next subsection, that assumption was certainly the near unanimous view of the major scholars who wrote about abrogation in the thirty years between 1965 and 1995.

This understanding came largely from four Supreme Court decisions. In one, Parden v. Alabama (1964), the Court upheld Congressional legislation abrogating state sovereign immunity. In the other three the Court denied the plaintiffs' claim of federal jurisdiction, affirming the state's sovereign immunity, but did so because Congress did not make its intent to abrogate sufficiently clear. The last two cases, however, did contain hints that the Court was prepared to use the Eleventh Amendment as the constitutional peg on which to hang a limitation of Congress' power to subject the states to private claims in federal court.

The question in *Parden* was whether the Federal Employees Liability Act[88] (FELA) allowed an employee of a state-owned railroad to sue his employer (the state) in federal court for injuries sustained as a result of his employment. Like *Hans*, the plaintiff in *Parden* was a resident of the defendant state, thus making the literal terms of the Eleventh Amendment inapplicable. Although he was later to advocate that *Hans* should be overruled (Atascadero State Hospital v. Scanlon, 1985), Justice Brennan, writing for the five-Justice majority, chose instead to rely on two theories of state waiver of sovereign immunity to provide relief for the plaintiff. These were treated previously and will not be reiterated here. Suffice it to say that both the plan waiver and the activity waiver theories are based less on the actions of Congress than on those of the state. Congress is not so much abrogating the state's immunity as the state is, through its actions, voluntarily accepting the dictates of federal law. In other words, the *Parden* majority was advocating a consent theory, not an abrogation theory.

To the four dissenters, however, *Parden* was clearly a case of congressional abrogation rather than one of voluntary consent. They did not dispute that Congress has the authority under Article 1 to abrogate state sovereign immunity in certain matters: "[We] agree that it is within the power of Congress to condition a State's permit to engage in the interstate transportation business on a waiver of the State's sovereign immunity from suits arising out of such businesses." Rather, the dissent questioned whether Congress intended by the FELA to subject states like Alabama to suits by employees injured while working for state-owned interstate railroads. In light of the Eleventh Amendment, the general grant of judicial jurisdiction to hear the suits of injured railroad employees was not a sufficient indication of congressional intent to abrogate Alabama's sovereign immunity.

Nine years later in Employees of Public Health and Welfare of Missouri v. Department of Public Health and Welfare of Missouri (1973), the reasoning of the dissent in *Parden* became the majority holding. Justice Douglas, who had dissented in *Parden*, wrote the opinion for the six-Justice majority. Like *Parden*, *Employees* presented the Court with an opportunity to reconsider *Hans* since the plaintiffs were residents of the defendant state. Moreover, the facts in *Employees* were much like those in *Parden*—Missouri had voluntarily engaged in an enterprise, owning and operating hospitals, that was covered by the Fair Labor Standards Act (FLSA). The FLSA conferred jurisdiction on federal courts to hear private claims by those paid less than the statutory minimums prescribed by the statute.[89] The United States, as *amicus curiae* (a nonparty who is granted permission to submit a brief and, infrequently, to present oral argument), urged the Court to go beyond *Parden*'s limited holding of voluntary waiver and decide that *Hans* should not be extended to cases in which Congress, pursuant to its Article 1 powers, had subjected states to suit in federal courts.

The Court, however, neither followed the government's suggestion nor adopted Justice Brennan's consent theory. Rather, the majority followed the reasoning of the *Parden* dissent and only addressed the issue of whether Congress *intended* to abrogate Missouri's sovereign immunity through FLSA's general grant of a private right of action in federal court against any person who violated its substantive provisions. The Eleventh Amendment certainly had an impact on the Court's decision, but only in determining how clear congressional intent to abrogate state sovereign immunity must be: "Recalcitrant private employers may be whipped into line....But we are reluctant to believe that Congress in pursuit of a harmonious federalism desired to treat the States so harshly." Yet, despite the strong federalism language, the Court questioned neither whether Congress subjected Missouri to the substantive provisions of the FSLA nor its authority to do so. That would come later. Moreover, the majority did not even suggest that the Eleventh Amendment placed any limits on Congress' authority to abrogate state sovereign immunity with respect to activities otherwise within its Article 1 authority. It only had to be clear about its intention to do so.

Justice Thurgood Marshall's concurrence in *Employees*, however, directly raised the constitutional dimensions of the abrogation issue and in doing so, rejected the United States' position on its merits. Disagreeing with the majority's conclusion regarding Congress' intent, Justice Marshall concluded that Congress indeed intended to subject states to private suits in federal court for violations of the FLSA. The question, as he saw it, was whether Congress had the power to make a state amenable to suit by one of its own citizens in federal court. Justice Marshall found the answer in Hans v. Louisiana which he interpreted as holding that Chisholm v. Georgia had misread the jurisdictional scope of Article 3. According to Justice Marshall, *Hans* held that the Eleventh Amendment only confirmed that Article 3 was never intended to waive the states' *common law* sovereign immunity from suits in United States courts. This common law immunity extended not only to cases in which federal jurisdiction derived from diversity of citizenship, that is, where a nonresident citizen sued a state, but included as well suits arising under the federal Constitution and laws. Justice Marshall argued, however, that the Eleventh Amendment did not deprive individuals of a federal judicial remedy. Since Article 3 affected only the jurisdiction of United States courts, Congress was not precluded from creating a private right of action in state courts. And Congress had done so in the FLSA.[90] Once Congress has granted a private right of action against a state in state court, that court is obliged under the

Supremacy Clause[91] to hear and decide the federal claim.[92] The failure to do so would place the state's own declaration of sovereign immunity in a superior position to the federal law, resulting in the federal law no longer being "the supreme law of the land." Justice Marshall thus reasoned that the Eleventh Amendment was limited to determining the forum in which federal claims could be heard. It did not either grant or confirm that states were entitled to a constitutional immunity from federal claims.[93]

In his dissent, Justice Brennan also discussed the constitutional issue. On two points he agreed with Justice Marshall: (1) that Congress had intended to abrogate the states' sovereign immunity with respect to the minimum wage/maximum hour provisions of the FLSA,[94] and (2) that the Eleventh Amendment did not immunize the states from liability when Congress chose to exercise its Article 1 powers. However, in all other respects Justice Brennan's view of the Eleventh Amendment differed sharply from that of Justice Marshall. Justice Brennan viewed the Eleventh Amendment as only applicable to those provisions of Article 3 that confer jurisdiction based on the character of the parties. In his view, it had no bearing on Congress' power to create private rights of action under its Article 1 powers, and thus did not deprive the federal courts of jurisdiction when the constitutional basis of that jurisdiction was the nature of the claim rather than the status of the parties. Justice Brennan, in other words, believed that the Eleventh Amendment was intended to apply only to diversity jurisdiction,[95] a far narrower view of the impact of the Eleventh Amendment on Congress' power to abrogate state sovereign immunity than that expressed by Justice Marshall.

It was in the third case that differences among the Justices with regard to the scope of the Eleventh Amendment began to assume center stage.[96] Welsh v. Texas Department of Highways and Public Transportation (1987), was a claim under the Jones Act by an individual who was employed to work on a state-owned ferry dock. Texas interposed the Eleventh Amendment as a defense. Justice Powell, writing for a plurality consisting of Chief Justice Rehnquist, and Justices O'Connor and White, never reached the question of whether Congress had the power to abrogate a state's sovereign immunity because, in the plurality's view, the Jones Act did not do so in "unmistakably clear language."[97] In so holding, however, the Court assumed that Congress could abrogate a state's sovereign immunity pursuant to its Article 1 powers, although its language was hardly a ringing endorsement of that ability: "[w]e assume without deciding or intimating a view on the question that the authority of Congress to subject unconsenting states to suit in federal court is not limited to § 5 of the Fourteenth Amendment."

The broader Eleventh Amendment issue arose as a result of Justice Brennan's dissenting opinion, joined by Justices Marshall, Blackmun, and Stevens, in which he leveled a broad-based attack on the Court's previous Eleventh Amendment decisions. He first argued that *Ex parte New York* (1911), which held that the Eleventh Amendment applied to admiralty jurisdiction, was wrongly decided and should be overruled. More importantly for present purposes, Justice Brennan mounted a frontal assault on Hans v. Louisiana. According to Justice Brennan and his dissenting colleagues, the only historical basis for the decision in *Hans* lay in the statements of Alexander Hamilton in *Federalist No. 81* and those of James Madison and John Marshall in the Virginia Ratifying Convention. Brennan argued that Hamilton's assertions in *Federalist No. 81* contradicted his arguments in *Federalist No. 80*, making it hard to pin down exactly his views on the matter. Further, the assurances of Madison and Marshall had to be read in the context of the near panic in Virginia that the federal judiciary, *pursuant to its diversity jurisdiction*, would be the vehicle by which nonresident war-bond holders would invade the state's treasury.[98] Because Justice Brennan read the history surrounding the adoption and ratification of the Eleventh Amendment to be limited to a concern that diversity jurisdiction would provide a forum for nonresident and foreign debt security holders to collect money from the states without their consent, *Hans* should be overruled. The Eleventh Amendment would therefore be no bar to Congress' abrogation of Texas' sovereign immunity, which Justice Brennan argued Congress did in the Jones Act.

The plurality's response to the dissent's call for overruling *Hans* was not nearly as strong as it could have been and was in later cases. First, as Justice Scalia noted in his concurring opinion, the plaintiff had not argued that *Hans* should be overruled. The issue was therefore not before the Court. Second, *Hans* was not central to the plurality's holding, based as it was on congressional intent and not congressional power. Regardless of what the context for the statements may have been, the plurality argued that three of the most influential of the framers, James Madison, John Marshall, and Alexander Hamilton, positively stated that the federal courts would not be open to suits by private individuals against states. The plurality admitted, however, that contrary statements from equally eminent founders such as Edmund Randolph and others, made the history ambiguous. The key for the plurality was *stare decisis* (the ordinary practice of a court to follow precedent). *Hans* had been the law for nearly one hundred years and numerous cases relied upon it. Given that long-standing precedent, the fact that *Hans* was a unanimous decision, and the ambiguity surrounding the Framers' intent, the plurality held that it would take some special justification to overrule *Hans*. The Court thus split 4–4 on the question of whether the Eleventh Amendment extended protection to states in cases that did not rest on diversity of citizenship jurisdiction.

Justice Scalia provided the fifth vote for the state. He did not enter the constitutional debate, not directly at least. Rather, he argued that regardless of whether *Hans* was correctly decided, a matter upon which he expressed no opinion, Congress must be held to have drafted the Jones Act in light of its holding. Since the Court cannot assume that Congress would intentionally enact a statute of questionable constitutionality, Justice Scalia opined that Congress could not have intended the Jones Act to abrogate the states' sovereign immunity. Justice Scalia's position seems eminently reasonable until, that is, one digs beneath the surface. Justice Scalia assumes that *Hans* said or implied something about Congress' power under the Necessary and Proper Clause to use the federal courts to enforce its substantive regulatory norms. (The Necessary and Proper Clause, Article 1, § 38, Clause 18, grants Congress the authority to adopt whatever means are "necessary and proper" to implement its constitutionally enumerated powers.) But as noted previously, *Hans* did not even hint that its holding might affect Congress' Article 1 authorities. Nor did the Court, before *Welsh*, say anything that would give Congress the least bit of concern about the Eleventh Amendment's restricting its Article 1 enforcement powers. Quite the contrary. Justice Scalia's approach therefore merely postponed the inevitable.

The inevitable came two years later. Pennsylvania v. Union Gas Company (1989) was the fourth and final pre-1996 case in which the issue of whether Article 1 conferred upon Congress the authority to abrogate state sovereign immunity came before the Court. *Union Gas* began as a suit by the United States against Union Gas to recover the costs of cleaning up a so-called superfund site. Union Gas impleaded (involuntarily joined) the state of Pennsylvania, claiming that the state was responsible for part of the clean-up costs because it was the "owner or operator" of the site within the meaning of the Comprehensive Environmental Response, Compensation, and Liability Act of 1980.[99] Pennsylvania moved to dismiss the attempt to add it to the defendant list, asserting that the Eleventh Amendment immunized it from suit. Unlike *Welsh*, in *Union Gas*, five Justices agreed that Congress had clearly indicated its intention to make states liable for their share of superfund site clean-up costs. This set the stage for an extensive discussion of two constitutional issues, (1) whether Hans v. Louisiana ought to be overruled, and (2) the narrower issue of whether, even if *Hans* was correctly decided, Congress has the constitutional authority under Article 1 to abrogate the states' sovereign immunity.

Justice Brennan, writing for a four-Justice plurality, avoided a lengthy discussion of the larger question of whether the Court should overrule *Hans* (larger because overruling *Hans* would limit the Eleventh Amendment to only diversity jurisdiction cases) in favor of addressing the narrower abrogation issue. His plurality opinion argued that Congress had the power to abrogate state sovereign immunity under Article 1. The argument rested on two distinct yet interrelated positions. The first was precedential. Both *Parden* and *Employees* established that Congress has the authority to abrogate state sovereign immunity under Article 1. In addition, Fitzpatrick v. Bitzer (1976) held that Congress has the authority under § 5 of the Fourteenth Amendment to abrogate state sovereign immunity. The plurality argued that there is no essential difference between Congress' powers under the Commerce Clause (Art I, § 8, Clause 3, which gives Congress the power to regulate commerce "among the states") and those under § 5 of the Fourteenth Amendment (granting Congress the authority to implement the rights guaranteed by the Fourteenth Amendment)—both are plenary grants of Congressional authority and until recently have been interpreted to give Congress wide discretion to determine appropriate regulation responses. Consequently, both, in their separate ways, limit state autonomy.

The second of the plurality's arguments was a return to Justice Brennan's plan waiver theory in *Parden*—that by joining the Union, states gave up their sovereignty with respect to those matters over which the Constitution gave Congress legislative authority, in this case the Commerce Clause. Moreover, because environmental harms are rarely limited by artificial state boundaries there are no legitimate concerns that the superfund legislation infringes on the states' autonomy. Finally, in response to Pennsylvania's argument that Congress has no authority to expand the jurisdiction of the federal courts beyond that permitted by Article 3, the plurality simply cited *Fitzpatrick*—if Congress can authorize suits against the states under § 5 of the Fourteenth Amendment without violating Article 3, it can do so under Article 1 as well.

Justice Scalia, joined by Chief Justice Rehnquist, and Justices Kennedy and O'Connor, dissented on constitutional grounds.[100] Justice Scalia first raised the question that the plurality had avoided—that *Hans* should be overruled. According to the dissent, if the United States enjoys sovereign immunity from individual claims for violations of the Constitution or federal laws, the states must have the same immunity: "[I]f private initiation of suit against the offending sovereign as such is essential to preservation of the structure, it is difficult to see why it would not be essential at both levels of government." In addition, Justice Scalia restated Justice Powell's *stare decisis* argument in *Welsh*; "*Hans* has been reaffirmed in case after case, often unanimously and by exceptionally strong Courts; its reversal 'would overrule at least seventeen cases, in addition to *Hans* itself' and cast doubt on 'a variety of other cases that were concerned with this Court's traditional treatment of sovereign immunity.'"

The dissent did not however rest only on these arguments. It asserted a view of the Eleventh Amendment that not only went well beyond its text, something that the Court had done consistently since *Hans*, but also well beyond the view of the Eleventh Amendment as a technical correction to the jurisdiction of the federal courts. "*Hans* was not expressing some narrow objection to the particular federal power by which Louisiana had been hauled into court, but was rather enunciating a fundamental principle of federalism, evidenced by the Eleventh Amendment, that the States retained their sovereign prerogative of immunity." "[S]tate immunity from suit in federal courts is a structural component of federalism, and not merely a default disposition that can be altered by action of Congress pursuant to its Article 1 powers."

The fifth and deciding vote was provided by Justice White. He disagreed with both the plurality justices and Justice Scalia with respect to the clarity of Congress' intent to abrogate the state's sovereign immunity.[101] But because he had been outvoted on that issue he conceded the point and proceeded to the constitutional issue. On this issue Justice White agreed with the plurality that "Congress had the authority under Article 1 to abrogate the Eleventh Amendment immunity of the States...." Thus, despite the fractured nature of the opinions in *Union Gas*, a majority of the Court held that Congress may abrogate state sovereign immunity when acting pursuant to its Article 1 powers, subject only to the requirement that it make its intention to abrogate sufficiently clear.[102]

The Scholars

As noted in the introduction to this discussion, there was very little scholarly disagreement with the constitutional proposition affirmed in *Union Gas* that Congress could abrogate state sovereign immunity when "necessary and proper" to enforce its Article 1 regulatory prerogatives.[103] This does not mean that these scholars necessarily believed that *Hans* was incorrectly decided and should be overruled. But as the plurality's opinion in *Union Gas* demonstrated, it is not necessary to argue that *Hans* should be overruled to believe that Congress has the power to abrogate state sovereign immunity pursuant to both Article 1 and § 5 of the Fourteenth Amendment.

It is difficult to accurately pigeonhole the various views of those scholars who agree that Congress has the power under Article 1 to abrogate a state's Eleventh Amendment sovereign immunity because there are some fundamental theoretical differences between them. For example, Laurence Tribe and John Nowak both believe that the Eleventh Amendment does not speak to congressional power at all but only circumscribes judicial power.[104] However, they reach this conclusion from different avenues. Professor Nowak relies primarily on historical arguments, while Professor Tribe relies on arguments based on the structural protections that participation in the congressional legislative process affords the states, making judicial intervention in disputes between the different levels of government less necessary.[105]

Other scholars reject the Tribe/Nowak reading of the Eleventh Amendment because, however supported, it accepts the argument that, absent congressional abrogation, the Eleventh Amendment recognizes a general *constitutional* immunity for states from federal judicial action. The lack of a general immunity is certainly the position of those who hold to the view that the Eleventh Amendment only prohibits the exercise of diversity jurisdiction. But again, there are a variety of views among even the diversity theorists as to how the Eleventh Amendment intersects with Congress' Article 1 powers. For Martha Field, who believes that the Eleventh Amendment only makes clear that Article 3 did not alter the states' common law immunity,[106] congressional abrogation presents no constitutional issue distinct from the scope of congressional authority over the particular activity regulated. There are simply no restrictions on legislative authority to alter judicially fashioned common law doctrines.[107] On the other hand, Vicki Jackson, while sharing several of Professor Field's views on the common law nature of state sovereign immunity, would narrow congressional abrogation power to a somewhat greater extent than would Professor Field. Finding it impossible to reconcile the Supreme Court's appellate jurisdiction established by Cohens v. Virginia with *Hans*' prohibition of original jurisdiction in lower federal courts even for federal constitutional claims, Professor Jackson concludes that the Eleventh Amendment provides constitutional protection of state sovereign immunity but only for cases in which the basis for jurisdiction is diversity of citizenship and only to the extent that the claim is asserted in federal court.[108] In other words, Congress could not grant jurisdiction to the federal courts in cases based on state law when a citizen of one state sues another state. There is no sovereign immunity bar, however, to Congress' creating a federal cause of action in either federal or state court since immunity from nondiversity based claims is only a matter of federal common law. Professor Jackson, therefore, ultimately agrees with the views expressed by Justice Thurgood Marshall in *Employees* that the Eleventh Amendment is not an immunity doctrine but rather a forum allocation doctrine. Other diversity theorists, would similarly have no problems with Congress' power to abrogate state sovereign immunity under Article 1 but, because they rely on what history reveals about the reach of the Eleventh Amendment, they do not take their analysis to the point of determining whether sovereign immunity exists beyond diversity jurisdiction, and if so, in what form.

Finally, Professor Carlos Manuel Vázquez has charted a course that differs from that of his colleagues.[109] Professor Vázquez categorizes the Eleventh Amendment as embodying two mutually exclusive theories: the forum allocation theory (Justice Marshall's *Employees* dissent) and the immunity from liability theory (the dissent in *Union Gas*). He posits that the former would pose no obstacle to Congress' creating a federal cause of action in favor of individuals against states. The Eleventh Amendment only determines the forum in which the claim can be heard. The latter, on the other hand, would limit Congress' power to create causes of action against the states. The immunity from liability theory, however, would pose a problem for the rule of law since one of the fundamental principles of a society governed by law is that for every wrong there must be a remedy (Marbury v. Madison, 1803). However, this is not the only thing necessary for the preservation of the rule of law. Stability and coherence of the law are also needed. These are provided by adherence to precedent, *stare decisis*. The difficulty is that the two principles conflict in Eleventh Amendment jurisprudence. Reconciliation can be found in the legal fiction created in *Ex parte Young* that individuals can sue state officers prospectively to prohibit continuing violations of federal law. This fiction not only provides a remedy for wrongs committed, upholding the sanctity and supremacy of federal law, but it also provides the needed stability by preserving Hans v. Louisiana and the cases that have relied upon its ruling. Professor Vázquez would thus leave Eleventh Amendment law where it stood in 1996, not because it is necessarily correct but because it is a satisfactory way of accommodating federal legislative authority with the *Hans* Court's concerns for state autonomy.[110]

The various approaches outlined previously only scratch the surface of the numerous approaches that scholars have explored in an attempt to make sense of an amendment whose doctrine is completely independent of its text and whose history is at best contestable and indeterminate and at worst outright manipulable.[111] It is no wonder that scholars have been unable to agree on a coherent theory of the Eleventh Amendment. And even those who do agree on a theory cannot agree on the fine points. The inability of both judges and scholars to firmly moor the Eleventh Amendment in any coherent normative or historical theory, more than any other single factor,[112] has opened the door to the Rehnquist Court's invalidation of Congress' Article 1 abrogation powers and the limitation on its seemingly plenary powers under § 5 of the Fourteenth Amendment.

The Demise of Article I Abrogation Authority—*Seminole Tribe* and Its Progeny

Seminole Tribe

In 1996 the Court decided two cases that limited federal legislative power to restrict the autonomy of the states. In one, the Court, for the first time in sixty years, struck down a federal commerce clause enactment (prohibiting the possession of a gun in a school zone) as beyond the scope of congressional legislative powers (United States v. Lopez, 1996).[113]

The other case, which over the long run will undoubtedly prove to be the more significant of the two in terms of curbing federal legislative authority vis-à-vis the states, was Seminole Tribe of Florida v. Florida (1996). The case evolved from a dispute between the Tribe and the state of Florida over gaming on Indian lands. Pursuant to its exclusive constitutional authority to regulate Indian commerce under Article 1, § 8, Congress, in 1988, enacted the Indian Gaming Regulatory Act[114] in order to establish a process that protected both the interests of the state in regulating gaming within its borders and those of the tribes desiring to establish gaming establishments. As part of that process, the Act required the states and the tribes to enter into a compact detailing their agreement, which then had to be approved by the Secretary of Interior. The provision that prompted the lawsuit provided that United States district courts would have jurisdiction over actions initiated by tribes in the event that the state failed to negotiate in good faith. If the tribe was able to demonstrate that the state had not negotiated in good faith, an elaborate set of possible judicial and administrative remedies were enumerated to force the states to do so.[115] Such an action was brought by the Seminole Tribe of

Florida against Florida. The district court denied the State's motion to dismiss for lack of jurisdiction. The Court of Appeals for the Eleventh Circuit reversed, holding that the Eleventh Amendment prohibited Congress from abrogating a state's immunity even under an Article 1 power that was exclusive to Congress.[116]

In a 5–4 opinion, the Supreme Court affirmed the Eleventh Circuit's ruling on Congress' ability to abrogate a state's Eleventh Amendment sovereign immunity.[117] In doing so, the Court specifically overruled *Union Gas*. Rejecting Florida's attempt to narrow the issue by arguing that a distinction can be made between the interstate commerce clause and the Indian commerce clause with respect to Congress' power to abrogate a state's sovereign immunity, the Court's majority confronted the reasoning of the *Union Gas* plurality directly. While recognizing that *stare decisis* ordinarily should "counsel strongly against reconsideration of our precedent" that principle did not apply to the decision in *Union Gas*. First, citing numerous times from Justice Scalia's dissent, the Court argued that it was that case which deviated sharply from prior precedent, and, as such, violated principles of *stare decisis*. "Never before the decision in *Union Gas* had we suggested that the bounds of Article III could be expanded by Congress operating pursuant to any other constitutional provision other than the Fourteenth Amendment. Indeed it had seemed fundamental that Congress could not expand the jurisdiction of the federal courts beyond the jurisdiction of Article III." The Court bolstered its argument that *state decisis* did not require adherence to *Union Gas* by noting that the power to abrogate a state's sovereign immunity, while supported by five Justices, rested on the (faulty) reasoning of only four. Justice White, who provided the fifth vote, agreed with the result, but specifically rejected much of the plurality's reasoning. Finally, the Court reaffirmed *Hans*, not simply on *stare decisis* grounds but on its own merits.

> The dissent mischaracterizes the *Hans* opinion. That decision found its roots not solely in the common law of England, but in the much more fundamental "jurisprudence in all civilized nations." The dissent's proposition that the common law of England, where adopted by the states, was open to change by the legislature is wholly unexceptional and largely beside the point: that common law provided the substantive rules of law rather than jurisdiction. It is also noteworthy that the principle of state sovereign immunity stands distinct from other principles of the common law in that only the former prompted a specific constitutional amendment. *Hans*—with a much closer vantage point than the dissent—recognized that the decision in *Chisholm* was contrary to the well-understood meaning of the Constitution. The dissent's conclusion that the decision in *Chisholm* was "reasonable...certainly would have struck the Framers of the Eleventh Amendment as quite odd: That decision created "such a shock of surprise" that the Eleventh Amendment was at once proposed and adopted.

The Court is clear that its ruling encompasses all of Congress' Article 1 powers, undercutting Justice Brennan's "plan waiver" rationale in *Parden*:

> [W]e reconfirm that the background principle of state sovereign immunity embodied in the Eleventh Amendment is not so ephemeral as to dissipate when the subject of the suit is an area, like the regulation of Indian commerce, that is under the exclusive control of the Federal Government. Even when the Constitution vests in Congress complete lawmaking authority over a particular area, the Eleventh Amendment prevents congressional authorization of suits by private parties against unconsenting States.

To Justice Stevens' concerns, expressed in his dissent, that individuals would be deprived of all remedies for claims over which the federal courts exercise exclusive jurisdiction, such as antitrust, bankruptcy, and copyright infringement, the Court responded in a footnote that gave little hint that these areas would be exempted from the *Seminole Tribe* ruling. First, the Court said that the remedial concern is answered by *Ex parte Young*'s holding that federal courts can enjoin state officers from violating these protections. Second, the Court suggested that the remedy prescribed by Congress in the Gaming Act was quite extraordinary: "there is no established tradition in the lower federal courts of allowing enforcement of those federal statutes against the States." The Court thus indicated both that the *Ex parte Young* remedy adequately ensured compliance with federal law, and that there was no need to add to that remedy an additional action against the state. Individuals have fared well enough for the one hundred years of *Hans* and will continue to fare well under a constitutional regime that makes clear that Congress has no authority to abrogate a state's sovereign immunity under Article 1.

Of these two dissents, the most extensive is that of Justice Souter, writing for himself and Justices Breyer and Ginsburg. Justice Souter's dissent covers some eighty-five pages in the United States Reports and is thus difficult, if not impossible, to summarize or condense. It is fair to say, however, that he mounts a broad attack on virtually the entirety of Eleventh Amendment jurisprudence. As he sees it, the Eleventh Amendment presents three distinct questions: (1) did the states enjoy sovereign immunity prior to the ratification of the Constitution? (2) if they did, were they entitled to assert this immunity in cases brought in federal court under either diversity or federal question jurisdiction? and (3) does Congress have the authority through its legislative powers to abrogate this immunity? For answers to these questions, Justice Souter turned to the historical record.[118] As to the first question, Justice Souter finds the historical record to be unclear, although he does concede that there is evidence that some Framers believed that immunity existed in a state's own courts.

The second question was somewhat easier for Justice Souter to answer. The question of whether states would be subject to suit in federal court for violating a federal law, constitutional or statutory, was never debated either in the constitutional convention or later in the state ratification conventions. The lack of historical record led Justice Souter to conclude that the states would enjoy no immunity from federal question jurisdiction. With respect to diversity jurisdiction, Justice Souter argued, as do the diversity theorists, that while the Eleventh Amendment overruled *Chisholm*, it did so without so much as mentioning sovereign immunity. It simply eliminated diversity jurisdiction where the state was a party defendant. This led Justice Souter to conclude that *Hans* was wrongly decided. As he articulated it, "[t]he *Hans* Court erroneously assumed that a State could plead sovereign immunity against a non-citizen suing under federal question jurisdiction, and for that reason held that a State must enjoy the same protection in a suit by one of its own citizens." This assumption, he argued, is clearly inconsistent with "the Founders' hostility to the implicit reception of common law doctrine as federal law, and with the Founders' conception of sovereign power as divided between the States and the National Government for the sake of very practical objectives."

The third question was even easier to answer. Justice Souter accused the majority of ignoring the "Founders' view that common law, when it was received into the new American legal system, was always subject to legislative amendment." His opinion concluded with the observation that the incorporation of the common law as constitutional law created constitutional turmoil around the turn of the twentieth century, and was likely to do so again: "It was the defining characteristic of the *Lochner* era, and its characteristic vice, that the Court treated the common-law background (in those days, common law property rights and contractual autonomy) as paramount, while regarding congressional legislation to abrogate the common law on these economic matters as constitutionally suspect."

Justice Stevens penned a far more narrow dissent. He was willing to assume the correctness of both *Hans* and Justice Iredell's dissent in *Chisholm*. However, he contended that neither led to the majority's conclusion that Congress lacked the power under Article 1 to subject states to individual claims in federal court. The question for Justice Stevens was "whether the relatively modest jurisdictional bar that the Eleventh Amendment imposes should be understood to reveal that a more general jurisdictional bar implicitly inheres in Article III." Justice Stevens read *Hans* to establish only a presumption against the exercise of federal jurisdiction when an individual sued a state. That presumption could be overcome by congressional action. The reason that the Judiciary Act of 1875 was insufficient to overcome the presumption in *Hans* was that it was not sufficiently explicit with regard to the claim being asserted or the status of the defendant. Analogizing the implicit constitutional postulates of federalism in the Eleventh Amendment to the Court's abstention doctrines, Justice Stevens argued that because abstention (the doctrine that admonishes a federal court to decline to hear, or postpone decision on, matters that are of particular interest to the states despite its jurisdiction over them) is founded on Tenth Amendment principles, it has never been thought to preclude Congress from prohibiting the federal courts from abstaining. Finally, Justice Stevens distinguished *Hans* on the grounds that, unlike *Seminole Tribe* in which the Tribe's claim was founded on federal law, the validity of the underlying contractual obligation of the asserted federal Contract Clause right in *Hans* was dependent upon state law.

Despite being the narrower of the two dissents, Justice Stevens' dissent is the more difficult of the two to accept. First, his concern for those cases wherein Congress has lodged exclusive jurisdiction in the federal courts is not a constitutional concern. Congress could amend the jurisdictional statutes to vest the state courts with concurrent jurisdiction. This may not be the best solution because it may add greater uncertainty and divergent viewpoints to an area that demands certainty and uniform policy. But as long as the holding in *Cohens* that the Eleventh Amendment does not preclude the Supreme Court's appellate jurisdiction when the state is a party remains good law, that difficulty is easily cured by the Supreme Court's exercise of appellate jurisdiction. Indeed, Congress can grant an automatic right of appeal to the Supreme Court in all cases where national policy objectives make reliance on discretionary Supreme Court review inadvisable. Second, and more importantly, Justice Stevens' attempts to distinguish *Hans* are rather thin. While it is true that *Hans* never discussed the relationship between Eleventh Amendment sovereign immunity and congressional Article 1 powers, it is not too difficult to read *Hans*, as did Justice Scalia in *Union Gas*, as standing for an immunity from liability interpretation of the Eleventh Amendment. Indeed it is far easier to read *Hans* in that light than in the overly narrow way that Justice Stevens did. The views of Professors Tribe and Nowak notwithstanding, once *Hans* is read to establish that the Eleventh Amendment creates an immunity for the states in federal courts, then the majority is correct that Congress lacks the power to grant any jurisdiction to the federal courts that is beyond that granted by Article 3 as amended by the Eleventh Amendment. In short, *Hans* is the key to understanding and rationalizing the Court's Eleventh Amendment jurisprudence.

Justice Souter's opinion recognizes this and it directly confronts the issue of whether *Hans* was correctly decided. There are several reasons to believe that his opinion may be the correct interpretation of the Eleventh Amendment. For one, the historical evidence he marshals is extensive and persuasive. True, he draws inferences from this historical material that may or may not be correct in an epistemological sense, but they are certainly logical and reasonable. The majority's response that Justice Souter simply "cobbled together" a theory out of "whole law review cloth" is no response at all. If *Hans* was correctly decided it was because it properly interpreted the historical understanding of state sovereign immunity before *Chisholm* and correctly characterized the popular reaction to that decision. Certainly, as Justice Powell pointed out in *Welsh*, there are legitimate *stare decisis* reasons for adhering to *Hans*, but the *Seminole Tribe* majority went far beyond that rationale for its decision. As Justice Souter himself points out, the majority's response to his arguments reduces the entirety of the historical record to the statements of Hamilton, Marshall, and Madison to the exclusion of all other evidence to the contrary. As previously noted, Hamilton's writings in *Federalist No. 80* contradicted his absolute immunity statements in *Federalist No. 81*. And Madison and Marshall were engaged in a debate to persuade doubting members of the Virginia Constitutional Convention that their fears regarding Article 3 were overblown and to vote for ratification. Put another way, their words were those of advocacy, not of interpretation. To use those statements as proof positive that the Framers understood that states could not be sued in federal court on any claim is, in light of contrary statements made by equally knowledgeable statesmen of the day, little more than an argument that Madison and Marshall were "hoisted on their own petard."

Closing the Waiver Gap—The College Savings Bank *Litigation*

Three years after deciding *Seminole Tribe*, the Court decided three cases, sometimes referred to as the *Alden* trilogy, that not only re-affirmed *Seminole Tribe*'s essential holding that Congress could not abrogate state Eleventh Amendment sovereign immunity when acting pursuant to its Article 1 powers, but built upon *Seminole Tribe* to establish a new role for the Eleventh Amendment as an equal (maybe senior) partner with the Tenth Amendment in the protection of state autonomy from federal legislative authority. Moreover, as will be explained in the subsections that follow, these three cases impact not only on Congress' Article 1 powers but on its § 5, Fourteenth Amendment powers as well.

Florida Prepaid Postsecondary Education Expense Board v. College Savings Bank (1999) and College Savings Bank v. Florida Prepaid Postsecondary Education Expense Board (1999) were companion cases decided on the same day. Both involved allegations that Florida Prepaid, a state agency established to assist students in financing their college education, violated various provisions of federal patent laws. The first case, *Florida Prepaid*, alleged that the state agency had infringed on College Savings Bank's patent by using the bank's financing scheme to assist college tuition payments. The second, *College Savings Bank*, alleged that the state agency had violated the Lanham Act by engaging in false and misleading advertising. The primary significance of *Florida Prepaid* is its ruling regarding Congress' power to abrogate a state's Eleventh Amendment immunity pursuant to § 5 of the Fourteenth Amendment, and will therefore be discussed in detail in that subsection. However, *College Savings Bank*, while also important to the Court's new § 5 analysis, is also significant in defining the scope of Congress' Article 1 powers.

The Bank argued that Congress had unmistakably abrogated the state's sovereign immunity for violations of the Lanham Act,[119] and in any event the state had waived its sovereign immunity by "voluntarily elect[ing] to engage in...federally regulated conduct that subjects it to suit." Writing for a five-Justice majority, Justice Scalia dismissed the abrogation claim in one short sentence: "[o]ur decision...in *Seminole Tribe*...held that the power 'to regulate Commerce' conferred by Article 1 of the Constitution gives Congress no authority to abrogate state sovereign immunity."

The majority had only a marginally more difficult time with the waiver issue: "[g]enerally, we will find a waiver either if the State voluntarily invokes our jurisdiction...or else if the State makes a 'clear declaration' that it intends to submit itself to our jurisdiction." As there was no contention that Florida had expressly waived its immunity, College Savings Bank was left with only the constructive waiver theory of *Parden*. The Court would have none of that argument. Determining that *Parden* had been substantially limited by *Edelman* and *Employees* and partially overruled by *Welsh*, the Court took the final step and overruled the constructive waiver theory, leaving nothing of *Parden* remaining. The Court went on to hold that constructive waiver would not be implied because the state was engaging in a for-profit activity and thus could realistically end the activity without endangering its essential sovereign functions. Characterizing the Eleventh Amendment as a constitutional right, the Court held that the robustness of the Eleventh Amendment would not be affected by the context in which it is asserted.

The only knotty issue for the Court seemed to be distinguishing Congress' ability to abrogate a state's sovereign immunity by conditioning its approval of an interstate compact (Petty v. Tennessee-Missouri Bridge Commission, 1959) or its grant of federal funds on a state's waiver of sovereign immunity. With respect to interstate compacts, Justice Scalia analogized congressional approval of them to a gift. And as a gift, Congress could grant or withhold approval at its pleasure. The Lanham Act did not present something that could similarly be compared to a gift. Rather, it provided sanctions for engaging in permissible activities in violation of congressionally imposed norms.

The Court's reaction to the Spending Clause, however, was far more equivocal. (The Spending Clause, Art I, § 8, Clause 1, gives Congress the power to "lay and collect taxes . . . and provide for the common defense and general welfare of the United States.") Since the relationship between Congress' discretion under the Spending Clause and a state's sovereign immunity had not been directly decided[120] the Court was not required to deal with the issue in the same way as the interstate compact question. Rather, the Court hinted that the Eleventh Amendment might indeed limit Congress' ability to condition the receipt of federal funds on a waiver of sovereign immunity, depending upon the impact a denial of the funds might have on the state's freedom to choose whether to accept or reject the funds.[121] That is the last word to date on the intersection of the Spending Clause and the Eleventh Amendment. The issue was briefed in a case decided late in the 2000 Term, but the Court chose to decide it on narrower grounds without a mention of the Eleventh Amendment (Alexander v. Sandoval, 2001).

Justice Breyer, writing for himself and Justices Ginsburg, Souter, and Stevens wrote the primary dissent in *College Savings Bank*. Justice Breyer made two arguments. The first attacked the Court's overruling of *Parden*. The second was a broader rejection of the holding in *Seminole Tribe*. With respect to the second argument, since Justice Breyer essentially reiterated, in an abbreviated way, the substance of Justice Souter's *Seminole Tribe* dissent, it will not be repeated here. With respect to the first argument, however, Justice Breyer distinguished two issues: (1) Congress' *power* to abrogate state sovereign immunity, and (2) the clarity with which Congress must speak when it attempts to abrogate that immunity. It was only with respect to the second issue that *Parden* had been limited by subsequent cases. Every other case prior to *Seminole Tribe* assumed that Congress had the power to abrogate if it unmistakably spelled out its intention to do so. Thus, overruling *Parden* in its entirety had no support in precedent. Moreover, the Court's decision was against the weight of authority, under both congressional statute and Supreme Court precedent regarding the assertion of sovereign immunity when a state is sued for wrongs committed while engaged in commercial activities. Citing by way of analogy the post-World War II law denying foreign state sovereign immunity with respect to those activities, Justice Breyer noted that "it is today's holding, not *Parden*, that creates the legal 'anomaly.'"

Seminole Tribe and *College Savings Bank* decided, albeit by the slimmest of majorities, that Article 1 does not confer upon Congress the authority to abrogate a state's Eleventh Amendment immunity in federal courts. The cases did not decide the two remaining issues regarding congressional abrogation power, the ability to subject states to suit in courts of their own jurisdiction and the power to abrogate a state's sovereign immunity pursuant to § 5 of the Fourteenth Amendment, a power previously upheld in Fitzpatrick v. Bitzer (1976). These two issues will be discussed in the sections that follow.

ARTICLE I, MANDATING FEDERAL CLAIMS BE HEARD IN STATE COURT, AND THE ELEVENTH AMENDMENT

Closing the Circle—Alden v. Maine

Justice Thurgood Marshall's concurring opinion in *Employees* argued that while the plain language of the Eleventh Amendment prohibited Congress from using its Article 1 powers to abrogate a state's sovereign immunity in federal courts, there was nothing in that amendment nor anywhere else in the Constitution to prohibit Congress from creating federal claims that could be asserted in state courts. The only question was whether this authority was within Congress' Article 1 powers. Justice Marshall's position was rejected in Alden v. Maine (1999). In doing so the Court thus rejected the idea that the Eleventh Amendment merely allocates the forum in which federal claims can be heard in favor of an interpretation that confers absolute immunity on states for federal causes of action founded on Article 1. (See also Federal Maritime Commission v. South Carolina Ports Authority, 2002, applying *Alden* to federal administrative tribunals.)

Alden v. Maine was without doubt the most significant of the trilogy decided in the spring of 1999. Not only did *Alden* hold that Congress could not rely on its Article 1 powers to abrogate state Eleventh Amendment immunity in any court, federal or state, but it fused state sovereign immunity theory with broader notions of state autonomy, previously the domain of the Tenth Amendment, and the assumptions therein regarding the division of authorities between the states and the federal government.[122] Eleventh Amendment sovereign immunity, in the majority's view, is no longer a doctrine whose sole purpose is the protection of states from an unelected federal judiciary over which they have no formal or structural influence. Rather, it has become *the* essential component of the constitutional design that insulates the states from the bulk of federal regulatory authority, leaving the states free to ignore individual statutory entitlements with little fear of significant monetary consequences.

The facts of *Alden* help illuminate the systemic importance of the case. In 1992, John Alden, a state probation officer employed by the state of Maine, filed suit in United States district court alleging that Maine had violated the overtime provisions of the Fair Labor Standards Act (FLSA). While the case was pending in the district court, the Supreme Court decided *Seminole Tribe*. The district court, citing *Seminole Tribe*, then dismissed the case for lack of jurisdiction. Alden, pursuant to the jurisdictional provisions of the FLSA that gave concurrent jurisdiction to state courts, refiled in state court. The state court, in turn, dismissed the case on sovereign immunity grounds. It was that state court decision which found its way to the Supreme Court.

The starting point of any analysis of *Alden* must be the Court's acknowledgment that Congress may bind the states to the substantive provisions of the FLSA. The Court recognized this in two ways. First, it did not even cite to, much less overrule, the 1985 case in which it upheld, as against a Tenth Amendment challenge, the application of the FLSA to the states, Garcia v. San Antonio Metropolitan Transit Authority (1985). Second, the Court noted three ways in which the FLSA could be enforced against the states, (1) a suit by the United States against the states; (2) a private claim against state officers seeking damages for violating the Act; and (3) a private claim against state officers to enjoin their continuing violation of the Act.[123] The constitutional question in *Alden* was thus only remedial, whether Congress may remedy a state's violation of federal law by creating a private damage action in state court in favor of the injured party.

Justice Kennedy, writing for himself and four other Justices, began the majority's analysis by dismissing as unimportant the Eleventh Amendment's text, which refers only to the power of the federal courts under Article 3.

> The Eleventh Amendment makes explicit reference to the States' immunity from suits "commenced or prosecuted against one of the United States by Citizens of another State, or by Citizens or Subjects of any Foreign State." [citation omitted] We have, as a result, sometimes referred to the States' immunity from suit as "Eleventh Amendment immunity."

The phrase is convenient shorthand but something of a misnomer, for the sovereign immunity of the States neither derives from nor is limited by the terms of the Eleventh Amendment. Rather, as the Constitution's structure, and its history, and the authoritative interpretations by this Court make clear, the States' immunity from suit is a fundamental aspect of the sovereignty which the States enjoyed before ratification of the Constitution, and which they retain today...except as altered by the plan of the convention or certain constitutional Amendments.

Moreover, by way of emphasis, the Court said that "[t]o rest on the words of the amendment alone would be to engage in the type of ahistorical literalism we have rejected in interpreting the scope of the States' sovereign immunity since the discredited decision in *Chisholm*." The message from the Court is clear. Not only is the text of the Eleventh Amendment merely exemplary of broader notions of state sovereign immunity, but the Eleventh Amendment Framers intended it to be such. From that jumping off point, the Court's analysis appears to head in at least two different directions. First, state sovereignty and the dignity that inheres in the very definition of sovereignty itself, insulates states from a higher authority's second-guessing. The second, while related to the first, is distinct. It rests on more general principles of the states' independent political decision making, autonomy if you will, that are derived from Tenth Amendment jurisprudence.[124]

To establish that state sovereign immunity is central to the maintenance of a "residuary and inviolable sovereignty" and that the states "are not relegated to the role of mere provinces or political corporations, but retain the dignity, though not the full authority, of sovereignty," the *Alden* Court relies on history. Much of what Justice Kennedy describes as the views of the original framers has been cited elsewhere in this book, and will not be repeated here. But one bit of history he did emphasize was the nearly uniform public outcry that followed *Chisholm* and the speed with which Congress reacted to that outcry, demonstrating that Charles Warren was correct when he noted that *Chisholm* "fell upon the country with a profound shock."[125] This, coupled with the text and history of the Eleventh Amendment (described previously in Part I) was, in the eyes of the majority, sufficient to "suggest that Congress [in proposing the Eleventh Amendment] acted not to change but to restore the original constitutional design." The limited immunity described in the Eleventh Amendment's text thus became perfectly logical: "[g]iven the outraged reaction to *Chisholm*, as well as Congress' repeated refusal to otherwise qualify the text of the Amendment, it is doubtful that if Congress meant to write a new immunity into the Constitution it would have limited that immunity to the narrow text of the Eleventh Amendment...."

While logical, the argument is largely unpersuasive because it allows as the only possible reason for the "shock" and "outrage" following *Chisholm*, the undifferentiated loss of the states' sovereign immunity. As other scholars have noted, however, the historical record equally, if not more plausibly, suggests that it was the fear of foreign and out-of-state creditors and their ability to sue the states in federal courts to collect for Revolutionary War debts under the diversity of citizenship clause of Article 3 that provoked the states' reaction to *Chisholm*, a far more narrow concern than that assumed by the majority.

Even if Justice Kennedy is correct that the states were shocked that their sovereign immunity was lost by *Chisholm*'s interpretation of Article 3, that does not address the issue of congressional abrogation authority, much less Congress' power to require that claims arising under federal law be heard in state courts. Indeed, one can even accept the holding in *Seminole Tribe* and still conclude that it does not answer the problem posed by *Alden*. As Justice Thurgood Marshall observed in his *Employees*' concurrence, to require a state to defend a claim, even a federal claim, in its own courts over which the electorate retains some measure of control is not the same affront to the state's dignity as requiring it to defend a claim in court of a different sovereign. To answer this distinction the Court turned to the second analytical head, that relating to autonomy. As the Court said:

> [t]his separate and distinct structural principle [sovereign immunity] is not directly related to the scope of the judicial power established by Article III, but inheres in the system of federalism established by the Constitution. In exercising its Article I powers Congress may subject the States to private suits in their own courts only if there is "compelling evidence" that the States were required to surrender this power to Congress pursuant to the constitutional design.

The Court found no such compelling evidence either in the original understanding, the historical practice of Congress with respect to mandating that federal claims be heard in state courts, or the previous cases interpreting the Eleventh Amendment.

Far more important than how the presumption was applied in *Alden*, is the enormity of the burden that the United States must meet in order to sustain legislation abrogating a state's sovereign immunity and the historical debate that this burden terminates. Given the Court's treatment of the historical record and the precedent, both of which it characterized as ambiguous at best, the *Alden* decision creates an irrerbuttable presumption against congressional Article 1 abrogation authority. The Court, in other words, uses the ambiguity of the historical record to *support* its claim of constitutional sovereign immunity.

In doing so, *Alden* relegates the historical debate regarding original intent to one of academic interest only. The Court did so by relying on a structural analysis of federalism, rather than a historical analysis of sovereign immunity. The Court determined that congressional power to subject a state to suit in its own courts would be inconsistent with the "essential principles of federalism and...the special role of the state courts in the constitutional design." Citing New York v. United States (1992), United States v. Lopez (1996), and Printz v. United States

(1997), all Tenth Amendment cases, the Court held that "[a]lthough the Constitution grants broad powers to Congress, our federalism requires that Congress treat the States in a manner consistent with their status as residuary sovereigns and joint participants in the governance of the Nation." To subject states to private claims, even in their own courts, would not only be an indignity to the states because it would treat them as "the disfavored status of a debtor, subject to the power of private citizens to levy on its treasury..." but would fracture the political accountability of the states to their citizens and "blur...the separate duties of the judicial and political branches of state government.... A State is entitled to order the processes of its own governance, assigning to the political branches, rather than the courts, the responsibility for directing the payment of debts."

Finally, the Court responded to the dissent's claim that states could now ignore federal law with impunity by noting that there are still limits to the states' ability to assert sovereign immunity. First, the states can consent to suit, which out of a "sense of justice," states have done on their own. Second, the states have consented, by the plan of the convention, to suits brought by other states or by the federal government. Third, Congress may act to abrogate state sovereign immunity under § 5 of the Fourteenth Amendment. Fourth, immunity from federal claims does not extend to political subdivisions of the state. And finally, sovereign immunity "does not bar *certain actions* against state officers" for prospective relief under *Ex parte Young*. These exceptions, according to the majority, preserve a "proper balance between the supremacy of federal law and the separate sovereignty of the states."

Justice Souter, writing for himself and Justices Breyer, Ginsburg, and Stevens, attacked the majority's holding that sovereign immunity was an essential element of statehood as conceived by the original framers. This holding, Justice Souter argued, makes much of the reasoning of *Seminole Tribe* and indeed the Eleventh Amendment itself, unnecessary since state sovereign immunity was always protected by the structural assumptions underlying federalism as recognized by the Tenth Amendment. Much of Justice Souter's opinion was taken up with disputing the historical evidence marshaled by the majority in support of its structural argument that sovereign immunity was an inherent right of statehood and was so understood by the framers. Repeating his characterization of the Court's sovereign immunity jurisprudence as a concept of natural law akin to the "liberty of contract" Justice Souter cited chapter and verse from Blackstone, Locke, the ratification debates, and *Chisholm*, even Justice Iredell's dissent, to demonstrate that sovereign immunity as conceived of by the Framers was a common law sovereign immunity, not one that was in any way constitutionalized. Moreover, Justice Souter noted that even if the natural law version of sovereign immunity was accepted, it is inapplicable to congressional abrogation: "Under the natural law theory, sovereign immunity may be invoked only by the sovereign that is the source of the right upon which suit is brought." In the case of federal law, that means the federal government.

Far more important, however, were Justice Souter's observations on the structural impact of the majority's holding on our federal system. First the dissent argues, the majority's opinion in *Alden* significantly alters the federal/state balance as it elevates the sovereignty of the states above that of the United States even when the United States is acting within its delegated authority under Article 1. As the dissent observed, "[t]he State of Maine is not sovereign with respect to the national objective of the FLSA. It is not the authority that promulgated the FLSA....That authority is the United States acting through the Congress, whose legislative power under Article I of the Constitution to extend FLSA coverage to state employees has already been decided...." The majority's political accountability argument thus seems not only out of place but perverse as well. When Congress acts within the substantive scope of its Article 1 powers, the states' ability to assert their sovereignty in opposition to that federal authority has less to do with the relationship between the state and its constituents than with the federal government and its constituents. Political accountability requires that national policy be set nationally, not locally. Consequently, if there is any attenuation of political accountability it is at the federal not the state level. It is true that the federal government can itself enforce its policy by suing the states. But in terms of the majority's apparent concern, political accountability at the state level, the Executive's decision to enforce the provisions of federal legislation is no more satisfactory than Congress' judgment to let that decision rest with the individuals harmed by the state action. The only distinction between the two is that the states probably have a greater influence on federal litigation decisions than on private ones. On the other hand, there is no reason to suspect that states have less influence on congressional decision making than on Executive decision making. If the assumption is that the Federal Executive will exercise greater restraint than a private litigant (not an unreasonable assumption), why isn't Congress rather than the Court, the appropriate body to weigh the costs and benefits of self-interested litigation?

Justice Souter's second concern is even more serious. Citing Lord Chief Justice Holt, William Blackstone, and Chief Justice Marshall's opinion in Marbury v. Madison (1803), the dissent concluded that "there is much irony in the Court's profession that it grounds its opinion on a deeply rooted historical tradition of sovereign immunity, when the Court abandons a principle nearly as inveterate, and much closer to the hearts of the Framers: that where there is a right, there must be a remedy." "[Chief Justice Marshall's] contemporaries might well have reacted to the Court's decision today in the words of Edmund Randolph when responding to the objection to jurisdiction in *Chisholm*: '[The Framers] must have viewed human rights in their essence, not their mere form.'" What the Court seems to have forgotten in its zeal to protect the states from the long arm of the federal government is that the state of Maine deprived individuals of rights conferred upon them by the federal government acting within its constitutional limits. These individuals were left with no remedy other than what the good will of the state might grant them or what the federal government, given its limited resources, might choose to enforce on their behalf. Describing the Court's assertion that the latter is sufficient to preserve the supremacy of federal law as being "on a par with closing the courthouse door to state tort victims unaccompanied by a lawyer from Washington," the dissent argued that "it is implausible to claim that enforcement by a public authority without any incentive beyond its general enforcement power will ever afford the private right a traditionally adequate remedy."[126] Put simply, Justice Souter's point was that a state's sovereign immunity pales in importance to concerns for ensuring that individuals receive justice. The majority, on the other hand, appears to view the rights of individuals in a classic Madisonian way. As Justice Kennedy argued in his concurring opinion in United States v. Lopez (1996), federalism and the decentralization of authority accomplished by the manner in which the Constitution divides authority between the states and the federal government and among the three branches of the federal government is essential to protecting individual liberty. The Court cannot, therefore, leave its guardianship of federalism to Congress.

If it is true that a court's ruling is to be judged solely by the persuasiveness of its reasoning, the majority opinions in *Seminole Tribe* and *Alden* do not fare well when compared to Justice Souter's dissents. Not only is Justice Souter's position consistent with the weight of historical scholarship, but the depth and detail of his research, the care with which he marshaled that research, and meticulous way that he analyzed the historical data he collected simply overwhelms the similar efforts of the majority. On the other hand, if *Seminole Tribe* is correct in its assertion regarding the broad scope of the holding in *Hans*—that the Constitution confirmed rather than abrogated the states' sovereign immunity—then *Alden* follows from *Hans*, if not inexorably, at least logically. Perhaps that is why Justice Souter chose to direct most of his dissenting comments to attacking the historical underpinnings of *Seminole Tribe*. However, he does not, at least not directly, answer three arguments put forward by the *Alden* majority that do not appear to be based upon what history teaches us about the views of the founding generation.[127]

First, Justice Kennedy argued that it would be anomalous to interpret the Constitution so as to allow "the National Government [to] wield greater power in the state courts than in its own judicial instrumentalities." This seems self-obvious particularly in light of the Court's federalism decisions since 1995 (United States v. Lopez (1995); Printz v. United States (1997); United States v. Morrison [2000]). But it is not. If the Framers contemplated that state courts would be the initial forum for the adjudication of federal claims, whether those claims arose from the Constitution, from federal treaties or from federal statutes, there is nothing anomalous at all about the plaintiffs' invoking the jurisdiction of the state court to hear their federal claims or about Congress' authority to permit them to do so. Indeed, until *Alden*, it was assumed that state courts would be open to federal claims, even those against the states themselves.[128] Moreover, the more central the claim is to important state interests, like the wages to be paid state workers *(Alden)* or the prerogative of the governor in the performance of his executive functions *(Seminole Tribe)* the more sensible it is that state courts act as the initial forum.[129]

Second, the Court agreed, albeit almost as an afterthought, that for Congress to essentially commandeer state courts to enforce federal law is a greater threat to the state's authority than forcing it to appear in the federal courts.[130] However, this argument, like the first, is circular. It assumes historical evidence the majority does not produce. As Justice Souter noted in a footnote, "the Court [is] in the position of supporting its view of what the Eleventh Amendment means by the 'historical' assertion that the Framers must have intended it to mean the same." Again, if the Framers understood that state courts would be the primary forum for the assertion of federal claims, subject to review by the United States Supreme Court (an understanding not contested by the majority), it would be no affront to their sovereignty, or their dignity for that matter, for the federal government to possess the authority to require state courts to hear claims arising under an otherwise constitutional assertion of federal legislative authority. Indeed, to the extent that the sovereign immunity doctrine is founded on the indignity the state would suffer if required to defend an individual claim in a court other than its own, *Alden* posed no threat whatsoever to the interests protected by sovereign immunity.[131]

But be that as it may, the historical argument has come full circle. Whether *Alden* was correctly decided depends upon how one assesses the relative persuasiveness of the majority and dissent's historical arguments. As noted previously, the sheer weight of the historical evidence presented by Justice Souter is impressive, if not overwhelming; the majority's efforts in this regard pale by comparison. This is particularly odd given the Court's opinion in another so-called "commandeering" case, involving Congress' authority to enlist the aid of state executive officers to enforce federal gun control laws (Printz v. United States [1997]). Agree or not with its historical analysis of the federal government's ability to enlist state officers to enforce federal law, the Court in that case marshaled its historical evidence with far more care and presented it in a far more persuasive manner than it did only two years later in *Alden*. One can only wonder why the Court in *Alden* was not as painstaking with its historical support. Perhaps it thought that everything after *Hans*, including congressional abrogation authority, was a foregone conclusion, requiring only a lawyer's *stare decisis*, not a historical justification. But *Alden* was not a forgone conclusion, as Justice Thurgood Marshall's concurring opinion in *Employees,* Justice Powell's dictum in

Pennhurst, and the plurality opinion in *Union Gas* attest. Maybe Justice Souter's historical evidence simply cannot be refuted.

A weak historical justification for the result in *Alden* is not only the basis for concluding that Justice Souter has the better of the argument. Of equal significance is the fact that the Court in *Printz* distinguished between a state court's responsibility to hear federal claims and a state executive's responsibility to enforce federal law on the basis that the Supremacy Clause, in so many words, requires state courts to apply federal law whereas no such responsibility rests on state executives. Maybe that explains why Justice Kennedy seemed so reluctant to make the anti-commandeering argument the centerpiece of the majority's opinion. In any event, the distinction in *Printz* between the exercise of federal authority with respect to the state executive and the state judiciary blunts the argument that "commandeering" the state courts to hear claims against the state is a greater threat to the states' sovereign interests than requiring them to appear in a federal court.

Finally, a congruity argument is apparent.[132] As Justice Kennedy stated, "it is unquestioned that the Federal Government [is immune] from suit not only in state tribunals, but also in its courts . . . [W]e are reluctant to conclude that the States are not entitled to a reciprocal privilege." Supporting this is the notion that the Constitution created a system of dual sovereignties, neither one entitled to greater respect or dignity than the other. But even if the majority is correct that what the Constitution created was co-equal sovereigns, a proposition not embraced by all,[133] the majority's argument ignores three countervailing interpretative arguments. First is the Supremacy Clause. If the Constitution created two co-equal sovereigns, each was limited in its sovereign prerogatives to its own sphere of authority. That means that just as the federal government cannot interfere with the states' exercise of their proper sphere of authority (United States v. Lopez, 1996; City of Boerne v. Flores, 1997), the state cannot interfere with the proper exercise of federal authority. And the Court has not yet held that the Fair Labor Standards Act and the extension of that Act to states and their political subdivisions was an improper exercise of federal authority. The anomaly is thus the distinction the Court apparently draws between Congress' substantive powers and its remedial powers, the latter being far less than the former.

Second, the Court's congruity argument assumes that there is indeed congruity. There is not. The federal government can sue the states *eo nominee* but the states do not have a similar prerogative, even if federal officers, under federal authority, violate state law. States are, by the Supremacy Clause, bound to obey federal law. There is no similar requirement imposed upon the United States. Finally, the Court's congruity argument assumes that the federal government's sovereign immunity is constitutional rather than common law. The Court has never held that the sovereign immunity of the United States is constitutional. Martha Field has opined that it is nothing more than a common law understanding.[134] If federal sovereign immunity is nothing more than a common law understanding, then, as

Justice Brennan argued in both *Employees* and in *Union Gas*, and Justice Souter argued in *Seminole Tribe* and *Alden*, the states' sovereign immunity is likewise only a common law immunity, subject to being waived not only by the state legislature but by Congress as well, in the proper exercise of its legislative authority.

One could, of course, read *Seminole Tribe* and *Alden* as indirectly holding that federal sovereign immunity is (now) constitutional but that would be hardly more than *ipse dixit* (something asserted but not proved). It certainly does not follow from any of the historical data that the Court has pointed to in any of its Eleventh Amendment cases, starting with *Hans* and ending with *Alden*. Nor is there anything that any legal historian has yet found that would support the argument that federal sovereign immunity is of constitutional dimension. To make the argument, the Court would have to work backwards from its conclusion in *Seminole Tribe* and *Alden*; since the states have a *constitutional* immunity from private suits, then the federal government *must* have the same constitutional immunity.

When all is said and done, whether the results in *Alden* and *Seminole Tribe* are defensible at all depend, not upon the majority's attempt to fit those rulings within the historical understanding of the Framers' conceptions of federalism, but rather on the far more pragmatic argument that given the totality of Eleventh Amendment jurisprudence, including the exceptions to state sovereign immunity, an acceptable accommodation between federal and state authority has been reached. That issue is explored in the final section.

Procedural Due Process and the Takings Clause—An Exception to Alden?

The Eleventh Amendment's proscription of retrospective relief against the state takes an interesting twist when the Takings Clause is considered. One can hypothesize a situation in which the state either physically dispossesses an individual from her property, for example, to widen a right of way along a state highway, or promulgates a regulation prohibiting owners of property used as nesting grounds for an endangered species of bird from destroying that habitat by building a home, logging, etc. The Takings Clause of the Fifth Amendment, as applied to the states through the Due Process Clause of the Fourteenth Amendment, requires on its face that the property owner be justly compensated for her loss.[135] Since the claim must be paid from the state's general fund, and the relief is retrospective in nature, the Eleventh Amendment prohibits a just compensation claim in federal court. Moreover, *Alden* protects the state from having to defend such a claim in its own courts. Thus, unless a state consents to claims for uncompensated takings, there would appear to be no remedy for a state's decision to take an individual's property rights without paying fair value for the property taken, other than that which a state has agreed to provide for violation of its version of the taking clause in its own judicial or administrative tribunals.

Like so much about constitutional sovereign immunity, what looks to be true is not always so. Some have argued that the Supreme Court in First English Evangelical Lutheran Church v. County of Los Angeles (1987) requires that the states provide a compensation remedy in their own courts. [136] The reason for this conclusion is the self-executing nature of the Takings Clause. The Clause itself both states the constitutional wrong and prescribes the remedy for that wrong.[137] But the issue of sovereign immunity never arose in *First English*. Nor should it have since the entity being sued was Los Angeles County which, under Lincoln County v. Luning (1890), could not claim the protection of the Eleventh Amendment. Moreover, California had waived its immunity for taking claims in its own courts.

Twelve years later, a plurality of the Court again suggested that Fifth Amendment takings claims filed in state court against state entities might not be subject to the ordinary rules of sovereign immunity (City of Monterey v. Del Monte Dunes at Monterey, Ltd., 1999). But that too was a case in which sovereign immunity was never raised because, like *First English*, the compensation was asserted against a local political subdivision, not the state. It may well be that when directly confronted with the issue of a state takings claim filed against the state itself in state court, the Supreme Court may turn its dictum into holding. That, however, is anything but clear. As Richard Seamon has argued, for the Court to do so would require it both to overrule a number of older precedents and undo the sovereign immunity symmetry between federal courts and state courts that *Seminole Tribe* and *Alden* so recently created.[138]

The answer may lie not with an attempt to reconcile the self-executing Takings Clause with the Eleventh Amendment but with the procedural requirements of the Due Process Clause of the Fourteenth Amendment and the extent to which, if at all, the Eleventh Amendment insulates a state from those requirements. In McKesson v. Division of Alcoholic Beverages and Tobacco, Department of Business Regulation of Florida (1990) the plaintiff contested, in the Florida state courts, the constitutionality of a Florida statute imposing an excise tax on liquor that McKesson Corporation claimed discriminated against interstate commerce. McKesson not only sought prospective declaratory and injunctive relief against the enforcement of the statute, which the state court granted, but also a retrospective claim for a refund of taxes already paid pursuant to the allegedly unconstitutional statute. In a unanimous opinion, the Supreme Court reversed the Florida Supreme Court's denial of the requested retrospective relief. The only specific mention of the Eleventh Amendment was in response to the state's assertion that state sovereign immunity deprived the federal courts, including the Supreme Court, of subject matter jurisdiction to review decisions of state courts when the state or one of its agencies is a party. The Court rejected the state's argument on the authority of Cohens v. Virginia.

With respect to the retrospective claim, the Court did not rule substantively on the state's obligation to refund taxes paid pursuant to an unconstitutional statute.

What the Court did say was that when a state requires a taxpayer to pay a tax when due, requiring her to file a postpayment claim for a refund, the Fourteenth Amendment's Due Process Clause requires the state, "to provide meaningful backward-looking relief to rectify any unconstitutional deprivation." And if the state chooses to relegate the taxpayer to a post-deprivation remedy[139] that remedy must be "'clear and certain.'" If the state is required to provide a remedy for illegally collected taxes, it might suggest *a fortiori* that the state must provide a remedy for a person's property that is seized by the state, physically or by means of excessive regulation. The self-executing nature of the Takings Clause plus the equitable argument that property taken for the public's benefit should require public compensation[140] only adds strength to that argument.

On the other hand, the Court has noted on several occasions, most recently in *Alden*, that if the federal government is protected by sovereign immunity from suits in its own courts without its consent, the states deserve no less from the constitutional structure. In other words respect for state sovereignty requires a parity of sovereign immunity between the federal government and the states. It is true that the federal government has waived its sovereign immunity with respect to takings suits via the Tucker Act.[141] (The Tucker Act, among its other provisions, gives the United States Court of Claims jurisdiction to hear damage claims against the United States founded upon the Constitution or federal and regulatory law.) But the Court is clear that absent that waiver, the federal government would be immune from takings claims (Lynch v. United States, 1934; Schillinger v. United States, 1894). To permit the Due Process Clause of the Fourteenth Amendment to override the states' immunity in their own courts would create an asymmetry between federal sovereign immunity and state sovereign immunity. Moreover, such a ruling would give the Due Process Clause of the Fourteenth Amendment more bite than the Due Process clause of the Fifth Amendment, creating an even more perplexing asymmetry. One resolution would be to look at the forum in which the right to seek compensation is afforded. There is nothing in *McKesson* that requires the post-deprivation remedy to be judicial. Indeed, in *Alden* the majority opinion specifically noted the possibility of a legislative remedy. So long as the remedy meets the requirements of fairness, clarity, and certainty, due process may be satisfied even if the state establishes a nonjudicial, indeed even informal, remedy to compensate those whose property has been taken without just compensation.[142]

The Anomaly of Nevada v. Hall

Alden held that state sovereign immunity, part of the constitutional design and inherent in the meaning of a sovereign state, prohibited Congress from requiring a state court to hear a federal claim. Only when state courts are generally open to a claim similar to the federal claim are they required by the Supremacy Clause to hear the federal cause of action (Testa v. Katt, 1947).[143] It would thus seem that the Constitution immunizes the states from having to defend retrospective individual claims in either federal or state courts without their consent. But once again appearances, particularly in the Alice-in-Wonderland of Eleventh Amendment jurisprudence, are deceiving. States are required to defend individual damage claims in the courts of *other* states.

Nevada v. Hall (1979) was a personal injury claim brought by California residents in California state court against the state of Nevada, the University of Nevada (a state agency for purposes of the Eleventh Amendment), and the administrator of the estate of a former employee of the University who was accused of negligently injuring the plaintiffs while traveling in California on official University of Nevada business. Nevada challenged the jurisdiction of the California court to require Nevada's appearance. This was turned aside by the California Supreme Court, as was a claim by Nevada that damages should be limited to $25,000, the maximum permitted by Nevada's sovereign immunity waiver statute for tort actions. The jury awarded the California plaintiffs $1,150,000. In the United States Supreme Court, Nevada argued that the "federal rule of law implicit in the Constitution...requires all of the States to adhere to the sovereign-immunity doctrine as it prevailed when the Constitution was adopted."

Writing for a six-Justice majority, Justice Stevens rejected Nevada's argument, holding that there was no such federal rule of law, either explicit or implicit. The Eleventh Amendment itself and the history of its adoption speak only to the power of the federal courts. It provides no basis for limiting the power of one state to exercise jurisdiction over another. With respect to implicit constitutional limitations deriving from the sovereignty of the states, the principle upon which *Alden* relied, the Court said:

> [O]urs is not a union of 50 wholly independent sovereigns. ...one State's immunity from suit in the courts of another State is [nothing] other than a matter of comity. Indeed, in view of the Tenth Amendment's reminder that powers not delegated to the Federal Government nor prohibited to the States are reserved to the States or the people, the existence of express limitations on state sovereignty may equally imply that caution should be exercised before concluding that unstated limitations on state power were intended by the Framers. The people of Nevada have consented to a system in which their State is subject only to limited liability in tort. But the people of California, who have no voice in Nevada's decision, have adopted a different system. Each of these decisions is equally entitled to our respect.

Rather than rejecting the Eleventh Amendment and its history as irrelevant, Justice (now Chief Justice) Rehnquist relied upon it in his dissent to argue that implicit in the constitutional scheme was an immunity of states from suit not only in federal courts but in the courts of sister states as well. To hold otherwise, as the Court did, was to deny the "important concepts of sovereignty that do not find expression in the literal terms of [the Eleventh Amendment], but which are of constitutional dimension because their derogation would undermine the logic of the constitutional scheme." "Ironically, and...wrongly, the Court transforms what it described as a constitutional right in Edelman v. Jordan...into an albatross."

Looked at one way, *Alden* and Nevada v. Hall are consistent. Sovereign immunity according to the majority in *Alden*, is a federalism value, one that is part and parcel of the way in which the Constitution distributes authority between the federal and state governments. The confluence of the Tenth and Eleventh Amendments evidenced by *Alden* places this in bold relief. Indeed, this distinction between federal/state disputes and state/state disputes is the basis upon which *Alden* distinguishes Nevada v. Hall. On the other hand, if *Alden* is correct that sovereign immunity is a constitutional concept that inheres in the very idea of statehood itself, the two cases are irreconcilable. It is hard to understand how a state's claim that it is constitutionally entitled to the respect and dignity of an independent sovereign can be recognized when sued under an otherwise valid law enacted by the general government which represents the people as a whole, and yet be ignored when sued under the laws of a sister state in which it has no right of participation, formal or informal, effective or ineffective. As I have said elsewhere, "[i]f the states were profoundly shocked by Chisholm v. Georgia, they would have taken up arms had they known that Nevada v. Hall was in the offing."[144] At the very least, sovereign immunity, as a constitutional principle, would require that states respect the sovereign immunity decisions of sister states as a matter of the Full Faith and Credit Clause, in *Hall* limiting any judgment against Nevada to $25,000.[145] (Article 4, § 1, the Full Faith and Credit clause, requires one state to recognize and apply the laws and judicial determinations of another state. For example, State A must respect a divorce decree entered by a court in State B.) Whether *Alden* will prompt the Court to reconsider *Hall* in the future and adopt Chief Justice Rehnquist's dissent remains to be seen. But Justice Kennedy's distinction of Hall in *Alden* gives no indication that it intends to do so.

SECTION 5 OF THE FOURTEENTH AMENDMENT AND CONGRESSIONAL POWER TO ABROGATE A STATE'S ELEVENTH AMENDMENT SOVEREIGN IMMUNITY

Congress' Constitutional Authority to Abrogate State Sovereign Immunity

Even as the Court expressed doubt about Congress' powers under Article 1 to abrogate state sovereign immunity and then denied that power altogether, it has steadfastly held to its 1976 holding in Fitzpatrick v. Bitzer that § 5 of the Fourteenth Amendment clearly confers upon Congress that power. *Fitzpatrick* was an action for both injunctive and damage relief. The plaintiffs alleged that

Connecticut's State Employees Retirement Act discriminated on the basis of gender and was thus a violation of Title VII of the Civil Rights Act of 1964,[146] the provision that prohibits employment discrimination. Connecticut argued it was immune from suit under the Eleventh Amendment. Writing for a unanimous Court, Justice Rehnquist noted that the Fourteenth Amendment, unlike the Article 1 powers that were at issue in Edelman v. Jordan and the *Alden* trilogy, represented a "shift in the federal-state balance":

> There can be no doubt that [the Court has] sanctioned Congress, acting under the Civil War amendments, [to move] into the judicial, executive, and legislative spheres of autonomy previously reserved to the states.... It is true that [none] of our previous cases presented the relationship between the 11th amendment and the enforcement power granted to Congress under § 5 of the 14th amendment. But we think that the 11th amendment, and the principle of state sovereignty which it embodies, are necessarily limited by the enforcement provisions of § 5 of the 14th amendment. ...that section [expressly grants Congress] authority to enforce "by appropriate legislation the substantive provisions of the 14th amendment, which themselves embody significant limitations on state authority. [portion omitted] We think that Congress may, in determining what is "appropriate legislation" for purposes of enforcing the provisions of the 14th amendment, provide for private suits against states or state officials which are constitutionally impermissible in other contexts.

In addition to that textual and structural argument, the Court also relied upon a chronological argument: Since the Fourteenth Amendment was adopted after the Eleventh Amendment, it must, under ordinary rules of textual interpretation, be held to have limited the terms of the Eleventh Amendment. The chronological argument is weak at best. Not only does it separate the Constitution into distinct and largely unrelated segments, but it assumes that in 1868 the Framers of the Fourteenth Amendment could have not only predicted Hans v. Louisiana but the extensions of *Hans* that occurred in *Seminole Tribe* and *Alden* as well. Nevertheless, the chronological argument, maybe because of its simplicity, has become the rationale by which the later cases have, for purposes of the Eleventh Amendment, distinguished Congress' Article 1 power to abrogate state sovereign immunity from its abrogation authority under § 5 of the Fourteenth Amendment. (Seminole Tribe of Florida v. Florida, 1996; Pennsylvania v. Union Gas Company, 1989 [Justice Scalia, dissenting]).

As a result, as long as Congress sufficiently expresses its intent to abrogate state sovereign immunity, an issue that will be discussed in the following subsection, individuals can hold the state liable not only for damages for violating Congress' substantive regulations, but for the litigation costs attendant to enforcing those regulations as well, including attorneys fees under the Civil Rights Attorney's Fees Awards Act of 1976[147] (Hutto v. Finney, 1978). While not limiting the general principle that § 5 permits Congress to abrogate a state's Eleventh Amendment immunity, more recent cases have drawn an ever-increasingly tight noose around what the Court will consider "appropriate legislation."[148]

The first indication that the Rehnquist Court was prepared, in the name of federalism, to restrict Congress' § 5, Fourteenth Amendment powers came in City of Boerne v. Flores (1997) in which the Court struck down the Religious Freedom Restoration Act of 1993 (RFRA). RFRA mandated that any action by a state or local government that adversely affected religious practice be strictly scrutinized to ascertain whether it was supported by a compelling state interest and whether the means were narrowly tailored to achieve that interest. This contradicted the level of scrutiny previously imposed by the Court for neutral regulations that had an adverse impact upon one's freedom of religious exercise (Employment Division, Department of Human Resources v. Smith, 1990). While the Court recognized that congressional determinations regarding what legislation was appropriate to secure the guarantees of the Fourteenth Amendment were "entitled to much deference," Congress did not have the constitutional authority to "decree the *substance* of the Fourteenth Amendment's restrictions on the States...." Admitting that the line between what is properly within Congress' remedial powers and what is an improper congressional determination of the substantive meaning of § 1 of the Fourteenth Amendment was opaque, the boundaries could be determined by analyzing whether there is "a congruence and proportionality between the injury to be prevented or remedied and the means adopted to that end." The Court found both parts of the test to be lacking in RFRA. The legislation was thus not "appropriate" within the meaning of § 5. First, the actions prohibited by RFRA went far beyond those the Court had determined to be unconstitutional. There was thus no congruence between the scope of RFRA and the constitutional harm. There was virtually nothing other than anecdotal evidence to support the proposition that there were widespread, national violations of individuals' religious freedoms resulting from the unintended actions of state and local governments. Second, since the evidence of Constitutional violation was so lacking, the RFRA was "so out of proportion to a supposed remedial or preventive object that it cannot be understood as responsive to, or designed to prevent, unconstitutional behavior."

The Court next spoke to the limits of Congress' § 5 powers two years later in the *Alden* trilogy, this time specifically in the context of the Eleventh Amendment.[149] Florida Prepaid Postsecondary Education Expense Board v. College Savings Bank (1999) was an action by the bank against the state agency alleging an infringement of its patented method of financing higher education. Jurisdiction was based upon the Patent and Plant Variety Protection Remedy Clarification Act,[150] enacted specifically to make clear Congress' intent to subject states to patent infringement actions by private individuals. The Bank argued that the Protection Act was a valid exercise of congressional § 5 power to protect the property rights of patent holders. Chief Justice Rehnquist's majority opinion disagreed. His analysis proceeded in two quite distinct directions, both of which have significant implications for the breadth of Congress' powers to enforce the Civil War Amendments. The first follows the "congruence and proportionality" reasoning of *City of Boerne*:

> In enacting the Patent Remedy Act...Congress identified no pattern of patent infringement by the states, let alone a pattern of constitutional violations. Unlike the undisputed record of racial discrimination confronting Congress in the voting rights cases...Congress came up with little evidence of infringing conduct on the part of the States. The House Report acknowledged that "many states comply with patent law" and could provide only two examples of patent infringement suits against the States. The Federal Circuit in its opinion identified only eight patent-infringement suits prosecuted against the States in the 110 years between 1880 and 1990.

There was, in other words, no pervasive constitutional problem that demanded the remedy imposed. Making states generally liable in damages for patent infringement was thus "out of proportion to a supposed remedial or preventative object [and thus] cannot be understood as responsive to, or designed to prevent, unconstitutional behavior."

More important than the application of the "congruence and proportionality" test to the particular facts of patent infringement is the factual burden the Court placed upon Congress before it can satisfy that test. The Court has consistently denied that it has the authority to require Congress to produce a factual record as a condition of sustaining the constitutionality of its Article 1 exercises (United States v. Lopez, 1996; Heart of Atlanta Motel v. United States, 1964). Indeed it repeats this in *Boerne*: "the lack of support in the legislative record is not determinative..." Yet in the same sentence, the Court questions the deference just extended: "identifying the targeted constitutional wrong or evil is still a critical part of our § 5 calculus because '[s]trong measures appropriate to address one harm may be an unwarranted response to another, lesser one....'" Consequently, congressional findings, indeed specific congressional findings, appear to be a condition of sustaining a § 5 enactment.

Maybe of greater consequence is the Court's second line of reasoning. The Due Process Clause of the Fourteenth Amendment protects property only from deprivations *without due process of law.* While admitting that patents are a species of property protected from infringement, the Court held that there was no denial without due process of law. It relied on two cases in which the issue was what process is due for an unauthorized and random deprivation of property by the state, Hudson v. Palmer (1984) and Paratt v. Taylor (1981). The *Florida Prepaid* majority reiterated the holdings in those cases that there is no deprivation of property without due process as long as the claimant remains able to assert a state post-deprivation remedy to compensate for the lost or damaged property. Only if that state remedy is nonexistent or inadequate is there a deprivation of property without due process. Despite extensive citation by the dissent that Congress had evidence that state remedies were likely to be inadequate, the Court concluded that Congress' findings with respect to the adequacy of the state remedies were insufficient to establish a nationwide problem. At best, the testimony established only that "the remedies in some States were uncertain." This uncertainty did not however, demonstrate a pervasive violation of § 1, which the Court says is necessary to satisfy the proportionality part of the test.[151]

At first blush, it might appear that the *Florida Prepaid* majority accepted Justice Kennedy's concurring opinion in *Coeur d'Alene* that the availability of federal remedies (in that case, a prospective suit against a state officer) should be dependent upon the adequacy of state remedies. But that reading would all but eviscerate *Fitzpatrick* whenever the state has enacted a remedial scheme similar to that of the federal government, which is generally true with respect to most civil rights claims. On the other hand, the Court in *College Savings*, the companion case, did hold that only when the congressional abrogation "was genuinely necessary" would it be upheld. And the argument could be made that where the state provides an adequate remedy for the particular claim, even if it is not as expansive as that provided by federal law, abrogation is not "genuinely necessary."[152]

Troubling as this possibility might be, the incorporation of a test to determine whether an individual has been deprived of procedural rights in a case in which the issue was whether Congress has appropriately protected the substantive property rights of individual patent holders has implications at least as far reaching as the previously noted possibility. The only possible explanation for the Court's conflating two seemingly disconnected analyses, other than judicial inattention, is the remedial rather than the substantive nature of Congress' § 5 powers. Indeed, the reason for the "congruence and proportionality" test is to flesh out whether Congress is acting substantively or remedially. Thus, if the Court is testing the propriety of Congress' remedial (or process) powers it might seem logical to apply process cases. But as Daniel Meltzer argues, the procedural due process cases are fact specific. Florida would be held to have satisfied the requirements of due process only if patent infringement was "random and unauthorized" *and* the State provided an adequate post-infringement remedy.[153] The Court in *Florida Prepaid* seemed unconcerned with determining whether either condition was present except by way of a passing reference in a footnote that Florida provides a legislative remedy for compensation as well as a judicial remedy for a taking. No effort was made to explore the practical adequacy of either remedy to College Savings Bank's specific harm. Nor did the majority even attempt to answer Justice Stevens' observation in his dissent that the Bank alleged a willful, not a random and unauthorized, infringement of its patent. Instead the Court avoided these factual nuances and struck the statute down on its face[154] reflecting, I suspect, the Court's view that state sovereign immunity is preeminent in the constitutional structure, apparently more so than Congress' ability to act in a prophylactic way to protect individual rights under the Fourteenth Amendment.

One year later, in a 5–4 opinion, the Court applied the *Boerne* "congruence and proportionality" test to strike down Congress' attempt to apply the Age Discrimination in Employment Act of 1967 (ADEA)[155] to the states (Kimmel v. Florida Board of Regents, 2000). The ADEA prohibits any employer, including a state, "to fail or refuse to hire or to discharge any individual or otherwise discriminate against any individual...because of such individual's age." The Court held that this prohibition was disproportionate to any unconstitutional acts of the states for two reasons. First, according to the majority, the ADEA, by creating a presumption that discrimination on the basis of age is unlawful, went well beyond the Court's equal protection jurisprudence on age discrimination. Age discrimination, according to the Court, is not per se unconstitutional but rather is, in most instances, rationally related to the legitimate objective of maintaining a competent and efficient workforce (Massachusetts Board of Retirement v. Murgia, 1976). Second, the majority conducted what can only be described as a *de novo* examination (a method of review by an appellate court in which no deference is paid by that court to the factual or legal findings made by the body being reviewed) of the congressional record and concluded that it contained no *direct* evidence of pervasive age discrimination *by states*.[156] Quotes from newspaper articles and letters from constituents regarding age discrimination by public employers were held to be an insufficient factual predicate for congressional action. Moreover, the one official report of age discrimination by states prepared by California was dismissed as not focusing on *unconstitutional*, that is, irrational age discrimination.

Kimmel was followed only thirteen months later by Board of Trustees of the University of Alabama v. Garrett (2001). *Garrett* was an action by an employee of the University of Alabama Hospital to recover damages against the state for being demoted from her position as Director of Nursing due to her having undergone surgery and chemotherapy for breast cancer. Garrett alleged that the University discriminated against her in violation of the Americans with Disabilities Act of 1990 (ADA).[157] The ADA explicitly provided a private individual with a right to sue a state and its local political subdivisions for damages for discriminating against those who have a medical disability or for not making a "reasonable accommodation" for those individuals. *Garrett* held that Congress exceeded its authority under § 5 of the Fourteenth Amendment by imposing retrospective relief on states for discriminating against the disabled.

In one sense, *Garrett* was an unexceptional application of *Kimmel*. Both were attempted exercises of congressional § 5 powers. And in both cases the Court held that discrimination against the protected class would be constitutional only if it were demonstrated that the discrimination were irrational. The major difference between the two (other than the characteristic that formed the basis of the protective legislation) was the extent of Congress' fact finding with regard to discrimination by the state. In *Kimmel* it was negligible. By contrast, in *Garrett* it was quite extensive. Indeed Justice Breyer attached a 42-page set of appendices to his dissent to document the instances of state and local discrimination unearthed by congressional committees. This was insufficient, in the majority's view, either to meet *Bourne*'s congruence and proportionality standard or to establish pervasive *state* (as contrasted with *local*) discrimination as required by *Florida Prepaid* and *Kimmel*.

For present purposes, however, *Garrett* is more important for what the Court suggests is the intersection between Congress' § 5 powers and the Eleventh Amendment. Put bluntly, the majority opinion hopelessly confuses the issue in two ways. First, Justice Breyer's dissent argued that evidence of local governmental discrimination ought to count as evidence of state discrimination for purposes of Congress' § 5 powers because local governments are states for purposes of the Fourteenth Amendment. Chief Justice Rehnquist responded very simply that "the Eleventh Amendment does not extend its immunity to units of local government." This implies that *Garrett* was, first and foremost, an Eleventh Amendment case—that the reason for Congress' inability to create a private right of action against the state was the sovereign immunity protections of the Eleventh Amendment.

Were this an exercise of Congress' Article 1 authority that would be truc. But it was not. It was an exercise of congressional § 5 Fourteenth Amendment authority and the Court analyzed it as such. The congruence and proportionality requirement was imposed in *Boerne* to assist the Court in determining whether the congressional legislation at issue was remedial (that is, permitted) or a substantive determination of the scope of the liberties protected by § 1 (that is, impermissible). Moreover, the necessity that Congress make specific findings of pervasive state discrimination, like congruence and proportionality, is a requirement peculiar to the Fourteenth Amendment. If the problem then is that Congress overstepped its Fourteenth Amendment authority, it should not matter whether it is legislating with respect to states or their local political subdivisions. Either way, Congress has no authority *under the Fourteenth Amendment* to protect those with medical disabilities from discrimination unless limited to those discriminatory practices that are patently "unreasonable."

However, that is not what the Court held. Indeed it appeared to hold just the opposite. To quiet concerns that the Court has deprived disabled individuals of their only remedy for discriminatory acts, the Court, in a footnote, assured those discriminated against that they maintained their right to sue the appropriate state officer to enjoin future violations in addition to the ability of the United States to sue on their behalf. These are the same assurances made in Alden v. Maine that the Eleventh Amendment did not leave individuals wronged by the state without a remedy. But it is hard to understand how a prospective claim against a state officer or an enforcement suit by the United States could proceed under a statute in which the liability is predicated upon an unconstitutional exercise of congressional power. One should be hesitant to accuse the Court either of being extraordinarily careless, or worse, so focused on the result that doctrinal confusion may well be a necessary biproduct. Maybe what the Court held in *Garrett* was that the Eleventh Amendment imposes upon Congress requirements that are not imposed upon it when the state is not a defendant. But the Court did not say that. Whether it will at some later time is unclear.

The doctrinal confusion created by *Garrett* may be eclipsed by a view of Congress that extends far beyond the rather narrow intersection of the Eleventh and Fourteenth Amendments. From the Civil War, through the Roosevelt and indeed the Nixon and Carter years, there was a general belief that the states were the enemy of progressive civil rights legislation and protections. The assumption was therefore if individual rights were to be protected at all, they must be protected at the national level, either by Congress or by the Court. The new "pro-state federalism" of the last decade suggests that precisely the opposite belief system is currently held by the majority of the Court. It is, as Ira Lupu recently argued, a "restoration of fundamentals as well as a reaction to the singularity of the rights paradigm that centrally occupied the Warren Court." [158] Convinced that it is returning to the Framers' view that concentrating power in a centralized federal government, even the power to protect individuals from state actions, is a greater threat to liberty than individual actions by the states themselves, the Rehnquist Court has created a new federalism paradigm, one that mistrusts Congress and its motives and prefers local autonomy unless there is some clear demonstration that autonomy has been abused. The result is the judicially imposed obligation that Congress must meet very exacting factual requirements in order to satisfy the judicially imposed congruence and proportionality test. If the same presumption against federal legislation washes over to other areas of congressional legislation that displace state policy prerogatives, regulation of private commercial behavior, for example, the impact could be enormous.[159]

Congressional Intent to Abrogate State Eleventh Amendment Immunity —The "Clear Statement Rule"

Statutory interpretation is a long-standing method by which the Court avoids the necessity of defining the constitutional limits of legislative power. If it can be reasonably argued that Congress (or a state legislature) did not intend to reach the limits of its constitutional authority, the Court avoids having to define what those limits are. Avoiding the constitutional issue therefore reduces the instances in which legislative and judicial power collide. The Eleventh Amendment is no exception, although the discussion of whether Congress intended to abrogate state Eleventh Amendment immunity is, since *Seminole Tribe* and the *Alden* trilogy, now limited to congressional abrogation attempts under § 5 of the Fourteenth Amendment and conceivably the spending clause.[160]

As discussed earlier in this section, the question of whether Congress made its intent to abrogate state sovereign immunity sufficiently clear was very much at issue in both *Parden* and *Employees.* Indeed, it was the basis of the majority's opinion in *Employees.* And while that case did not set forth any specific criteria for determining congressional intent to abrogate, it did hold that a general grant of jurisdiction over claims filed against any person engaged in a particular activity was insufficient, given the Eleventh Amendment, to indicate Congress' intent to abrogate a state's sovereign immunity.

The most authoritative statement of what it takes for Congress to declare its intent to abrogate state Eleventh Amendment sovereign immunity came in Atascadero State Hospital v. Scanlon (1985), a suit by individuals against a California state hospital for damages and other relief under the Rehabilitation Act of 1973. Section 504 of the Act provides remedies to individuals for violations by "*any* recipient of Federal assistance."[161] Based on Hutto v. Finney (1978), in which the Court relied on the breadth of the statutory language and the legislative history to determine congressional intent, the plaintiffs argued that both the natural inferences from the language "*any* recipient" and the legislative history of that language was sufficient to make clear Congress' intent to abrogate California's sovereign immunity. In a 5–4 opinion, Justice Powell, writing for the majority, disagreed:

> We...affirm that Congress may abrogate the States' constitutionally secured immunity from suit in federal court only by making its intention unmistakably clear in the language of the statute. The fundamental interests implicated by the Eleventh Amendment dictates this conclusion.
>
> In view of [Congress' authority under § 5 to alter the federal/state balance] it is incumbent upon the federal courts to be certain of Congress' intent before finding that federal law overrides the guarantees of the Eleventh Amendment. The requirement that Congress unequivocally express this intention in the statutory language ensures such certainty.

The principle of *Atascadero* seemed on its way to being well entrenched, leaving as the only question the strictness of the principle's application. But consistency has not been the hallmark of Eleventh Amendment jurisprudence, even when the issue is the seemingly easy one of determining congressional intent after *Atascadero*. Only two years later, in *Welsh*, a plurality of four Justices held that rights accorded seamen by the Jones Act generally against *any* persons engaged in particular maritime activities was insufficient to conclude that Congress intended to abrogate Texas' Eleventh Amendment sovereign immunity. Justice Scalia, the fifth vote for holding that the statute did not grant jurisdiction over the plaintiff's claim, rested his theory on the fact that Congress' knowledge and acceptance of *Hans* precluded a finding of congressional abrogation, an approach quite distinct from the clarity of expression theory of *Atascadero*.

Two years after *Welsh*, however, there was a spirited debate in *Union Gas* about whether CERCLA (the Comprehensive Environmental Response, Compensation and Liability Act—"Superfund") expressed Congress' intent to abrogate with sufficient clarity. Justice Brennan, writing for himself and four other Justices, one of whom was Justice Scalia, held that the specific inclusion of states as "persons" and as "owners and operators" in some provisions of the Act, coupled with provisions that exempted states from liability in certain situations while permitting citizen suits to the extent consistent with the Eleventh Amendment in others, met the clear statement rule of *Atascadero*. On the other hand, Justice White, writing for himself, Chief Justice Rehnquist, and Justices Kennedy and O'Connor, argued that because the majority mined congressional intent from two distinct, albeit related statutes, there was no "unmistakable language in *the* statute itself."

On the same day that the Court decided *Union Gas* it also decided Dellmuth v. Muth (1989), a case in which the plaintiffs sued the state of Pennsylvania under The Education of the Handicapped Act.[162] There the Court made plain that only textual statements were relevant to determine Congress' intent to abrogate: "[l]est *Atascadero* be thought to contain any ambiguity, we reaffirm...that in this area of the law, evidence of congressional intent must be both unequivocal and textual." With respect to how unequivocal the language must be, the Court held that neither numerous references in the act to states, their obligations under the statute, and private rights of judicial review, nor a specific section providing that attorneys fees for violating the act would not be reduced if the court found that the "State...unreasonably protracted the final resolution of the action" were sufficient to meet the unmistakable clarity requirement. This was true despite the fact that state liability was, according to the court of appeals, essential to the statutory scheme.

Yet just two years after *Union Gas* and *Muth*, in a surprising opinion written by Justice Kennedy and joined by Chief Justice Rehnquist and Justice White, as well as Justices Stevens and Souter, the Court refused to overrule the holding in *Parden* that Congress intended to abrogate state sovereign immunity in the FELA even though there was no explicit reference to the state at all, much less a reference that might meet the level of specificity required in *Muth* and apparently satisfied in *Welsh* (Hilton v. South Carolina Public Railways Commission, 1991). *Hilton*, like *Alden* that followed, was a suit in state court. Only the statute was different—the FELA in *Hilton* and the FLSA in *Alden*. Decided as it was before *Alden*, the majority in *Hilton* held that since the clear statement rule of *Atascadero* and *Welsh* was dictated by the Eleventh Amendment, and since the Eleventh Amendment did not by its terms apply to federal causes of action in state court, the application of the clear statement rule was not constitutionally compelled but only discretionary. Consequently, *stare decisis* (the decision in *Parden*) trumped any concern for doctrinal consistency and symmetry. The majority's approach prompted a spirited dissent from Justice O'Connor, joined by Justice Scalia, a dissent that presaged Justice Kennedy's opinion in *Alden.* [163]

> The Eleventh Amendment spells out one instance, but not the only one, in which respect and forbearance is due from the national to the state governments, a respect that cements our federation in the Constitution. The clear statement rule assumes that Congress will show that respect by not lightly abridging the powers or sovereignty retained by the States. From this standpoint, it makes little sense to apply the clear statement rule to congressional enactments that make the States liable to damage suits in federal courts, but not to apply the clear statement rule to congressional enactments that make states liable to damages suits in their own courts. Sovereign immunity, a crucial attribute of separate governments, is infringed in both cases. The suggested dichotomy makes even less sense if we consider the remarkable anomaly that these two canons of statutory construction create: a statutory scheme in which *state* courts are the exclusive avenue for obtaining recovery under a *federal* statute.

Justice Kennedy's majority opinion in *Hilton* downplaying the Eleventh Amendment is curious given the important role the Eleventh Amendment played in two earlier statutory interpretation cases, Quern v. Jordan (1979) and Will v. Michigan Department of State Police (1989). Both cases involved the exercise of congressional § 5, Fourteenth Amendment powers and raised essentially the same question, whether Section 1983 of the Civil Rights Act of 1871[164] made the state liable to a suit by private individuals. The major difference between the two was that the claim in *Quern* was filed in federal court while the claim in *Will* was filed in state court. Both cases decided that since Congress did not intend to abrogate a state's sovereign immunity when it enacted the 1871 Civil Rights Act, the word "person" did not encompass states. "Given the importance of the States' traditional sovereign immunity, if in fact the Members of the 42d Congress believed that § 1 of the 1871 Act overrode that immunity, surely there would have been lengthy debate on this point....Instead...not one Member of Congress mentioned the Eleventh Amendment or the direct financial consequences to the States of enacting § 1." Having decided that "person" did not include states, it took little to extend the *Quern* rationale to claims asserted in state courts. The only thorny issue in *Will* was whether Monell v. New York City Department of Social Services (1978), which held that municipalities were persons within the meaning of Section 1983, required rethinking the holding in *Quern*. Relying largely on the distinction between states and local governments for purposes of the Eleventh Amendment, the Court held that it would take far more evidence that Congress intended to hold states liable than the evidence marshaled in *Monell* to hold local political subdivisions accountable.

There is a strange air of unreality to these Section 1983 cases. Why should the 42d Congress in 1871 have made explicit its intent to abrogate states' Eleventh

Amendment sovereign immunity nearly twenty years before the Court decided *Hans*, holding that the Eleventh Amendment prohibited suits against the states even when founded on federal law? Even if the decision in *Hans* was not created from whole cloth, it was certainly not a forgone conclusion from prior cases. Indeed, the precursors of *Hans* appeared only in dissenting opinions. Thus, there was no reason for Congress to clearly express its intent to hold states liable for violations of individual rights, much less do so in a way that corresponded to a test developed a century later. Moreover, the distinction between states and their political subdivisions for Eleventh Amendment purposes was not part of Eleventh Amendment jurisprudence until *Lincoln County*, decided on the same day as *Hans*. Consequently, it is not illogical to conclude that if Congress intended to include local political subdivisions as persons it meant to include states as well. But be that as it may, the rule that the Eleventh Amendment requires a strict reading of "persons" is firmly entrenched and is unlikely to be overturned in the foreseeable future, even if *Seminole Tribe* and *Alden* are someday reconsidered.

Given its somewhat checkered past, it is hard to predict where the clear statement rule will go in the future. Certainly there is less reason for the Court to engage in an analysis of legislative intent now that the constitutional rules for congressional abrogation authority are, for the moment at least, more clearly established. There are, in other words, fewer knotty Eleventh Amendment issues that are best left to be decided another day. On the other hand, it might be easier for the Court to resolve some issues on statutory grounds than to enter the quagmire of the inherently indeterminate congruence and proportionality analysis. Perhaps that explains Justice Thomas' concurring opinion in *Kimmel.* Justice Thomas, joined only by Justice Kennedy, argued that Congress did not meet the *Atascadero* clarity test because (1) the ADEA was not absolutely clear that when it incorporated the remedial provisions of the FLSA (struck down in *Alden)* that it incorporated as well the provision that made states liable; and (2) when the ADEA described the forum for individual suits as "any Federal or State court of competent jurisdiction" it was not clear whether that was meant to include courts whose jurisdiction was precluded by the Eleventh Amendment. The other seven Justices preferred to tackle the constitutional issue head on. Even the four dissenting Justices, apparently seeing the constitutional handwriting on the wall, preferred to renew their criticism of the majority's Eleventh Amendment jurisprudence rather than join Justice Thomas in hopes of biding some time for Congress to express itself in even more unmistakable terms, and for the Court to loosen its tight grip on congressional § 5 remedial powers.

A Retrospective and Critique

Nearly thirty years ago Clyde Jacobs, in the first comprehensive book on the Eleventh Amendment,[165] criticized the Court's sovereign immunity jurisprudence on two scores. First, he characterized the jurisprudence as incoherent because it rested on a set of historical assumptions that ranged in accuracy from questionable to simply incorrect. Consequently, as the doctrine developed and was applied in contexts beyond the textual proscription of using of federal courts to open state treasuries to non-resident creditors, the errors became more glaring. Second, and more importantly, the Court's Eleventh Amendment jurisprudence focused more on preserving the sovereignty of the states than on ensuring the supremacy of federal law, thus threatening the rule of law itself.

With regard to the first criticism, little has improved in the thirty years since Professor Jacobs made these observations. Only once since Hans v. Louisiana has the Court come close to reconsidering its assumptions about the founding era's views of state sovereign immunity in a federal system (Pennsylvania v. Union Gas Company, 1989). As noted in the previous section, however, the Court was split in that case. As discussed in the previous section, Justice Brennan's plurality opinion found it unnecessary to consider the issue of whether *Hans* should be overruled because the Commerce Clause permitted Congress to abrogate a state's sovereign immunity. Only Justice Stevens, separately concurring, concluded that *Hans* should be overruled.

Since *Union Gas*, the Court has marched boldly forward, extending the reach of *Hans* in an ever-widening arch first to deprive Congress of the ability to abrogate state sovereign immunity under *any* of its Article 1 powers (College Savings Bank v. Florida Prepaid Postsecondary Expense Board, 1999) and then specifically overruling *Union Gas* (Alden v. Maine, 1999). In addition, the Court has further extended the prohibition on congressional abrogation authority to include the state judiciary as well (Alden v. Maine, 1999). The same reasoning supported an extension of states' sovereign immunity from a federal administrative agency with authority to issue relief that resembled retrospective relief at the behest of a private claimant (Federal Maritime Commission v. South Carolina

Ports Authority, 2002). Only in the sense that the Court's Eleventh Amendment doctrine is somewhat more predictable and thus may be more consistently applied in the future has it been improved since Professor Jacobs' seminal work. But even that predictability has become somewhat frayed around the edges with the *Coeur d'Alene*'s, "essential to the states' sovereign interests," exception to *Ex parte Young*, the holding in *Seminole Tribe* that the failure of Congress to spell out a remedy against state officers precluded a suit against the Governor, and the dictum in *Seminole Tribe* regarding possible limits on the Supreme Court's appellate jurisdiction. It is these extensions of *Hans* and the apparent attempts to impose new limits on recognized exceptions to the Eleventh Amendment that raise Professor Jacobs' second concern regarding the rule of law. Indeed, the problem may be more serious than Professor Jacobs imagined. These decisions have the effect of shifting substantial responsibility for ensuring the protections provided by federal law, certainly federal statutory law, from the state and federal judiciaries to the state legislatures.

Seminole Tribe, the *Alden* Trilogy, and the restrictions on Congress' § 5 Fourteenth Amendment powers in cases like *Boerne*, *Kimmel*, and *Garrett* are part of a larger pattern that has seen the Rehnquist Court reasserting the federal judiciary as the "umpire of the federal system." United States v. Morrison (2000) and United States v. Lopez (1995) limited the extent to which Congress could regulate noncommercial activities because of the effect of those activities on interstate commerce. Not only has the Court drawn a tighter noose around congressional ends in the name of preserving state autonomy, but it has, for the same reasons, limited the means by which Congress can enforce policies that are otherwise within its constitutional domain. It has held that concerns for state autonomy prohibit Congress from mandating that the states use their legislative (New York v. United States, 1992) or executive (Printz v. United States, 1997) resources to enforce federal law. The constitutional basis for these substantive limitations on federal legislative authority is the Tenth Amendment, or at least the spirit of state autonomy that amendment embodies.

The latter two cases restricting congressional means lie at the heart of the Court's rulings regarding congressional power to abrogate a state's Eleventh Amendment sovereign immunity. The doctrinal difference between the two lines of cases is that the constitutional rationale for the abrogation decisions is not the Tenth Amendment, usually thought to circumscribe federal legislative action that treads on state autonomy, but the Eleventh Amendment, usually thought to limit judicial power under Article 3. Two distinct yet related reasons were asserted for applying the Eleventh Amendment in this way. First, the Court reasserted its adherence to Hans v. Louisiana and its holding that state sovereign immunity was part of the original constitutional design. Second, the Court stated that sovereign immunity is more than an outmoded relic of a by-gone era of quiescent government; it is a necessary element of a larger structural principle that protects state autonomy from federal authority. Taking a page from its Tenth Amendment jurisprudence, the Court said in *Alden* that a rule that permits Congress to abrogate state sovereign immunity at will would be "an unwarranted strain on the States' ability to govern in accordance with the will of their citizens." The Tenth and Eleventh Amendments have thus been conflated—fused may be more descriptive. Indeed, it would appear that the Eleventh Amendment has displaced the Tenth Amendment as *the* constitutional hook by which congressional authority over the states can be monitored. What Chief Justice John Marshall said made our system a "government of laws and not of men" (Marbury v. Madison, [1803]), the principle that for every wrong there must be a remedy, has been compromised in the name of protecting the states from the exertion of federal power. The impact of that, compromise, however, falls less on the federal government's power vis à vis the states than it does on individuals who are the beneficiaries of federal legislative protections. While the Eleventh Amendment, from its inception, deprived individuals of a federal forum through which they could remedy wrongs committed by the states, until *Alden* a state forum remained available. And if a state court rejected a federal claim, review was available in the Supreme Court.[166]

One might, at this juncture, object that this analysis significantly overstates the problem. Federalism issues have never been determined by absolutes. The history of Eleventh Amendment jurisprudence, like that of the Tenth Amendment, has been an attempt by the Court to accommodate two conflicting structural norms, the supremacy of federal law and the autonomy of the states.[167] Justice Kennedy asserted in *Alden* that this goal has been accomplished. Private rights of action to make individuals whole are not needed because there is no reason to question the states' good faith compliance with federal directives. To the extent that the states do not live up to those good faith expectations, current Eleventh Amendment doctrine adequately ensures the supremacy of federal law through the judicially created exceptions to the sovereign immunity bar.

One can draw her own conclusions about whether, historically, the actions of the states in following federal norms justifies the confidence that the Court has placed in them. Certainly with respect to the states' judicial systems and their role in ensuring the supremacy of the federal Constitution there is some difference of opinion.[168] But there is no indication that the Framers placed much hope in the states' living up to the Court's expectations of good faith, voluntary compliance with federally enacted standards. Actually, quite the contrary is true.[169] Moreover, with a few exceptions,[170] the history of Eleventh Amendment litigation should give some pause to those who would contend that the states can be counted on to "do the right thing." (Virginia Coupon Cases, 1885; Hans v. Louisiana, 1890).

Whether or not current Eleventh Amendment doctrine reaches the elusive "acceptable accommodation" is therefore wholly dependent upon whether the judicially created exceptions sufficiently protect the supremacy and uniformity of federal law. There are five such exceptions. First, federal supremacy is ensured by permitting an individual to enjoin a state officer from enforcing a statute that violates federal law (*Ex parte Young*, 1908). Second, the United States can sue a state to enforce federal law both prospectively and retrospectively (United States v. Texas, 1892). Third, Congress can abrogate a state's sovereign immunity when exercising its powers under § 5 of the Fourteenth Amendment (Fitzpatrick v. Bitzer, 1976). Fourth, decisions on matters of federal law can be appealed to the United States Supreme Court (Cohens v. Virginia, 1821). Finally, the Eleventh Amendment does not bar federal jurisdiction when the defendant is one of the state's political subdivisions (Lincoln County v. Luning, 1890).

Certainly the exception for suits against political subdivisions, given the increased activity of local governments since the turn of the century and the broad acceptance of municipal home rule, does indeed give individuals the right to sue those levels of government with which they have the most significant day-to-day contact. Yet the protective cloak of this exception must be considered in light of (1) the Court's refusal to apply the doctrine of vicarious liability (the legal doctrine that permits an individual to sue an employer for the acts of its employees) to local governments (Monell v. Department of Social Services, 1978); (2) the absolute immunity of some local officials such as prosecutors, judges, and legislators from private damage claims (Imbler v. Patchman, 1976 [prosecutors]; Tenney v. Brandhove, 1951 [legislators]); and (3) the qualified good faith immunity of all other local (and state) officials (Pierson v. Ray, 1967).

The scope of the other exceptions is likewise limited.[171] The major exception to a state's Eleventh Amendment immunity is, of course, *Ex parte Young*. As explained earlier, however, the *Ex parte Young* exception has been whittled to its bare core. *Couer d' Alene* may be a very narrow exception, one that will rarely arise outside of a dispute between an individual (or group of individuals) and a state over the state's title to land. Or it may portend a balancing away of an individual's right to sue a state officer whenever a significant interest of the state (however defined) is at stake. In addition, Professor Jackson has speculated that the Court's reasoning in *Seminole Tribe* could well lead to a narrowing of *Ex parte Young*, particularly when a state statute or policy violates only a federal statute.[172] Finally, the Court in *Seminole Tribe* clearly held that an *Ex parte Young* remedy to prospectively prohibit a state officer from violating federal law will not be implied with respect to any statute in which Congress has provided for a different private remedy. Consequently, if it wishes to preserve the *Ex parte Young* cause of action, Congress may well be required to amend every statute in which a private right of action against the state, other than an *Ex parte Young* action, is granted to specifically provide for that latter claim.

Second, the ability of the federal government to sue the states is not unlimited despite dictum in *Alden* to the contrary. When the states of New York and New

Hampshire sued Louisiana to recover monies owed by the latter state on bonds held by residents of the plaintiff states, the Court held that since the real parties in interest were the individuals and not the plaintiff states, the suit was precluded by the Eleventh Amendment (New Hampshire v. Louisiana, 1883; and most recently, Kansas v. Colorado, 2001) made plain that where the United States is only a surrogate plaintiff to enforce what is, in fact, a private right of action, the United States would be barred just as the states of New Hampshire and New York were. The United States would then be limited to only those suits in which it has a direct interest in the outcome of the litigation, one over and above ensuring that the individuals protected by its legislation receive their just deserts. Consequently, retrospective relief in cases like *Employees*, Edelman v. Jordan, and Alden v. Maine might arguably be barred unless the money damages sought from the states would wind up first in the federal treasury, subject to the uncertainties of congressional budgetary processes, rather than to those who the federal statute says are entitled to them.[173]

Third, even if the speculations about the Court's limiting its appellate jurisdiction never come to pass, there are severe and obvious practical limitations on Supreme Court review as a means to ensure the supremacy of federal law. Appeal to the Supreme Court from state courts is limited to certiorari, a discretionary writ.[174] Supreme Court Rule 17 defines the limits of the Court's discretion. Only when a state court of last resort (generally the state Supreme Court) decides a matter that is inconsistent "with the decision of another state court of last resort or a federal court of appeals" or "when a state court...has decided an important question of federal law which has not been settled by...or [is] in conflict with [a decision] of this Court" will it even consider granting writ of certiorari.[175] Given the number of state court decisions involving federal law, both constitutional and statutory, the number of state court systems (fifty), the number of instances in which various state courts of appeals are, in any given case, the courts of last resort, and the limited number of certiorari petitions that can be granted each year, it is apparent that the Supreme Court will review only those cases that fall well outside the acceptable range. Others will simply fall through the cracks. State adherence to federal law is thus enforced only at its outer, pathological perimeters.

Finally, as explained in the previous section, Congress' powers to remedy state actions under § 5 of the Fourteenth Amendment have been limited in two ways. First, the conduct remedied must be reasonably congruent with actions judicially declared to be unconstitutional (City of Boerne v. Flores, 1997; Kimmel v. Florida Board of Regents, 2000). Second, it appears that Congress' remedial powers, once thought to be rather broad, are now limited to those instances in which Congress has made specific findings of *pervasive* state violations of constitutionally protected rights (Florida Prepaid Postsecondary Education Expense Board v.

College Savings Bank, 1999). Lacking this finding, Congress' remedial scheme is likely to be found to be disproportionate to the states' wrongs.

Arguably that is the price one must pay for living in a system that divides political authority between two "sovereigns." If all individual interests were determined at the federal level, states would indeed be relegated to the status of municipal corporations and the federal government's power would be unlimited. But that truism does not help in deciding whether, in the language of *Alden*, "(t)he principle of sovereign immunity as reflected in our jurisprudence strikes the proper balance between the supremacy of federal law and the separate sovereignty of the states."[176] One can evaluate whether the Court has reached an acceptable accommodation by looking at history, or original understanding, if you will. This is essentially the lynchpin of the majority's opinions in the cases starting with *Seminole Tribe*. Unfortunately, the dissents too rely on history to support their views. And while it is true that the overwhelming weight of scholarly authority does not support the Court's current approach to sovereign immunity, it is nevertheless true, as William Marshall noted, that the text of the Eleventh Amendment makes no exception for federal claims, making the dissenters' interpretation as atextual and arguably judgmental as that of the majority.

One need not rely on the ambiguities of history, however, to measure the acceptability of the federalism balance drawn by the Court in its Eleventh Amendment jurisprudence. One could wonder whether the cost to the individual of being deprived of a full panoply of remedies is greater than the loss of the state's right to govern according to its own judgments. At first blush, the conclusion reached after analyzing this question appears at least as, if not more, judgmental as the simple conclusion reached by Justice Kennedy in *Alden* that an acceptable accommodation has been achieved. First impressions may be wrong, however. In *Seminole Tribe*, *Alden*, and *Florida Prepaid* there was no question that Congress had the authority, indeed in *Seminole Tribe* and *Florida Prepaid* the *exclusive* authority, to regulate. Nor was there any question that Congress had the power to impose its substantive norms on the states without violating the states' autonomous right to govern. The only question was whether the Constitution imposed a limit on the means by which Congress could choose to remedy a state's violation of those substantive norms—enlisting the aid of the federal and/or state judicial system.

From where then, does the restriction on means derive? No one argues that the Eleventh Amendment's *text* imposes a limit on Congress' ability to enlist the aid of the judiciary to enforce laws that it is constitutionally entitled to enact. This is particularly true with respect to *Alden*; the text says nothing about the jurisdiction of state courts. It comes, says the Court, from generalized principles of federalism that underlie the constitutional sovereign immunity memorialized by the Eleventh Amendment. The result is that individuals must rely largely on the good faith of the states' elected political representatives to make good on the protections afforded them by federal law. This is the wrong result, not because scholars and dissenting Justices say it is, but because it alters the federal/state balance in a way that has not been seen since the Articles of Confederation were replaced by the Constitution.

Two things are clear about what our founders did. First, they rejected the Articles of Confederation because a stronger federal government was needed. And they did this, not by tinkering with the existing structure, but by replacing it with one wholly new, one that gave the federal government powers to act directly upon and for the benefit of individuals, a power previously held exclusively by the states. Second, they rejected the objections of the anti-federalists that the powers granted the federal government to act upon and for the benefit of individuals were unwarranted invasions on the state's sovereignty.

It is indeed ironic for a Court that relies so heavily on original understanding to justify reading its Eleventh Amendment jurisprudence, to place the interests of individuals, constitutionally declared by federal law, largely at the mercy of state charity. To do so is a direct threat to the supremacy of federal law, a constitutional value at least as explicit as the constitutional value of state autonomy. As the Court held in Martin v. Hunter's Lessee (1816), the uniformity and supremacy of federal law cannot be left to the state courts. And if federal supremacy cannot be left to the state courts, it most certainly cannot be left to the state legislatures or state executives.

NOTES

1. U.S. Constitution, amend. 11.
2. U.S. Constitution, art. I, sec.10.
3. Monaco v. Mississippi, 292 U.S. (1934) 313, 322.
4. *McCulloch* upheld the constitutionality of congressional legislation creating the Second Bank of the United States against a claim that that legislation was beyond Congress' powers and thus impinged on the states' reserved powers.
5. *Martin* sustained the constitutionality of Section 25 of the Judiciary Act of 1789 giving the United States Supreme Court appellate jurisdiction over decisions of state courts wherein a claim or defense was based on federal law and the decision of the state court denied that claim or defense. The state's claim was that to give the United States Supreme Court the right to revise the decisions of the highest court of a state was to impinge on that state's sovereignty.
6. *Cohens* and *Hans* will be discussed below in this section. *Ex parte Young* is discussed in the section that follows.
7. The case is actually far more complicated, and interesting, than set out in the text. Its history and context are described in Jacobs, *Eleventh* 77–81. *See also* Orth, *Judicial* 34–37.
8. U.S. Constitution, art. 4, sec. 2.
9. A far more complete history is documented in Jacobs, *Eleventh* 97–103.
10. As will be noted below, this aspect of Davis v. Gray is no longer good law.

11. Clyde Jacobs does not disguise his disdain for the majority opinion in *Davis*, describing the decision as "an extreme expression of the nominal party rule" and hinting that it may have been more a reflection of the anti-state sovereignty mood of the time than good legal reasoning. Jacobs, *Eleventh* 112.

12. Jacobs, *Eleventh* 114. John Orth recounts some of the same history of this period but with a decidedly more political slant. *See* Orth, *Judicial* 58–71. For a more extensive political/historical explanation of the Court's post-Civil War cases, *see* Gibbons, *Eleventh* 1968–2003.

13. Jacobs, *Eleventh* 114–15.

14. The Virginia Coupon Cases actually consists of seven cases decided by the Supreme Court between 1881 and 1890. Three, those reported in 114 U.S., were decided the same day; Poindexter v. Greenhow (114 U.S. [1885] 270), White v. Greenhow (114 U.S. [1885] 307), and Chafin v. Taylor (114 U.S. [1885] 309). An extensive history, both judicial and political, is recounted by John Orth in Orth, *Judicial* 90–109 and Gibbons, *Eleventh* 1991. A briefer history, one that concentrates exclusively on the legal history of *The Virginia Coupon Cases*, can be found in Jacobs, *Eleventh* 126–30. There seems to be some minor dispute between Professors Orth and Jacobs regarding the total amount of the debt affected by The Funding Act of 1871. Orth claims that it exceeded $47 million (Orth, *Judicial* 91) while Jacobs claims the amount to be $33 million. Jacobs, *Eleventh* 192 n.52. For arbitrary reasons, I have used Professor Orth's figure in the text.

15. Antoni v. Wright, 63 VA. 296 (1872).

16. Jacobs, *Eleventh* 182, 183, n.14.

17. 19 U.S. (6 Wheat.) 305–06 (argument of Senator Philip Barbour); 315 (argument of Alexander Smyth). This argument later became part of the rationale for the holding in *Hans*.

18. Jacobs, *Eleventh* 88–91.

19. Fletcher, *Historical* 1033, 1084. Gibbons, *Eleventh* 1952–53. Vicki C. Jackson, "The Supreme Court, the Eleventh Amendment, and State Sovereign Immunity," 98 *Yale Law J.* (1988) 24.

20. *See* Marshall, *Diversity* 1372, 1387.

21. Jacobs, *Eleventh* 89.

22. Fletcher, *Historical* 1084; Gibbons, *Eleventh* 1959.

23. Jackson, *Supreme* 24.

24. Students of Constitutional Law may recognize this reasoning as being similar, if not identical, to the Court's first interpretation of the Fourteenth Amendment seventeen years earlier in *The Slaughter House Cases* (1873). In that case the Court declined to interpret the Privileges or Immunities Clause of the Fourteenth Amendment to include rights not previously recognized as federally protected because to do so would "radically [change] the whole theory of the relations of the State and Federal governments...."

25. *See, for example,* Jacobs, *Eleventh* 160–64. Amar, *Of Sovereignty* 1484–91. Jackson, *Supreme* 3–4. Fredric S. Le Clercq, "State Immunity and Federal Judicial Power—Retreat From National Supremacy," 27 *Florida Law Rev.* (1975) 361. Scholarship criticizing *Hans* for failing to give sufficient weight to rule of law concerns is not limited to contemporary commentary. John Norton Pomeroy described the pre-*Hans* decisions (of which *Hans* is an extension) that abandoned the strict formal pleading rule of *Osborne* as "a national disgrace" for their failure to provide a remedy for clear constitutional viola-

tions by states. John Norton Pomeroy, "The Supreme Court and State Repudiation—The Virginia and Louisiana Cases," 17 *American Law Rev.* (1883) 684, 684–85.

26. *See, for example,* Jacobs, *Eleventh* 110, 161.

27. Field, *Eleventh* 515. William A. Fletcher, "The Diversity Explanation of the Eleventh Amendment: A Reply to Critics," 56 *University of Chicago Law Rev.* (1989) 1261. The leading diversity theory advocate on the Supreme Court was Justice William Brennan. His most articulate defense of that theory was his dissenting opinion in Atascadero State Hospital v. Scanlon 473 U.S. (1985) 234, 247–302 (Justice Brennan, dissenting).

28. Calvin R. Massey, "State Sovereignty and the Tenth and Eleventh Amendments," 56 *University of Chicago Law Rev.* (1981) 61 (concluding that the pre-Eleventh Amendment history supports the conclusion that it was designed to "provide a party status basis for *denial* of jurisdiction," but arguing that Justice Bradley totally misread history in concluding that the Eleventh Amendment granted general sovereign immunity).

29. *Compare, for example,* Fletcher, *Diversity Explanation* (Eleventh Amendment meant only to prohibit non-citizens from suing state in federal courts) *with* Pfander, *History* 1269 (Eleventh Amendment meant to prohibit only those suits to enforce pre-Constitution state indebtedness).

30. *Compare* Jackson, *Supreme* 19 (sovereign immunity has constitutional dimensions) *with* Field *Eleventh* (Eleventh Amendment only preserves states' common law immunity). *See also* John Nowak, "The Scope of Congressional Power to Create Causes of Action Against State Governments and the History of the 11th and 14th Amendments," 75 *Columbia Law Rev.* (1975) 1413. Laurence Tribe, "Intergovernmental Immunities in Litigation, Taxation, and Regulation: Separation of Powers Issues in Controversies About Federalism," 89 *Harvard Law Rev.* 682 (agreeing that state sovereign immunity is not constitutional but arguing that *Chisholm*'s remedial creativity raised constitutional federalism and separation of powers concerns).

31. *See, for example,* Marshall, *Diversity*. *Cf.* Jacobs, *Eleventh* 110 (while objecting to *Hans* on "rule of law" grounds nevertheless argues that there exists no evidence that anyone "contemplated the possibility that a state could be sued in federal court by one of its own citizens under the federal-question clause").

32. Orth, *Judicial* 74–81 (arguing that *Hans* was decided for "political" reasons. *See also*, Massey, *State* 135–37.

33. Suzanna Sherry, "The Eleventh Amendment and State Decisis: Overruling Hans v. Louisiana," 57 *University of Chicago Law Rev.* (1990) 1260.

34. For a concise history of this period, Jacobs, *Eleventh* 132–49. A less detailed but still informative history is recounted in Orth, *Judicial* 127–35.

35. Jacobs, *Eleventh* 146–49. Orth, *Judicial* 130–31.

36. Jacobs, *Eleventh* 144.

37. But *see* Michael Gerhardt, "Confronting the Fictions of the Eleventh Amendment: Pennhurst State School and Hospital v. Halderman," 60 *Washington Law Rev.* (1985) 407 (arguing that *Ex parte Young* ought to be abandoned in favor of suing state officers under sec. 1983 of the Civil Rights Act).

38. Orth, *Judicial* 132–35.

39. The most comprehensive discussion to date of the prospective/retrospective discussion is Carlos Manuel Vázquez, "Night and Day: *Coeur d' Alene, Breard,* and the

Unraveling of the Prospective-Retrospective Distinction in Eleventh Amendment Doctrine," 87 *Georgetown Law J.* (1998) 1.

40. *Compare* Marshall, *Diversity* 1372 (arguing that the Eleventh Amendment's overriding concern is protecting the state's treasury from the claims of creditors).

41. The first case reached the Supreme Court on the issue of whether the district court could order a cross-district remedy which required that children from the Detroit district be bussed to suburban schools and vice versa. Oversimplified, the Court held that remedy was impermissible absent a finding that the suburban districts contributed to the segregation of the Detroit schools. Milliken v. Bradley (I), 418 U.S. (1974) 717.

42. The Court had previously upheld the award of "notice relief" in a sequel to Edelman v. Jordan, Quern v. Jordan, 440 U.S. (1979) 332.

43. Vázquez, *Night* 34.

44. The Court's treatment of the injunction against the county officials will be treated in the discussion of Eleventh Amendment immunity for political subdivisions.

45. This aspect of the Court's decision is extensively, critically, and thoughtfully treated in David L. Shapiro, "Wrong Turns: The Eleventh Amendment and the *Pennhurst Case*," 98 *Harvard Law Rev.* (1984) 71–76.

46. Congressional abrogation of state sovereign immunity is the subject of separate and extended discussion below.

47. The Court has consistently held that a state's sovereign immunity under the Eleventh Amendment and the federal government's sovereign immunity under either the common law or the constitutional structure (the Court has never been absolutely clear about which) are *co-terminus*. Trindal v. Wesley, 167 U.S. (1897) 204, 213.

48. Nathan C. Thomas, "Note The Withering Doctrine of *Ex Parte Young*," 83 *Cornell Law Rev.* (1998) 1110–11.

49. Vicki C. Jackson, "*Seminole Tribe*, The Eleventh Amendment and the Potential Evisceration of *Ex parte Young*." 72 *New York University Law Rev.* (1998) 495. *See also* Thomas, *Note*. For a more sanguine view of *Ex parte Young*'s continued vitality, *see* Meltzer, *Seminole Decision* 1.

50. 25 U.S.C. sec. 2701 (1988).

51. Jackson, *Potential* 520–22.

52. *See generally* Durchslag 577, 582–91. Fletcher, *Historical* 1033, 1099–1109.

53. The balance of the *Lincoln County* opinion (approximately one half of the opinion) was devoted to whether the bonds were issued in contravention of the state constitution, whether presentation of the coupons for payment was properly pleaded and whether the statute of limitations had run by the time the suit was filed.

54. The Court said that "we are less sure than was the District Court that Ohio had consented to suit against entities such as the Board in the federal courts." 429 U.S. 279–80.

55. The Court also reversed the district and circuit courts on the merits, holding that the First Amendment was not violated if the Board had a reason for dismissing the plaintiff unrelated to his protected speech activities.

56. These included the School itself, an arm of the state, those who administered the School, state employees, the Pennsylvania Department of Public Welfare, also an arm of the state, and several officials of that department. The "school," unlike the one in *Mt. Healthy*, was not independent but was part of the State Hospital for the Mentally Retarded.

57. Interstate compacts are agreements between two or more states, usually for joint undertakings. These must be approved by Congress. U.S. Constitution, art. 1, sec. 10, clause 3.

58. Perhaps the most focused critique is that of Fletcher, *Historical* 1099–1107. Others, however, have also registered their dissent. *See, for example,* Orth, *Judicial* 119 (the distinction between states and their political subdivisions "produces bizarre results"). Gerald E. Frug, "The Judicial Power of the Purse," 126 *University of Pennsylvania Law Rev.* (1978) 715, 756. Vicki C. Jackson, "One Hundred Years of Folly: The Eleventh Amendment and the 1988 Term," 64 *Southern California Law Rev.* 51, 57 n.23 (1990). But *see* Durchslag, *Political Subdivisions*.

59. According to Professor Fletcher, the change in how we view municipal corporations occurred even before *Lincoln County*. The Court simply chose to ignore it. *See* Fletcher, *Historical* 1101–02.

60. Fletcher, *Historical* 1106.

61. H. Jefferson Powell, "The Oldest Question of Constitutional Law," 79 *University of Virginia Law Rev.* (1993) 633, 653. Chief Justice Jay argued in *Chisholm* that states under the Constitution were not sovereign. They were more analogous to "municipal corporations." 2 U.S. (2 Dall.) 472–73.

62. The United States Constitution imposes no restraint on the states' prerogatives to structure their local governments in any way they please, granting them whatever powers and imposing whatever constraints on those powers they think necessary. Hunter v. City of Pittsburgh, 207 U.S. (1907) 161. The *states'* sovereignty in this regard is thus protected by substantive constitutional doctrine unrelated to the Eleventh Amendment.

63. For a description of those elements essential to sovereignty that are absent from the powers of local political subdivisions, see Durchslag, *Political Subdivisions* 597–602 n.1.

64. Local political subdivisions are "persons" within the meaning of sec. 1983 of the Civil Rights Act, 42 U.S.C., sec.1983 (1994). Monell v. New York City Dept. Social Serv., 436 U.S. (1978) 658. The state, however, is not. Will v. Michigan State Police, 491 U.S. (1989) 58. Yet, one might dispute the magnitude of the potential loss to civil rights enforcement. Local political subdivisions cannot be sued vicariously for the acts of their officers but must be found independently liable either for negligent training or supervision or for adopting an unconstitutional policy. Municipal liability, in other words, is difficult to establish. Further discussion of municipal liability under sec. 1983 is beyond the scope of this work. *See generally*, Peter W. Low and John C. Jeffries, Jr., *Civil Rights Actions: Section 1983 and Related Statutes* (Westbury: Foundation Press, 2d ed. 1994) 112–87.

65. Jacobs, *Eleventh* 108.

66. "No state shall, without the consent of Congress . . . enter into any argument or compact with another state . . ." U.S. Constitution, art. 1, sec. 10, clause 3.

67. 46 U.S.C., sec. 688(a) (1994) provides a cause of action in federal court for seamen injured in their employment.

68. 45 U.S.C., sec. 51 *et. seq.* (1994).

69. Justice Brennan's dissent asserted that this argument was raised in *Parden* but rejected by majority.

70. Assistance for the aged, blind, and disabled is administered by the state pursuant to the federal Social Security Act and regulations promulgated by the United States Department of Health and Human Services, formerly known as the Department of Health,

Education, and Welfare. Operative provisions are currently found in 42 U.S.C., secs. 801–05 (1994)

71. 15 U.S.C., sec. 1125(a) (1994). The Lanham Act provides a civil damage remedy against any person who, through advertising or otherwise, creates confusion about the origin or connection of one person and another or of one product or another. States were made subject to the Lanham Act by the Trademark Remedy Clarification Act, 106 Stat. 3567, currently codified in 15 U.S.C., sec. 1125(a)(2) (1994).

72. Marshall, *Diversity* 1372, 1384.

73. Professor Marshall agrees with this conclusion. For contrary views, *see* Atascadero State Hospital v. Scanlon, 473 U.S. (1985) 234, 263–80 (Justice Brennan, dissenting). Gibbons, *Eleventh* 1899, 1899–1914.

74. For an analysis of the breadth of the *Cohens* exception to the Eleventh Amendment. *See* Jackson, *Supreme* 19–25.

75. Emphasis added.

76. *Alden* is discussed at length below.

77. For a comprehensive analysis of when a state will be held to consent to a suit for purposes of the Eleventh Amendment, *see* Vázquez, *Eleventh* 1683.

78. Evan H. Caminker, "State Immunity Waivers for Suits by the United States," 92 *Michigan Law Rev.* (1999) 116. As Professor Caminker argues this requirement is consistent with the Court's holdings with respect to suits brought by one state against another invoking the original jurisdiction of the Supreme Court. Caminker, *State* 113–14.

79. Jonathan R. Siegel, "The Hidden Source of Congress' Power to Abrogate State Sovereign Immunity," 73 *University of Texas Law Rev.* (1995) 113–114. However, Caminker, *State* 117–19, expresses some doubt about Professor Siegal's conclusions.

80. *See* Melvyn R. Durchslag, "Accommodation by Declaration," 33 *Loyola of Los Angeles Law Rev.* (2000)1375, 1388–89.

81. U.S. Constitution, art. 1, sec. 8, clause 18.

82. U.S. Constitution, art. 1, sec. 8, clause 7.

83. The textual assertion somewhat overstates the Court's precise holding. The Court did concede that the state could have taxed the Bank had the tax been uniformly assessed against all entities in the state. Consequently, a tax assessed against the value of the Bank's real estate would have likely withstood a challenge based on federal supremacy. 17 U.S. (4 Wheat.) (1819) 436.

84. U.S. Constitution, art. 1, sec. 8, clause 8.

85. Typically, state actions that interfered with the major post-Civil War national concern, oiling the tracks of the industrial revolution, were disposed of by the Court in one of two ways. If there was no federal legislation touching upon the subject matter of the state regulation, the Court acted pursuant to the "national unified market" assumptions of art. 1, sec. 8, clause 3 of the Constitution, the Commerce Clause. *See, for example,* H. P. Hood & Sons v. DuMond, 336 U.S. (1946) 525. If Congress had spoken with respect to the area or field regulated by the state, and if the state regulation was inconsistent with the federal legislation, the state law was invalid under the Supremacy Clause. *See* Cooley v. Board. of Wardens, 53 U. S. (12 How.) (1851) 299. Gibbons v. Ogden, 22 U.S. (9 Wheat.) (1824) 1. The coincidence of the increased role of the federal government in regulating matters once considered local because they "affected commerce," and the more active role of state and local governments in matters once thought to be the exclusive domain of the private sector, not only in some general way increased the tension between the federal government

and the states, but also raised the fundamental question posed by the abrogation cases—to what extent will the states be treated as private individuals for purposes of federal economic regulation.

86. The Judiciary Act of 1875 (18 Stat. 470). The statute says nothing specific regarding the nature or status of the parties. It simply confers jurisdiction over a certain class of claims. Justice Brennan was later to use the generality of that jurisdictional grant to distinguish it from statutes in which Congress specifically conferred jurisdiction to hear claims asserted by individuals against states. Welsh v. Department of Highways and Public Transportation (1987).

87. Fitzpatrick v. Bitzer will be discussed in-depth later in this section.

88. 45 U.S.C., sec. 45 *et. seq.* (1994).

89. 29 U.S.C., sec. 201 *et. seq.* (1994). The act, which had previously excluded employees of federal, state, and local governments, was amended in 1966 to include employees of state and local governments working in a number of institutions, including hospitals that Congress determined affected interstate commerce. *Employees* 411 U.S. (1973) 282–83.

90. 29 U.S.C., sec. 216(b) (1994).

91. U.S. Constitution, art. 6, sec. 2. "This constitution, and the Laws of the United States which shall be made in Pursuance thereof...shall be the supreme Law of the Land; and the Judges in every state shall be bound thereby, any Thing in the Constitution or Laws of any State to the Contrary notwithstanding."

92. Justice Marshall relied principally on Testa v. Katt, 330 U.S. (1947) 386. *Testa* was a case brought in Rhode Island state court under the Emergency Price Control Act, 54 Stat. 34, for damages and attorney's fees, the plaintiff claiming that he purchased an automobile for more than the federally established ceiling price. The Court held that since the Rhode Island courts had jurisdiction to hear state claims of this sort, they were obligated to hear this claim. Justice Marshall likely overreads *Testa*. The question in *Testa* under the facts was not whether state courts were obligated by the Supremacy Clause to hear all claims that Congress might empower them to decide, but rather whether, having jurisdiction under state law, the state could *discriminate* against federal claims.

93. For an extensive treatment of the difference between the "forum allocation" and "immunity" views of the Eleventh Amendment as well as a critique of both views, *see* Vázquez, *Eleventh* 1683.

94. Consistent with his opinion in *Parden*, however, Justice Brennan disagreed that an explicit indication of congressional intent was necessary. 411 U.S. 300–01 (Justice Brennan dissenting).

95. For a powerful critique of the "diversity theory" of the Eleventh Amendment, *see* Marshall, *Diversity* 1372. Professor Marshall's conclusion is that the "diversity" theory fails to account for the primary reason why the Eleventh Amendment was adopted, the fear that federal courts would be the vehicle by which state treasuries would be open to private claims. *See also* Redish, *Federal Jurisdiction* 191–193; Lawrence Marshall, "Fighting the Words of the Eleventh Amendment," 102 *Harvard Law Rev.* (1989) 1342 (arguing that the plain language of the Amendment encompasses more than diversity jurisdiction and cannot be ignored, as the diversity theory does). Other scholars, however, have marshaled some impressive historical evidence supporting the diversity theory. *See, for example,*

Amar, *Of Sovereignty* 1425; Gibbons, *Eleventh* 1889; and Pfander, *History* 1269. *See also* Jackson, *History*.

96. There was one case in between, County of Oneida v. Oneida Indian Nation of New York, 470 U.S. (1985) 226. This was an action by the Oneida Indian Nation of New York to recover lands it claimed were illegally held by several upstate New York counties. Because counties are not protected by the Eleventh Amendment, the Eleventh Amendment became relevant only because the county attempted to implead the state in order to get reimbursement for the money spent to acquire the disputed land. Since that claim was not founded on federal law, the Court dismissed the counties' attempt to join the state because the Eleventh Amendment precluded the exercise of ancillary jurisdiction. Justice Brennan, dissented on the ground that the Eleventh Amendment only precluded the exercise of diversity jurisdiction, the same position he took in *Employees*. What is interesting is that Justice Marshall, who expressed a different view of the Eleventh Amendment in *Employees*, joined Justice Brennan's diversity theory dissent. He did not provide an explanation for this apparent change of opinion.

97. The Court also overruled *Parden* to the extent that it implied that less than clear and unmistakable language could abrogate state sovereign immunity. The Court's standards in this regard are discussed in detail below.

98. This history is recounted in Part I.

99. 42 U.S.C., sec. 9601 *et. seq.* (1994). The Act's acronym, which is how it is more colloquially known, is CERCLA. It is also known (or derided) as the Superfund legislation.

100. Justice Scalia agreed with the plurality that Congress had made its intent to abrogate sufficiently clear. The Chief Justice and Justices O'Connor and Kennedy, however, did not concur with this part of Justice Scalia's dissent.

101. Chief Justice Rehnquist and Justices Kennedy and O'Connor joined this part of his concurrence.

102. The "clear statement" requirement will be separately discussed below..

103. Some has since cropped up. *See, for example,* William P. Marshall and Jason S. Cowart, "State Immunity, Political Accountability, and Alden v. Maine," 75 *Notre Dame Law Rev.* (2000) 1069 (arguing that requiring state courts to adjudicate federal claims fractures political accountability). William P. Marshall, "Understanding *Alden,*" 31 *Rutgers Law J.* (2000) 803. *Cf.* Jay Tidmarsh, "A Dialogic Defense of *Alden*," 75 *Notre Dame Law Rev.* (2000) 1161 (arguing that denying Congress the authority to *require* state courts to hear federal claims was not inconsistent with the respective roles of the federal and state court systems to "converse" with each other about the "other system's rights, obligations, and entitlements.").

104. Nowak, *Congressional Power* 1413 and Tribe, *Intergovernmental Immunities* 682.

105. This theory of modest or slight judicial review in federalism disputes was first and most forcefully articulated by Professor Herbert Weschler nearly fifty years ago. Herbert Weschler, "The Political Safeguards of Federalism: The Role of the States in the Composition and Selection of the National Government," 54 *Columbia Law Rev.* 543 (1954). It was later expanded upon and refined by others. *See, for example,* Jesse Choper, *Judicial Review and the National Political Process* (Chicago: University of Chicago Press, 1984); John Hart Ely, *Democracy and Distrust* (Cambridge: Harvard University Press, 1980); and Larry Kramer, "Understanding Federalism," 47 *Vanderbilt University Law Rev.* (1994) 1485.

106. Field, *Eleventh* 515

107. Martha A. Field, "The Eleventh Amendment and Other Sovereign Immunity Doctrines: Congressional Imposition of Suit upon the States," 126 *University of Pennsylvania Law Rev.* (1978) 1203.

108. Jackson, *Supreme.*

109. Vázquez, *Eleventh* 1683.

110. Developments since *Seminole Tribe*, particularly those decided in 1999, have given Professor Vázquez some cause for concern. Carlos Manuel Vázquez, "Eleventh Amendment Schizophrenia," 75 *Notre Dame Law Rev.* (2000) 859.

111. Ann Althouse, "The *Alden* Trilogy: Still Searching for a Way to Enforce Federalism," 31 *Rutgers Law J.* (2000) 631.

112. Except perhaps the Justice's individual ("political") views of the appropriate spheres of federal and state authority. *See* Frank B. Cross, "Realism about Federalism," 74 *New York University Law Rev.* (1999) 1304, 1308–13.

113. Discussion of *Lopez* is beyond the scope of this book. It is, however, discussed extensively and in its broader federalism context in Vicki C. Jackson and Elaine Combs, *Federalism: A Reference Guide To the U.S. Constitution* (forthcoming) and Steven McAllister and Christopher Drahozal, *The Reserved Commerce Power: A Reference Guide to the U.S. Constitution* (forthcoming).

114. 25 U.S.C., sec. 2702 (1994).

115. 25 U.S.C., sec. 2710(d)(7) (1994).

116. Seminole Tribe of Florida v. Florida, 11 F3d (Eleventh Cir. 1994) 1016.

117. How the Court disposed of the question of whether *Ex parte Young* permitted an action against the Governor to compel him to negotiate in good faith was discussed previously in this Part.

118. Much of that record is set forth in Part I. It will not be repeated here.

119. The explicit congressional intent to abrogate occurred in the Trademark Remedy Clarification Act, 106 Stat. 3567, *codified in* 15 U.S.C., sec. 43(a) (1994).

120. Edelman v. Jordan involved a federal grant program but Congress had not expressly conditioned the receipt of federal funds on a waiver of the state's sovereign immunity.

121. The notion that Congress' power to condition the receipt of federal funds is limited by a principle of coercion comes from the Tenth Amendment. *See* New York v. United States, 505 U.S. (1992) 144; South Dakota v. Dole, 483 U.S. (1987) 203, 211–12.

122. The *Alden* Trilogy generated significant academic commentary, most of which focused on *Alden*. A sampling includes "Symposium, State Sovereign Immunity and the Eleventh Amendment," 75 *Notre Dame Law Rev.* (2000) 817; "Symposium, New Directions in Federalism," 33 *Loyola, Los Angeles Law Rev.* (2000) 1245; "Symposium, Federalism after *Alden*," 31 *Rutgers Law J.* (2000) 631; and "Shifting the Balance of Power? The Supreme Court, Federalism, and State Sovereign Immunity," 53 *Stanford University Law Rev.* 1115 (2001).

123. Daniel J. Meltzer, "State Sovereign Immunity: Five Authors in Search of a Theory," 75 *Notre Dame Law Rev.* (2000) 1011, 1015–16.

124. It is difficult to determine which of the two strains are predominant, but if I had to choose it would be the second. But *see* Meltzer, *Five Authors* 1038.

125. Charles Warren, *The Supreme Court in United States History, Vol. 1* (Boston: Little, Brown and Co., 1922), (rev. ed. 1926).

126. Perhaps the most complete analysis to date of the adequacy of the Court's alternatives to a private right of action can be found in Meltzer, *Five Authors* 1016–27.

127. These are explored in William P. Marshall, "Understanding *Alden*," 31 *Rutgers Law J.* (2000) 803.

128. Louise Weinberg, "Of Sovereignty and Union: the Legends of *Alden*," 76 *Notre Dame Law Rev.* (2001) 1113, 1141, 1163–1165.

129. Vicki C. Jackson, "Seductions of Coherence, State Sovereign Immunity, and the Denationalization of Federal Law," 31 *Rutgers Law J.* (2000) 691, 692–699 and David Shapiro, "The 1999 Trilogy: What is Good Federalism?" 31 *Rutgers Law J.* (2000) 753, 754–760.

130. The major scholarship extensively discussing the issue of commandeering state courts to hear federal claims include Daniel J. Cloherty, "Exclusive Jurisdiction and the Eleventh Amendment Recognizing the Assumption of State Court Availability in the Clear Statement Compromise," 82 *University of California Law Rev.* (1994) 1287. Martin H. Redish and Steven G. Sklaver, "Federal Power to Commandeer State Courts: Implications for the Theory of Judicial Federalism," 32 *Indiana University Law Rev.* (1998) 71; and Richard H. Seamon, "The Sovereign Immunity of States in Their Own Courts," 37 *Brandeis University Law J.* (1998) 319.

131. Jackson, *Seductions*; Shapiro, *Trilogy*.

132. The most extensive treatment of the congruity argument appears in Richard H. Seamon, "The Asymmetry of the State Sovereign Immunity," 76 *University of Washington Law Rev.* (2001) 1067.

133. *See, for example,* Amar, *Of Sovereignty* 1425.

134. Field, *Eleventh* (1978) 515, 544.

135. ... "nor shall private property be taken for public use, without just compensation." U.S. Constitution, amend. 5.

136. *See, for example,* Richard H. Fallon, Jr., "The Ideologies of Federal Courts Law," 74 *Virginia Law Rev.* (1998) 1141, 1211, n.318. Vázquez, *Eleventh* 1683, 1709–10.

137. The characterization of a taking as a constitutional wrong is misleading and is done only for simplicity's sake. There is nothing wrong with the government's taking private property as long as it is done for a public use. What is wrong is the failure to provide just compensation. The wrong and the remedy are thus indistinguishable. This only underscores the self-executing nature of the Takings Clause.

138. Seamon, *Asymmetry*. But *see* Carlos Manuel Vázquez, "Sovereign Immunity, Due Process, and the *Alden* Trilogy," 109 *Yale Law J.* (2000) 1927, 1952–53 (arguing that the Court has seemingly taken contradictory positions with respect to the sovereign immunity of the federal government from takings claims [immune] and that of state governments [not immune].

139. The Court noted that the state could give the taxpayer a pre-deprivation remedy either in the form of an action to prevent the state from collecting the tax or by allowing the taxes to be withheld and then giving the taxpayer the ability to defend a subsequent state effort to collect the unpaid taxes. *McKesson*, 496 U.S. 36–37. These actions, however, are prospective.

140. Frank I. Michelman, "Property, Utility, and Fairness: Comments on the Ethical Formulations of 'Just compensation' Law," 80 *Harvard Law Rev.* (1967) 1165.

141. 28 U.S.C., secs. 1346(a), 1491 (1994).

142. *See* Seamon, *Immunity*. Daniel J. Meltzer, "Legislative Courts, Legislative Power, and the Constitution," 65 *Indiana Law J.* (1990) 291, 298. *Cf.* Florida Prepaid Postsecondary Education Expense Board v. College Savings Bank, 527 U.S. (1999) 627, 644 n.9 (noting the availability of a private bill remedy for patent infringements by this state).

143. Vicki Jackson has written that because Maine permitted claims against the state under its own wage and hour legislation to be heard in state court, *Alden* is inconsistent with Testa v. Katt and thus throws doubt on *Testa*'s continuing vitality. Vicki C. Jackson, "Principle and Compromise in Constitutional Adjudication: The Eleventh Amendment and State Sovereign Immunity," 75 *Notre Dame Law Rev.* (2000) 953, 965–66. The *Alden* majority does not even cite to *Testa*, much less answer Professor Jackson's argument. Maine's brief, however, asserted that *Alden*'s claim was one for overtime. Maine had no provision for its courts to hear such claims.

144. Durchslag, *Accommodation* 1375, 1384–85, n.36. *See also* Gary J. Simon, "The Role of History in Constitutional Interpretation: A Case Study," 70 *Cornell University Law Rev.* (1985) 253, 263–64.

145. U.S. Constitution, art. 4, sec. 1. This was the basis of Justice Blackmun's dissenting opinion in Nevada v. Hall.

146. 42 U.S.C., sec. 2000(e) (1994)

147. 42 U.S.C., sec. 1988 (1994).

148. A complete review of Congress' sec. 5 enforcement powers is beyond the scope of this work. It is the subject of a separate book in this series,

149. The Eleventh Amendment was not at issue in *Boerne* since the offending governmental body was a city, and cities are not protected by the Eleventh Amendment.

150. 35 U.S.C., secs. 271(a), 296(a) (1994).

151. Articles discussing proportionality include Douglas C. Laycock, "Conceptual Gulfs in City of Boerne v. Flores," 39 *William and Mary University Law Rev.* (1998) 743; Elizabeth S. Malloy, "Whose Federalism?" 32 *Indiana University Law Rev.* (1998) 45. Ann Woolhandler has argued that some looser form of proportionality might be sufficient when Congress is attempting to protect what she describes as "old property" (land, traditional personal property, and the like) than similar attempts to protect so-called "new property" (patent rights, intangible property, and other statutorily created property rights) Ann Woolhandler, "Old Property, New Property, and Sovereign Immunity," 75 *Notre Dame Law Rev.* (2000) 919. But *see* Jackson, *Principle* 979–84.

152. *See, generally*, Vázquez, *Schizophrenia* 894–900

153. Metzger, *Five Authors* 1059–60.

154. Metzger, *Five Authors* 1057–59.

155. 29 U.S.C., sec. 623(a)(1) (1994).

156. The Court dismissed evidence of age discrimination by private employers as irrelevant to the question of unconstitutional discrimination by the states.

157. 42 U.S.C., sec. 12111 *et. seq.* (1994). There was a separate claim filed under the ADA against the University of Alabama by Milton Ash who was diagnosed with chronic asthma and sleep apnea and requested daytime work and a work environment that did not

aggravate his asthma. Ash's claim was consolidated with that of Garrett and the cases were argued as one in the Supreme Court.

158. Ira C. Lupu, "Why the Congress was Wrong and the Court was Right—Reflections on City of Boerne v. Flores," 39 *William and Mary Law Rev.* (1998) 793, 811.

159. Professor Lupu, for one, doubts that the regulation at issue in Perez v. United States, 402 U.S. 146 (1971) or indeed McCulloch v. Maryland, 17 U.S. (4 Wheat.) 316 (1819) could pass muster under the Court's "new federalism." He doubts, however, the Court will go that far. Lupu, *Congress* 815.

160. U.S. Constitution, art. 1, sec. 8, clause 1.

161. 29 U.S.C., sec. 794(a) (1994) (emphasis added).

162. 20 U.S.C., sec. 1400 *et. seq.* (1994).

163. Justice Blackmun separately concurred in the judgment but wrote no opinion. Since Justice Thomas did not participate in the decision, the decision was 6–2.

164. 42 U.S.C., sec. 1983 (1994) provides in part: "every person who, under color of any statute, regulation, custom, or usage, of any State...subjects, or causes to be subjected, any citizen of the United States...to the deprivation of any rights...secured by the Constitution and laws shall be liable to the party injured in an action at law, suit in equity, or other proper proceeding for redress."

165. Jacobs, *Eleventh.*

166. 12 U.S.C., sec. 1257 (1994).

167. H. Jefferson Powell, "The Oldest Question of Constitutional Law," 79 *University of Virginia Law Rev.* (1983) 633.

168. *Compare* Burt Neuborne, "The Myth of Parity," 90 *Harvard Law Rev.* (1977) *with* Paul M. Bator, "The State Courts and Federal Constitutional Litigation," 22 *William and Mary Law Rev.* (1981) 605.

169. *Federalist No. 15* 88–91 (Alexander Hamilton) (Henry Cabot Lodge, ed. 1902). It may also be true that the federal government cannot be trusted to respect state autonomy concerns. *See* Lewis B. Kaden, "Politics, Money and State Sovereignty: The Judicial Role," 79 *Columbia Law Rev.* (1979) 847 and William Marshall, "American Political Culture and the Failures of Process Federalism," 22 *Harvard J. of Law and Public Policy* (1998) 139. But *see* Larry Kramer, "Understanding Federalism," 47 *Vanderbilt Law Rev.* (1994) 1485. The latter problem, however, can be adequately remedied under the Tenth Amendment. Neither *Seminole Tribe* nor *Alden* is required. *See* Calvin R. Massey, "State Sovereignty and the Tenth and Eleventh Amendments," 56 *University of Chicago Law Rev.* (1989) 61.

170. Ironically, one of these notable exceptions may be Alden v. Maine. *Alden* involved a dispute between the state and its probation officers regarding whether these employees were covered by the Fair Labor Standards Act at all, and if they were covered, whether they fit within the category of law enforcement personnel whose overtime was computed differently from other government employees. As soon as the Federal District Court ruled that the employees were covered and that they were not law enforcement personnel, the state complied with the federal law. It did not, however, pay them their back wages.

171. My views on the efficacy of these exceptions are also set forth in Durchslag, *Accommodation* 1375.

172. Jackson, *Seminole* 530–538.

173. *Cf.* Caminker, *State* 113–19.

174. 28 U.S.C., sec. 1257 (1994).

175. Rules of the Supreme Court, 445 U.S. 983, (1980) 1003.

176. A number of empirical studies demonstrate that federalism doctrine ebbs and flows with the "political" makeup of the Court, suggesting either that there are no neutral criteria by which one can evaluate whether the accommodation is acceptable or that the Court adheres to none. *See* Cross, *Realism* 1304, 1308–13. If either is true, the threat to the rule of law is even greater than that feared by Professor Jacobs.

Bibliographic Essay

It is difficult, if not impossible, to isolate scholarly works that focus upon the history of the Eleventh Amendment from those that focus on the doctrinal conclusions that flow from that history. As this book makes clear, Eleventh Amendment jurisprudence conflates history with doctrine in a way unequaled by any other single subject of constitutional jurisprudence in the past half century. With that caveat, however, I have chosen to organize this brief bibliographic essay in just this way, describing first those essential works that have as their core an analysis of the history of the Eleventh Amendment and then noting those that analyze and critique the Court's doctrinal conclusions and analyses. The scholarship noted in this essay is by no means exhaustive, as a brief scan of the endnotes demonstrates. The past twenty-five or so years have seen an explosion of scholarship exploring the constitutional dimensions of state sovereign immunity, and the end appears nowhere in sight. Indeed, the works listed here do not necessarily represent all of what might be described as seminal or groundbreaking works in this area. Some scholars might argue that the list is either under- or over-inclusive. The works noted are, however, those that proved essential to my understanding of the Eleventh Amendment—those, if you will, that permitted me to move to the next steps.

HISTORICAL WORKS

Two excellent books have been written on the Eleventh Amendment, both of which are essential to begin to understand its political and doctrinal history. The first, published in 1972, is Clyde E. Jacobs, *The Eleventh Amendment and Sovereign Immunity* (New York: Doubleday, 1972). The other, published fifteen years later, is John V. Orth, *The Judicial Power of the United States: the Eleventh Amendment in American History* (New York: Oxford University Press, 1987). Both authors excel in their analysis of the judicial history of the Eleventh Amendment. Professor Orth's book is notable for its controversial (albeit probably correct) conclusion that the seminal case of *Hans v. Louisiana* (1890) was prompted more by the politics of the post-Reconstruction era and a concern for the reputation of the federal judiciary than by precedent, sound legal reasoning, or historiography.

In addition, a number of law review articles document much of the early, pre-constitutional history that led to the enactment of the Eleventh Amendment. Four, however, stand out both for their detail and the clarity of presentation:

Martha A. Field, "The Eleventh Amendment and Other Sovereign Immunity Doctrines: Part One,"126 *University of Pennsylvania Law Journal* (1977) 1260.

William A. Fletcher, "A Historical Interpretation of the Eleventh Amendment: A Narrow Interpretation of an Affirmative Grant Rather than a Prohibition of Jurisdiction," 35 *Stanford Law Review* (1983) 1033.

John J. Gibbons, "The Eleventh Amendment and State Sovereign Immunity: A Reinterpretation," 83 *Columbia Law Review* (1983) 1899.

James E. Pfander, "History and State Suability: An "Explanatory" Account of the Eleventh Amendment," 83 *Cornell Law Review* (1998) 1269.

I would be remiss not to mention two recent books that contribute significantly to understanding the tensions between the federal government and the states—tensions that produced the Eleventh Amendment and culminated some seventy years later in the Civil War:

Forest McDonald, *States Rights and the Union: Imperium in Imperio, 1776–1876* (Lawrence: University Press of Kansas, 2000)

Bernard A. Weisberger, *America Afire: Jefferson, Adams, and the Revolutionary Election of 1800* (New York: Harper Collins, 2000)

As these works make plain, the Eleventh Amendment was but one small piece of a much larger and more complex puzzle.

DOCTRINAL ANALYSES

Broadly (and for that reason somewhat inaccurately) stated, there are two camps of Eleventh Amendment scholars: those who subscribe to the *diversity* theory and those who subscribe to the *immunity* theory. In addition to Judge (formerly Professor) William Fletcher, Judge John Gibbons, and Professors James Pfander and Martha Field (whose-works are cited above), the following authors provide excellent insights into the theory that holds that the Eleventh Amendment only prohibits the exercise of federal jurisdiction and then only in those instances when the basis of jurisdiction is diversity of citizenship (that is, when a non-resident plaintiff sues a state):

Akhil Reed Amar, "Of Sovereignty and Federalism," 96 *Yale Law Journal* (1987) 1425.

Vicki C. Jackson, "The Supreme Court, The Eleventh Amendment. and State Sovereign Immunity," 98 *Yale Law Journal* (1988) 1.

On the other side, the "immunity" theory is not without its strong advocates. Two of the works are of particular significance:

William P. Marshall, "The Diversity Theory of the Eleventh Amendment: A Critical Evaluation," 102 *Harvard Law Review* (1989) 1372.

Carlos Manuel Vázquez, "What is Eleventh Amendment Immunity," 106 *Yale Law Journal* (1997) 1683.

I recommend Professor Marshall's article for its lucidity and simplicity and Professor Vázquez's work for the scope of its research, and its meticulous analysis. Moreover, Professor Vázquez has a different take on the immunity position, relying largely on arguments of the need for stability and coherence in order to preserve the rule of law.

The most significant nuance of the diversity/immunity debate is whether Congress has the authority to abrogate a state's Eleventh Amendment immunity. For some, congressional authority does not alter their conclusions, one way or the other. The congressional power cases either confirm that the Court is adhering to the original principles of the Eleventh Amendment (Professor Marshall's and to a more limited degree Professor Vázquez's position) or is moving down the wrong road (Professor Jackson). For others, however, congressional legislative authority alters whatever immunity the Eleventh Amendment otherwise provides:

Martha A. Field, "The Eleventh Amendment and Other Sovereign Immunity Doctrines: Congressional Imposition of Suit upon the States," 126 *University of Pennsylvania Law Review* (1978) 1203. (The Eleventh Amendment merely confirms that the states were not deprived of their common law immunity, and gives Congress the power to abrogate that immunity.)

John E. Nowak, "The Scope of Congressional Power to Create Causes of Action Against State Governments and the History of the Eleventh and Fourteenth Amendments," 75 *Columbia Law Review* (1975) 1413. (History supports congressional power to abrogate state sovereign immunity.)

Laurence Tribe, "Intergovernmental Immunities in Litigation, Taxation, and Regulation: Separation of Powers Issues in Controversies About Federalism," 89 *Harvard Law Review* (1976) 682. (Congressional power to abrogate state sovereign immunity is supported by the states' representation in the federal legislative process, making judicial action to protect state sovereign immunity from federal legislative actions unnecessary.)

Finally, several symposia have recently been published exploring the Court's most recent decisions on Congress' power to abrogate state sovereign immunity. These include:

"Symposium, New Directions in Federalism," 33 *Loyola, Los Angeles Law Review* (2000) 1245.

"Symposium, State Sovereign Immunity and the Eleventh Amendment," 75 *Notre Dame Law Review* (2000) 817.

"Symposium, Federalism After Alden, 31 *Rutgers Law Journal* (2000) 1245.

"Shifting the Balance of Power?: The Supreme Court, Federalism, and State Sovereign Immunity," 53 *Stanford Law Review* (2001) 1115.

A number of articles from these symposia are cited in the notes to Part II. Since they cover a wide range of sovereign immunity issues from an even wider set of opposing views, I have not noted these here. I commend each symposium. The authors represented are all recognized scholars whose contributions are noteworthy. However, if I had to choose one symposium that one should read to get an understanding of the impact of the Court's 1999 *Alden* trilogy cases, it would undoubtedly be the symposium in the *Notre Dame Law Review*.

Table of Cases

A
Alden v. Maine, 527 U.S. 706 (1999)
Alexander v. Sandoval, 531 U.S. 1049 (2001)
Atascadero State Hospital v. Scanlon, 473 U.S. 926 (1985)

B
Beers v. Arkansas, 61 U.S. 527 (1857)
Blatchford v. Native Village of Noatak, 501 U.S. 775 (1991)
Board of Trustees of the University of Alabama v. Garrett, 531 U.S. 356 (2001)
Breard v. Greene, 523 U.S. 371 (1998)
Brown v. Board of Education of Topeka, 349 U.S. 294 (1955)

C
Chisholm v. Georgia, 2 U.S. 419 (1793)
City of Boerne v. Flores, 512 U.S. 507 (1997)
City of Cleburne v. Cleburne Living Center, Inc., 473 U.S. 432 (1985)
City of Monterey v. Del Monte Dunes at Monterey, Ltd., 526 U.S. 687 (1999)
Clark v. Barnard, 108 U.S. 436 (1883)
Cohens v. Virginia, 19 U.S. 264 (1821)
College Savings Bank v. Florida Prepaid Postsecondary Education Expense Board, 527 U.S. 666 (1999)
Cowels v. Mercer County, 74 U.S. 118 (1868)
Cutting v. South Carolina, unreported

D
Davis v. Gray, 83 U.S. 203 (1872)
Dellmuth v. Muth, 491 U.S. 223 (1989)
Dred Scott v. Sanford, 60 U.S. 393 (1851)

E
Edelman v. Jordan, 415 U.S. 651 (1974)
Employment Division, Department of Human Resources v. Smith, 494 U.S. 872 (1990)

Employees of Dept. of Public Health & Welfare of Missouri v. Department of Public Health and Welfare, 411 U.S. 279 (1973)
Ex parte Young, 209 U.S. 123 (1908)

F

Federal Maritime Commission v. South Carolina Ports Authority, 70 U.S.L.W. 4464 (U.S. May 28, 2002)
First English Evangelical Lutheran Church v. County of Los Angeles, 482 U.S. 307 (1987)
Fitzpatrick v. Bitzer, 427 U.S. 445 (1976)
Florida Department of Health and Rehabilitative Services v. Florida Nursing Home Association, 450 U.S. 147 (1981)
Florida Department of State v. Treasure Salvors Inc., 458 U.S. 670 (1982)
Florida Prepaid Postsecondary Education Expense Board v. College Savings Bank, 527 U.S. 627 (1999)
Ford Motor Company v. Department of Treasury, 323 U.S. 459 (1945)

G

Garcia v. San Antonio Metropolitan Transit Authority, 469 U.S. 528 (1985)
Garrett v. Trustees of the University of Alabama, 531 U.S. 356 (2001)
Governor of Georgia v. Madrazo, 26 U.S. 110 (1828)
Grayson v. Virginia, 3 U.S. 320 (1796)
Great Northern Life Insurance Company v. Read, 322 U.S. 47 (1944)
Green v. Mansour, 474 U.S. 64 (1985)

H

Hagood v. Southern, 117 U.S. 52 (1886)
Hans v. Louisiana, 134 U.S. 1 (1890)
Heart of Atlanta Motel v. United States, 379 U.S. 241 (1964)
Hess v. Port Authority Trans-Hudson Corporation, 513 U.S. 30 (1994)
Hilton v. South Carolina Public Railways Commission, 502 U.S. 197 (1991)
Hollingsworth v. Virginia, 3 U.S. 378 (1798)
Hudson v. Palmer, 408 U.S. 517 (1984)
Hutto v. Finney, 437 U.S. 678 (1978)

I

Idaho v. Coeur d'Alene Tribe of Idaho, 521 U.S. 261 (1997)
Imbier v. Patchman, 424 U.S. 409 (1976)

K

Kansas v. Colorado, 121 S. Ct. 2023 (2001)
Kawananakoa v. Polyblank, 205 U.S. 349 (1907)
Kennecott Copper v. State Tax Commission, 409 U.S. 973 (1972)
Kimel v. Florida Board of Regents, 528 U.S. 62 (2000)

L

Lake County Estates Inc. v. Tahoe Regional Planning Agency, 440 U.S. 391 (1979)
Lapides v. Board of Regents of the University System of Georgia, 122 Sup. Ct. 1640 (2002)
Larson v. Domestic and Foreign Commerce Corp., 337 U.S. 682 (1949)
Lincoln County v. Luning, 133 U.S. 529 (1890)
Lochner v. New York, 198 U.S. 45 (1905)
Louisiana ex rel v. Jumel, 107 U.S. 711 (1882)
Lucas v. South Carolina Coastal Council, 505 U.S. 1003 (1992)
Lynch v. United States, 292 U.S. 571 (1934)

M

Malone v. Bowdoin, 369 U.S. 643 (1962)
Martin v. Hunter's Lesse, 14 U.S. 304 (1816)
Massachusetts Board of Retirement v. Murgia, 427 U.S. 307 (1976)
McCulloch v. Maryland, 17 U.S. 316 (1819)
McKesson v. Division of Alcoholic Beverages and Tobacco, 496 U.S. 18 (1990)
Milliken v. Bradley, 418 U.S. 717 (1977)
Minnesota v. Hitchcock, 185 U.S. 373 (1902)
Missouri v. Fiske, 290 U.S. 18 (1933)
Monell v. New York City Department of Social Services, 436 U.S. 658 (1978)
Moultrie v. Georgia, unreported
Mt. Healthy City Board of Education v. Doyle, 429 U.S. 274 (1977)

N

National League of Cities v. Usury, 426 U.S. 833 (1976)
Nevada v. Hall, 440 U.S. 410 (1979)
New Hampshire v. Louisiana, 108 U.S. 76 (1883)
New York v. United States, 505 U.S. 144 (1992)

O

Osborne v. Bank of the United States, 86 U.S. 577 (1824)
Oswald v. New York, 2 U.S. 402 (1792)

P

Papasan v. Allain, 478 U.S. 265 (1986)
Parden v. Terminal Railway of Alabama, 377 U.S. 184 (1964)
Parratt v. Taylor, 451 U.S. 527 (1981)
Pennhurst State School and Hospital v. Halderman, 451 U.S. 1 (1984)
Pennoyer v. McConnaughy, 140 U.S. 1 (1891)
Pennsylvania v. Union Gas Company, 491 U.S. 1 (1989)
Petty v. Tennessee–Missouri Bridge Commission, 359 U.S. 275 (1959)
Pierson v. Ray, 386 U.S. 547 (1967)
Poindexter v. Greenhow, 114 U.S. 270 (1885)
Port Authority Trans-Hudson Corporation v. Feeney, 495 U.S. 299 (1990)
Principality of Monaco v. Mississippi, 292 U.S. 313 (1934)
Printz v. United States, 521 U.S. 898 (1997)

Q

Quern v. Jordan, 440 U.S. 332 (1989)

R

Reagan v. Farmers' Loan and Trust Company, 154 U.S. 362 (1894)
Rhode Island v. Massachusetts, 37 U.S. 657 (1838)

S

Schillinger v. United States, 155 U.S. 163 (1894)
Seminole Tribe of Florida v. Florida, 517 U.S. 44 (1996)
South Dakota v. North Carolina, 192 U.S. 286 (1904)

T

Tenney v. Brandhove, 341 U.S. 367 (1951)
Testa v. Katt, 330 U.S. 386 (1947)

U

United States v. Lee, 455 U.S. 252 (1982)
United States v. Lopez, 514 U.S. 549 (1995)
United States v. Morrison, 529 U.S. 598 (2000)
United States v. Peters, 9 U.S. 115 (1809)
United States v. Texas, 143 U.S. 621 (1892)

V

Vanstophorst v. Maryland, 2 U.S. 401 (1791)
Vassal v. Massachusetts, unreported
Verizon Maryland, Inc. v. Public Service Commission of Maryland, 122 Sup. Ct. 1646 (2002)

W

Welch v. Texas Department of Highways and Public Transportation, 483 U.S. 468 (1987)
Will v. Michigan Department of State Police, 491 U.S. 58 (1989)

Index

ABOUT THE AUTHOR

MELVYN R. DURCHSLAG is Professor of Law at Case Western Reserve University School of Law.